INSHORE CRAFT OF GREAT BRITAIN

INSHORE CRAFT
OF GREAT BRITAIN

In the Days of Sail and Oar

by EDGAR J MARCH

New Introduction by John Leather

VOLUME ONE

CHATHAM PUBLISHING

LONDON

Copyright © Edgar J March 1970
Introduction copyright © John Leather 2005

Published in Great Britain in 2005 by Chatham Publishing,
Lionel Leventhal Ltd, Park House, 1 Russell Gardens,
London NW11 9NN

First published in 1970 by David & Charles, Newton Abbot

British Library Cataloguing in Publication Data
March, Edgar J.
Inshore craft of Britain in the days of sail and oar
1. Work boats—Great Britain—History   2. Sailboats—Great Britain—History
3. Coastwise shipping—Great Britain—History
I. Title   II. March, Edgar J.. Inshore craft of Great Britain in the days of sail and oar
387.2′0426′0941

Two-volume set ISBN 1 86176 254 2
Vol I ISBN I 86176 264 X
Vol II ISBN 1 86176 269 0

Originated by MRM Graphics Ltd
Printed and bound in Thailand

CONTENTS

LIST OF ILLUSTRATIONS

8   LIST OF ILLUSTRATIONS

INTRODUCTION

O n a summer's day at Southend-on-Sea in 1948, I was leaving the central station by a street where a bookshop window displayed many new titles. One stood out because of its garish dustjacket and sizeable format. Its title immediately appealed; *Spritsail Barges of the Thames and Medway*. Living in Essex by the River Colne I was accustomed to seeing numbers of the brown sailed coastal cargo barges and particularly during weekends and holidays when I sailed my boat in their company. Minutes later I was in the shop and the book in my hands, with its bold postwar printing, numerous photographs as well as plans of a number of barges. The author's name, Edgar J March, was unfamiliar and the price was high for those days—two guineas (£2-2-0) when most good books cost about 15 shillings—but I could not resist so much information on sailing barges and the book went home with me and many years and readings later remains on my study shelves.

But who was this Edgar March? Some clues appeared in the book. In 1913 he was articled to the District Surveyor of the part of north Kent where he lived for many years at Westgate-on-Sea, facing the lower estuary of the Thames, just west of Margate. He was, I believe, later employed by Kent County Council as a land and civil works surveyor. By inclination he was a maritime historian. He seems not to have owned or used boats himself but had perhaps made a few short trips on board sailing barges in the Thames and Medway, from the small coaster, barge and fishing port of Whitstable, on the north Kent coast. He was an enthusiastic modeller of small-scale models of sailing barges and perhaps some other sailing craft and for this he draughted his own plans from dimensions and notes taken from the craft to be modelled, or from half models and builders' plans. At that time, as an apprentice ship draughtsman, I could see he had not been trained in the detail and style of draughting plans and presenting data as is necessary in ship design and construction; but the drawings were clear and the reproduced lines fair, the whole intention being to aid and encourage modelmakers as well as making what became a major contribution in recording the spritsail barge, and which merited a second printing.

During the late 1940s March began collecting data on the once large numbers of sailing drifters which worked from many British ports until made obsolete by steam and, later, motor propelled drift vessels. This too was a major work which, because of the scattered coastwise positions of the ports involved, needed visits far from March's home. As I believe he did not drive a car, this must have involved aid from friends and also many rail journeys, besides considerable correspondence with the owners, builders, skippers and crews of sailing drifters, by then all ageing survivors of a once vast and complex industry. The resulting book, *Sailing Drifters*, appeared in 1952, also with many photographs, illustrations and plans. In size it greatly surpassed his *Spritsail Barges* and with its even more arcane subject it is not surprising that it was priced at the substantial sum of three guineas (£3-3-0). It was and remains an important historical record of sailing drifters.

Undeterred by the amount of work involved and the difficulties of contacting people who had been directly involved, Edgar March pressed on with yet another major book, this time *Sailing Trawlers*, his third work to be published by Percival Marshall and, in this case, describing the many smacks which trawled for bottom fish from British ports. Again the work was profusely illustrated with photographs and many plans drawn or re-drawn by the author and it commended itself to small craft enthusiasts and marine modelmakers alike and provided an enduring record of the subject. It was published in 1953.

During the writing of *Sailing Trawlers*, Edgar March moved house from Westgate to the village of Colwell Bay, at the west end of the Isle of Wight, almost suburban in atmosphere and architecture. With a beach facing across the Solent's west channel entrance between the island and the Hurst Spit shore, it probably suited his interests and temperament.

Shortly after publication of *Sailing Trawlers* the indefatigable March embarked on another, much larger and more complex work which was unfortunately beyond his experience and true interest. By means unknown he was tempted into writing a major book entitled *British Destroyers 1893–1953* to be published by Seeley Service & Co. The subject was alien to his scholarly interests in old-time working small craft. It needed the training and experience of a naval architect or shipbuilder concerned with warship design to successfully appraise and evaluate this very complex subject. After the first 'torpedo boat destroyers' were designed and built in 1893, the Royal Navy had scores of successive classes of this fast and constantly evolving warship type. It was a specialised field into which an amateur historian should perhaps not have ventured.

He was allowed access to the plans, specifications and other technical data and reports on many British destroyers from the 1890s to the 1950s, when the type ceased to be built for its primary role and was subsumed into one of the various types of modern frigates. If it is astonishing he should have been asked to write such a book it is more so that he completed his version of British destroyer development at all. It was published in 1966. Soon after, Edgar March was living in the Isle of Wight village of Freshwater at a house named Green Acre, suggesting trim lawns, colourful mixed borders and contented domesticity rather than the rough and tumble of the seaways which were backdrop to his books.

Besides his venture into warship history Edgar March was

busy corresponding with more old timers all around the coasts for a book to be entitled *Inshore Craft of Britain—In the Days of Sail and Oar.* March had, since the early years of the twentieth century, observed local craft of many types and collected information on them and brought this together for a two-volume work with the usual supporting photographs and plans he prepared or re-drew. One of the most interesting and authentic aspects of it was the extensive use he made of detailed correspondence with those who had owned or worked the craft mentioned or with others who had studied them in detail. Although not obvious to the average reader much of the text of this book was taken verbatim from those letters, and some of it was, perhaps, not quite fairly acknowledged. However, it had the merit of providing authenticity, rather than relying largely on author's opinion, and for this reason alone the work is enormously valuable. Years after the deaths of many of those who sailed and worked the vessels we can read genuine first-hand accounts.

Inshore Craft of Britain was published in 1970 and, at a time of surging interest in traditional craft of most types, was well received. It quickly became a classic work and so it remains today. Through its pages the reader can take a voyage around the British coasts a century or more ago, meeting the craft and men who owned and manned them, and the builders and sailmakers. They earned usually a poor and uncertain living from the fickle catches and trades of our inshore waters before the arrival of the compact marine motor that so eased the burden of their labours, and in some measure eventually enabled many of them to achieve modest prosperity.

Amongst the many works published on small working craft during the past eighty years the writings of Edgar March will endure, and this book, now happily republished, was perhaps his best.

John Leather C.Eng. FRINA
Fingringhoe, Essex, 2005

PREFACE

FROM the dawn of civilisation to the opening years of the twentieth century, beachmen and inshore fishermen depended upon the wind and the strength of their arms to propel their boats by sail and oar. Today, those of us who are in the evening of life look back on an era that seems as remote as that of the Pharoahs. The invention of the internal-combustion engine, driven by paraffin, petrol or diesel oil, completely changed a pattern of life which had existed for centuries and standardised hull design to a great extent. Different areas had developed boats to a design suitable for the local beaches and waters, or for the occupation of their owners, individualists of independent character. Within a few miles could be found totally different types, the majority open boats, with others half- or fully-decked, whose names were so varied and picturesque: sixerns, scaffies, fifies, nobbies, cobles, bawleys, lerrets, to name but a few. Seen in hundreds, their tanned sails of varied hues patterned the sea off many a fishing station. Lads soon learned to recognise them at a glance as the youths of today know the makes of cars, types of aircraft and, until a few years ago, steam locomotives.

The numerous drawings which illustrate this work will enable a comparison to be made of body plans, some shaped like a dish, others like a wineglass. There was a great diversity in rig between a Thames bawley and a Morecambe Bay prawner—yet both trawled for shrimps—and in hull form between a coble, a Sheringham crabber and one from Cornwall, all setting pots for crabs and lobsters.

Between us and those now far-distant days of Victorian and

11

Edwardian England lies a great gulf, so deep and wide that few can bridge it. As so little was ever committed to paper, only the quavering voices of aged men, or letters, often written in beautiful copperplate writing, can span that dividing line between our atomic age and the days of sail and oar.

It has been my pleasure and privilege to know many men who have only recently slipped their moorings for that eternity where there is no more sea, men who lived to see changes beyond the wildest dreams of their fathers. In their youth many handled huge racing yachts in summer, their small fishing boats in winter. They manned yachts owned by wealthy men who had not the sea in their blood, and those of a nation unable to produce men capable of such sailing until taught by our fishermen. In middle age they saw war sweep away that life for ever. Many were reservists who served their country well in the Grand Fleet or in the dangerous work of minesweeping; others helped to man the merchant ships bringing vital supplies through waters infested by mine and submarine, while their grandfathers carried on fishing. Between the wars came a struggle to earn a meagre living. In old age, the homes of many were bombed by the sons and grandsons of men to whom they had taught seamanship.

Thriving seaside towns were not so long ago tiny villages, and harbours now often deserted or crowded with small yachts were once thronged with fishing craft. Overhead wing huge jet airliners which can reached far distant lands in a time less than that in which the old generation could row or sail to fishing grounds only a few miles to seaward.

To ensure accuracy, I have obtained my facts from those who knew the life of which I write, and for over half a century I have been noting items of interest and collecting photographs. For earlier times, I have studied contemporary models in museums and waded through many Government Reports which sometimes yielded valuable scraps of information, as did old guide books. Searches in boatyards, now derelict, have perhaps produced a penny notebook in which a craftsman scribbled a few items—length of spars or sail dimensions—while old ledgers, torn and flung away, have given me priceless information concerning costs in terms of golden sovereigns.

My grateful thanks go to all those mentioned in the text who gave me such wonderful help. Alas, most of them are no longer with us. I am also indebted to many enthusiasts who placed information at my disposal and I would especially like to mention John Smith, John Leather and R. H. C. Gillis who sent me notes of inestimable value, R. W. Malster, Professor A. W. Brogger of Oslo University, Professor Haakon Shetelig of Bergen University for data on Viking ships, H. Oliver Hill, P. A. Rumbelow, the late E. C. Pain whose records of Deal boats were a goldmine, the late J. Hornell for notes on Hastings craft, the late P. J. Oke and others whose drawings prepared for the Coastal Craft Sub-Committee of the Society for Nautical Research have preserved the lines of many craft. I consulted *Deepsea Fishing and Fishing Boats*, c 1874, by E. W. H. Holdsworth, an early edition of Dixon Kemp lent by Bruce Jones, and a few facts came from the researches of the late R. C. Leslie.

Whenever possible I have given the source of photographs, but all too often it could not be traced and I have acknowledged the name of the donor.

Possibly I have spread my net rather widely by including under the title 'Inshore Craft' such vessels as the big Colne smacks and pilot cutters which frequently worked far out to sea, but I felt that such data should be recorded.

Shiplovers will appreciate that my joint British publishers, David & Charles (Publishers) Ltd and Fishing News (Books) Ltd accepted my two-volume work in its entirety and I thank them most warmly. It was Arthur J. Heighway of Fishing News (Books) Ltd who, after acceptance, thought it merited general distribution beyond fishing and nautical circles and arranged for joint publication with David & Charles.

Green Acre   EDGAR J. MARCH
Freshwater
Isle of Wight

CHAPTER ONE

HISTORICAL

JUST how and when primitive man first attempted to
catch fish swimming at or near the bottom of the sea is lost
in the mists of antiquity. Possibly sharp thorns, or pointed
pieces of bone or stick, were the first hooks used, but by Roman
times the design had developed into a hook very similar to that
used today. This is evidenced by specimens found in excava-
tions of Roman camps on the banks of the Humber, a place
which became the centre of deep-sea fishing about the middle
of the nineteenth century, 2,000 years later.

Fishing lines were probably made from the sinews of animals,
hair, strips of hide, or even certain creepers—indeed the word
'line' suggests some connection with 'liana', the name given to
climbing and twining plants. Then followed the making of
lines by twisting certain fibres together to form a fine rope.

Such fishing was of necessity confined to lakes, rivers and
estuaries, as the frail coracles then in use were totally unfitted to
face the open sea, which must have been of a terrifying im-
mensity to our shaggy forefathers. Coracles and skin boats,
known in Britain before the time of Julius Caesar and the
Roman invasions, were probably round wicker craft similar to
those still used today by salmon fishermen on the Severn and
certain Welsh rivers. Others, no doubt, were made of a framing
of light timbers covered with skins, a design surviving in the
curraghs of the Irish coast.

The round coracle, being unsuited to coastal waters, must
have been used only on lakes and rivers, progress being by
drifting down stream, steered by a paddle; but its shape prevented much advance against the current—a point of little

importance as its light weight allowed it to be easily transported along the bank. For sea use, the skin-covered curragh was superior, but its frailty and liability to damage by sharp rocks were a definite drawback.

These types were not confined to Britain. In Norway, rock carvings dating back to the Bronze Age depict boats with ribs of wood, two keels—an upper and an under—with skins going round the upper keel to the gunwale, the under keel protecting the hide from stones and the like, when landing or being hauled up the beach. Other carvings show skin boats similar to the Eskimo 'umiack', 30 to 40 ft long, with bone or timber ribs and a sealskin covering.

Being very narrow, such boats were easy to row but had poor sea-going ability, hence were suitable only for coasting in fair weather. Skin boats predominated in treeless Arctic wastes where only driftwood was available.

Despite their drawbacks, such primitive boats were undoubtedly used by fishermen. Stone Age carvings in Norway show lines weighted with oval pebbles and heavy, solid hooks for catching deep-water fish. Actual sinkers found weighed from $10\frac{1}{2}$ oz to 53 oz, suitable for all depths up to 90 fathoms.

In the period now known as the Stone Age, our ancestors discovered that by putting a cutting edge on a suitable piece of stone or flint it was possible to make an axe capable of felling a full-grown oak tree and hollowing the trunk into a dugout boat. Vast forests then covered the land and the fight for existence in the dim, tangled masses of closely growing trees made the oak grow straight to a great height before its branches could spread out to light and sunshine.

Dugouts have been found in varying stages of preservation in bogs and marshy ground all over Europe—even in Swiss lakes, where a very ornate one was discovered. Early in the eighteenth century one such boat was unearthed in the Clyde containing a ground stone axe of the late Stone Age; another found in Kent had a flint axe and scrapers, while in one in Cambridge was a knife of the late Bronze Age.

Page 17 (*above*) Fembӧring, rowing 10 or 12 oars, used in Northern Norway for cod fishing about 1900. The square sail is similar to that set in the early Shetland sixerns; (*below*) what a harbour to enter in a gale! West Ayr, Fethaland, *c* 1870. Note old sixerns, fourerns, weighing scales and vats

Page 18   (above) Sixerns at East Ayr, Fethaland, c 1870. Note lodges, weighing scales and vats; (below) more old sixerns at Stennis, c 1870

Log boats were crank and very heavy to row or paddle, so
that the next development was the erection of 'washstrakes' to
increase their freeboard. Cutting these planks with an axe was
a wasteful process, as never more than two boards could be cut
out of the same tree. The trunk was split down the middle, then
all the outer wood was cut away, an important feature being the
making of cleats all in one piece with the plank. This was a re-
finement necessary when the keel was made of a broad flat
piece of timber, the overlapping planks being sewn together
with bast or twisted gut, and the seams caulked with wool, or
bark, impregnated with oil, tar or resin. The absence of a
vertical keel meant weakness in a seaway.

A dugout found in 1833 near the river Arun in Sussex
measured 35 ft in length, 4 ft in width and was 2 ft in depth,
the sides being 4 to 5 in thick. Another, 42 ft long, came to
light in 1876 near Dumfries, but it was left to Hitler, Goering
and his myrmidons to destroy the finest relic of all, a boat
which had survived the vicissitues of possibly 3,000 years
only to be incinerated when Hull Museum was bombed in
1942.

Years before, I had stood beside that dugout, which was
black with age, and thought of the uncivilised men who had
hollowed it out with crude tools only a few miles from where I
was standing. How many long and slow centuries of development had culminated in the creations of the brains of their
descendants who can build the 'Queens', mighty battleships and
other vessels with but one factor—the sea—to connect them with
that early effort.

Similar thoughts had passed through my mind when I held
in my hand a silver coin found with others in an earthenware pot
turned up by a ploughman in the Middle East. Struck when
Darius was king of Persia, it bore on one side, beautifully de-
lineated, his chariot with captives chained to the wheels as
recorded in the Book of Daniel; on the other a ship, undoubtedly
carvel built, similar to that used by the Phoenicians. Down
what a long and dusty road have the legions of mankind trod

B

since that coin was minted, and how short is man's span compared with the thousands of years it has existed.

In May 1886 workmen excavating for a new gasholder at Brigg, on the banks of the river Ancholme, unearthed an enormous dugout 48 ft 6 in long, perfectly straight, with a beam of 6 ft and a depth of 2 ft 9 in. It had been hollowed from a huge oak log and the tree must have been at least 18 ft in circumference with no branches until about 50 ft from the ground. It is extremely doubtful if such a tree could be found today and one must admire the skill of the men who could fell it with axes made of stone.

The sides were 2 in thick, the bottom 4 in, the bow being rounded off; but the stern was made with a separate transom, 4 ft wide at the top, 2 ft 6 in deep, fitted into a groove cut across the floor, the caulking being moss. At some time it would seem that the boat had run on rocks as a rift 12 ft long had been patched with lengths of oak, the biggest 5 ft 8 in long, 6½ in wide, tapering to a point at each end, and let in from the outside until flush. On the inner sides were three cleats, each about 1 ft long and 4 in deep, with a hole in the centre through which pins were passed. The sides were sewn to the hull with thongs made from sinews, no metal being used anywhere.

During the Bronze and Iron Ages, the invention of the adze meant that planks could be made more easily than with an axe, and there is evidence that this tool was known somewhere between 150 and 100 BC. Ancient Egyptian wall paintings also show this tool in use.

In the later Bronze Age a broad bottom keel had two planks with thickened edges meeting in a lofty prow and stern, planks were added and strengthened internally by frames, and such a boat, c 300 BC, was found in South Jutland. The limewood planks were very broad, quite thin, sewn together and caulked with resin glue. Inside were slender hazel branches secured to the planking by lashings to cleats made in the boards which were all in one piece, with cross struts and props under

each thwart. Propulsion was by 20 paddle oars, no oar holes or
rowlocks being fitted.

In 1937 a boat was discovered at North Ferriby on the
Humber by E. V. and C. W. Wright. The outbreak of war in
1939 put an end to investigations but a certain amount had
been salved and placed in Hull Museum, only to be destroyed
by enemy action in 1942. In 1941, a second boat was discovered
but it was not until 1946 that the work of recovery could really
begin, the cost being met by the trustees of the National Maritime Museum, where the remains were finally taken.

The site was uncovered for only four or five hours according
to wind and tide, the excavation silting up and flooding daily,
necessitating constant pumping. The boat had a centre keel
plank with another on either side made of solid oak with the
axis of the trunk below the level of the boards. The tree had
been split in two, turned on the flat face and the curved side
adzed down. The two halves of the keel were joined with a very
short scarph, the overlap being only 3 in; the edges had a V-
shaped groove to take the bevelled edges of the outer planks
which were about half the thickness of the keel.

These planks, 35 ft long and 3 to 5 in thick, were secured to
the keel by stitching thin yew branches, twisted and cracked to
give the necessary flexibility, through holes 1¼ in square, 7 to 14
in apart and countersunk to avoid abrasion. The holes were
caulked with some powdered wood, probably yew, the seams
with moss, and sealed by a lath of oak passed under the stitches.
This tightened up the joint and was completed by swelling after
immersion in water.

The whole bottom structure was stiffened by a system of
transverse bars made of ash passing horizontally through holes
in the cleats left standing on the upper faces of the planks.
These bars, being a loose fit in the holes, were secured by
wedges. The boat was obviously flat-bottomed with hard
chines, three strakes a side, the edges of the planks being
grooved and caulked with moss. The ends were probably punt-
shaped, the total length about 50 ft with a beam of 8 ft 6 in; in

all probability ribs strengthened the inside as lugs on the keel suggested that possibility. The boat was propelled by paddles, one blade being found near the first boat. A possible connection with fishing is the broken fragment of baked clay with part of a hole showing, suggesting it might have been a sinker for line or net.

Here is evidence that the invention of the adze had increased the ability of men to build a boat of planks, a definite improvement on the dugout found at Brigg, only a few miles away. Tool marks on certain planks clearly showed the use of an adze as well as a broad chisel.

The invention of the saw allowed planks to be produced with greater economy than with axe or adze, and thin planking built up clinker fashion was the next development. The planks were fastened to stems attached to the keel, not to an inserted crosspiece. This construction can be seen in rock carvings at Roskar, Sunnmore, and a boat c 200 AD was found at Halsnoy, Hordaland, built of light, thin pine planks sewn with root fibres and sewn to the stems with coarse tarred thread. The joints were caulked with strips of red woven material dipped in tar, the planks had cleats with holes for lashing the frames, and rowlocks were fitted on the top strake. A Danish boat found at Nydam, in Slesvig, was of similar construction, but the planks overlapped and were riveted with iron nails, but still no vertical keel. This craft dated from c 300 to 350 AD.

Riveted planking made a very resistant hull but the ribs, previously sewn, no longer kept the planking together—they solely reinforced the hull and preserved its shape. The wonderful elasticity of a sewn hull was lost and the frames had to be much heavier to take the nails. In the course of time the planks became narrower and a vertical keel was introduced, adding greatly to the strength of the hull and making long sea voyages now practicable.

During July 1939, one of the great barrows at Sutton Hoo, near Woodbridge, Suffolk, was opened, and within was found the remains of a burial ship dating back to about AD 630. The spot was the graveyard of the family of the Uffings, the pagan rulers of the kingdom of the East Angles. A trench some 90 ft long, 16 ft wide and 8 ft deep, oriented east and west, had been dug in the sand and the ship lowered into it with its bow towards the open sea about six miles away. After the body of the chieftain had been laid to rest in the burial chamber set up amidships, the vessel was filled in with sand and a mound some 12 ft high raised above the surface.

The passage of years saw the gradual decay of all the timber, but the sand below and at the sides was leached white by the acids liberated by the rotting wood, in some places the grain being imprinted. Thus a perfect replica remained of the shape of the original ship, even the position of hundreds of clench nails being accurately preserved. Only amidships, where the burial chamber had collapsed, was the symmetry marred.

As may be imagined, the greatest care was needed in removing the sand from the inside to preserve the precious outline as intact as possible. Then the lines were carefully taken off by surveyors from the Science Museum, South Kensington. The vessel was a large, open, clinker-built, rowing-boat about 80 ft long, of 14 ft beam and 5 ft depth, built entirely of oak. It was flat-keeled with nine strakes of planking a side, including the gunwale.

While similar in many respects to the Nydam ship, the greater length necessitated the strakes being made up of four to five pieces, averaging 15 in in width and 1 in in thickness, joined by four or five clench nails about 1 in long in what must have been flush scarph joints. The position of the scarphs joining the stem and sternpost to the keel was clearly to be seen, each secured by three nails $6\frac{3}{4}$ in long, riveted over rooves. The keel plank may have been about $7\frac{1}{2}$ in wide and $2\frac{1}{8}$ in deep, its length between scarphs being some 60 ft.

Twenty-six ribs, spaced about 3 ft apart, went across the keel from gunwale to gunwale, and although only black dust remained it was possible to see they were of rectangular cross section, varying from 3 to $5\frac{1}{2}$ in in width and 3 in in depth. They were secured to the gunwales by iron nails 4½ in long, clenched over rooves and probably lashed to cleats left standing on the inside of the strakes—the usual Viking practice. Outlines in the sand showed that the tholes were of the same clawlike form found at Nydam and placed one between each pair of ribs. There being at least 19 tholes a side, it is reasonable to assume 38 rowers to propel the boat.

The clench nails were of varying length with domed heads of 1⅛ in diameter and riveted over diamond-shaped rooves, 2 in by 1¼ in, carefully ranged with all their long axes neatly in line. No rowing oars, steering oar or equipment were found.

A much smaller boat, 18 ft long and of 4 ft beam, was found under the second largest barrow. It appeared to have been clinker built, but the most important feature was a bluntly rounded stern, with a beam of some 3 ft 6 in, bound with an iron band, the first evidence of a breakaway from the typical pointed stern. The boat contained the remains of a cremation burial and, judging by the ornaments, dated back to the sixth or seventh century.

In 1920, a boat *c* 600 AD, with 10 pairs of oars was discovered in Heroy, Sunnmore, of similar build but having an external keel in one piece on the underside along the middle of the bottom plank, thus strengthening the hull and acting as a runner when beaching. Here again, instead of broad strakes in one piece, the planks were narrower and in several pieces, thus giving more elasticity. An important addition was a rudder attached to the starboard side with a tiller crosswise into the ship, making it possible to carry a mast and sails. This boat, about 59 ft long, of 9 ft 10 in beam and 2 ft 7 in deep, had fine lines and a proud stem.

Now began the great age of the Viking migrations to the western isles, and from 600 AD to 900 AD many improvements in construction were made. A vertical keel was solid enough to take a mast scottle and partners and a large square sail could be set; the rigging was simple as the boat sailed better when the mast had give in it. The planks were nailed to knees attached to

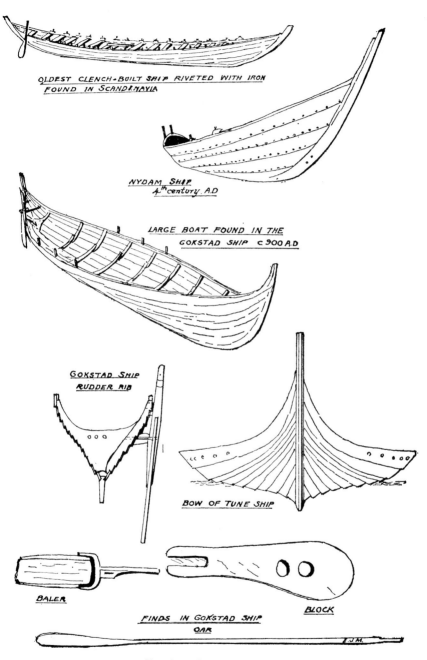

OLDEST CLENCH-BUILT SHIP RIVETED WITH IRON
FOUND IN SCANDINAVIA

NYDAM SHIP
4th century. A.D

LARGE BOAT FOUND IN THE
GOKSTAD SHIP c 900 A.D

GOKSTAD SHIP
RUDDER RIB

BOW OF TUNE SHIP

BALER

BLOCK

FINDS IN GOKSTAD SHIP
OAR

E.J.M.

Sketches of Viking ships

the thwarts and the higher sides necessitated oar holes instead of rowlocks. Stem and stern swept up in graceful curves.

Finality had now been reached in the art of boat-building and the magnificent ships found at Gokstad and elsewhere cannot be surpassed. In the Oseberg ship, c 800 AD, found in 1904, not one piece of wood had rotted and the baler was practically the exact shape of that used in the Shetland sixerns down to the end of the nineteenth century and called an 'auskerri'.

Extolled in sagas and recorded by historians, these superb longships were not so vital to the life of the community as were the humble working boats upon which the farmer-fishermen depended for their very existence. To wring a living in a harsh climate, a boat was a necessity to carry produce across the fjords, bring back supplies and above all to engage in fishing.

In the Gokstad vessel, discovered in 1880, were three small boats, the largest 31 ft 11½ in long, beam 6 ft 1 1/5 in, oak-built throughout with five strakes a side, incredibly thin, with six ribs and a method of transverse connections very similar to that still employed in west and north Norway. The loose thwarts rested on the frames, floorboards were of thin pine, there were three pairs of oars in rowlocks, no mast, and the boat was steered with a rudder. Here surely is the prototype of the sixern.

In many a bog were found numerous stems, keels, frames, oar blades, balers and other fittings, probably placed there for seasoning, to see the sun again in the 1920s.

Two boats were dug up in 1940-1, one rowing 12 oars with its 'eptirbatr' [after boat]—a four-oared dinghy, riveted with iron nails. Two years later another bog find in Herdla, north of Bergen, revealed two boats smashed to pieces, each of which had strong oak mast partners. The mast was raised obliquely from the after end and the heel slipped down into a socket in the step. It was then raised vertically and secured with one or two square wooden blocks. The mast was probably lowered in head winds or calms, or the men raised it after rowing a short distance up into the wind and then set sail, as is still done today with the square-sail boats in Norway. If the boat has to go a few miles across a fjord 'and the wind is scarce', the boat is rowed a little into the wind, then the whole stretch is made under sail. Tacking takes longer in a narrow sound than rowing.

Oak is found only in south Norway, pine in the north, but the islands off the coast north of Tromso had no pine forests and for centuries the Sea Finns supplied the whole of Lofoten, Vesteralen, Vaerog and Rost with boats, rowing up to twelve oars a side, their planks sewn with sinews, no nails, and knees of willow. Such a boat was found in 1931 at Barset, although some authorities think it was Norwegian built, of early Iron Age origin.

Hundreds of finds thus give invaluable evidence of the early development of the clench-built, open boat. A list prepared by Prof. H. Shetelig, of Bergen University, gives over 500 known boat graves. The smaller boats were well stabilised long before the Viking period—in the west, this tradition dates back 1,400 years.

Down to recent times whole parishes in Norway were occupied in boat building. If a builder owned a forest, a buyer had to order a year ahead. The timber was felled in the winter, hauled home by sledge, sawn and cut up, then left to season, the buyer finally collecting the finished boat. Many builders would, however, tow up to five boats long distances in the hope of a sale to a fisherman.

Ship- or boat-building was always done during the winter when farm work was at a minimum and labour easily procurable, the keel being laid in the autumn. A boat never stood from one season to another—even big ships could be built in about three months.

Cross beams, knees, frame timbers, stem and stern pieces were selected from crooked trees. To be absolutely sound, the whole strake was best made from the same tree, boards of equal thickness then having the same elasticity. Father and sons worked together on every farm, building perhaps five or six boats a year. For the bigger boats, several builders combined and when the last Nordfjord 'jekt' was building in 1881, four masters, each with his assistant and smith, worked together, twelve men in all. Many of the boats were in use for 100 to 150 years. In the 1930s, 10 to 12 boat builders in Sogn were building four and six-oared boats similar to those found in graves of the Viking era. For reefing the square sail, strips of walrus hide were still used. The length of the mast to the sheave equalled the girth of the boat at the mast thwart—the masthead was not counted.

Construction, building methods, tools, measurements, and rig had remained virtually unchanged for well over a thousand years; even the names for the different parts were the same from age to age. The reason? 1,400 years ago perfection was reached and the hull, being elastic, worked with the sea.

The longships vanished with the end of the Viking wars, but the small boats were and still are bound up in the life of the peasantry.

CONSTRUCTION

The master was the shipwright—'to erect a ship' was the common expression; the slip where the ship was built was the 'stocks'; the tools—the axe, gouge and auger as mentioned in the sagas. A good ship was oak throughout, ribs natural-grown timber, knees, planking and all timber prepared well in advance and kept in water to stay fresh and supple.

Boats were built by eye with few standard proportions. The 'joiner' formed the keel, bow, stern, ribs and beams; the 'filungar' prepared the planks, each calculated to fit into the ship's lines. His being the chief responsibility, his pay was twice that of the others.

The keel was laid on the stocks with the stem and stern riveted with heavy nails to each end and securely propped up in the correct position. Next, the planking was built up, clinker fashion, the first strake, the garboard, being riveted to the keel; then following strake by strake, riveted on, with each end nailed into a rabbet in the stems. The planks were built up before the ribs were put in, possibly a few moulds might be used to keep a symmetrical balance, but many builders scorned their use, except perhaps for one amidships.

When the strakes were up to the waterline, the ribs—frames —were put into place, spaced about 3 ft apart. The frames arched over the keel to which they were never attached, but connected only by the garboard strakes. This opening formed a 'limber hole' through which water taken inboard could freely pass from room to room and so facilitate baling. On each strake, and cut in one piece with them, were cleats. By making grooves of varying depth in the cleats each strake was made to fit exactly into its place. When all the ribs were in place and fastened to the planking, a transverse beam was placed over each rib from top to top and at each end a knee was fastened. The upright end, flush with the side of the ship, served as a hold for the planking above the waterline. Finally, the narrow strakes which continued in a rising curve to stem and stern were secured, and decorative pieces were fastened to the bow, the posts, the span and the 'tingl'. Inboard, the keelson and mast partners were secured, and a block of oak was nailed outside as a support for the rudder on the 'stjernbordi' or steering side, the origin of our word 'starboard'. Being now complete, the hull was tarred.

In Viking terminology the difference between a ship and a boat was one of size. The biggest to be called a boat was the 'twelve' with six pairs of oars; over that the craft was always called a ship. A longship had over 15 thwarts and her size was given by the number of thwarts or spaces between the ribs, equivalent to the number of pairs of oars; ie 30 thwarts or 'rooms' had 60 oars. The usual size had 20 to 25 thwarts, but the ships of kings and chieftains were larger.

The 'measure' of a ship depended upon how many 'rooms' it had, the rowlocks being between the frames. In the thirteenth century, when more peaceful times came, the measure was so many 'lasts', a loading capacity of about two tons, and a name commonly used in East Anglia as a herring measure until the introduction of the cran.

In the ships, the pine oars averaged about 18 ft, the length varying because the distance to the water was greater towards the bow and stern. The rowers had to have loose seats.

A replica of the Gokstad ship sailed across the Atlantic in 1893, making 10 to 11 knots at times under sail. In heavy seas the bottom rose and fell as much as $\frac{3}{4}$ in but not a drop of water came inboard; the hull remained tight as a bottle although the gunwale twisted up to 6 in out of line. The hull slipped through the water easily, leaving no wake until a speed of about four knots was reached. When it is remembered that this ship was 76 ft 6 in long, one appreciates just how superlative was the skill of those early Viking shipwrights.

When another replica of the Gokstad ship sailed or was rowed to Broadstairs in 1949, seats of the leather breeches worn by the rowers were no more after their strenuous efforts, and the boat had to lie out of sight of land until the Navy came to the rescue and the magnificent Norsemen were able to come ashore in all their glory.

The clench-built boat is typical in all countries where Viking influence introduced this method of construction, and it has prevailed down the centuries to modern times with only slight modifications.

CHAPTER TWO

THE SHETLAND ISLANDS

THE Shetlands, the northernmost fishing station in Britain, lie some 120 miles to the north of Scotland, as near to Bergen in Norway as to Aberdeen. They consist of about 100 small islands, many uninhabited. The 'mainland' is a low, narrow neck of land, about 70 miles from north to south. In places, only two to three miles separate the Atlantic from the North Sea, yet the herring caught off one coast differ considerably from those captured off the other.

The islands are almost devoid of trees. The lower slopes provided a poor living for the crofters whose chief occupation was fishing, the higher hills being bare, brown moorland frequently swept by fierce gales. The coastline is rocky, and in the northern part of the western side precipitous cliffs rise sheer out of the sea to heights of 1,000 ft in places. The erosion of countless centuries has fretted the coast into innumerable fjords, called 'voes', which afford some shelter for small craft but frequently prove wicked places in certain winds when great waves crash against the cliffs and spray flies across to the opposite coast.

The finest natural harbour, Lerwick, lying 187 miles from Aberdeen, is about half-a-mile wide and sheltered from the north and east by the Isle of Bressay. Here enormous fleets of drifters of every nationality once gathered for the herring fishing and the little grey town rang with the laughter and talk of a dozen tongues and more.

The summer days are long and have little darkness. Fog is prevalent, especially in June; but the cold winds then sweeping in from the Arctic wastes mean it is often warmer in winter, when southerly winds prevail.

Few coastlines take a more fearful hammering as huge seas with all the fetch of the Atlantic behind them, and lashed at times by winds of upwards of a 100 miles an hour, fling themselves against the cliffs standing in their path as the cyclonic storms race eastward. Gale succeeds gale as the depressions pass, accompanied by violent shifts of wind, awe-inspiring to see, terrible to experience in an open boat. Now and again a terrific tempest brings death and destruction in its train, to be spoken of in hushed voices for generations to come, as was the gale of 1881. Rocks weighing many tons are lifted from the seabed and hurled about like a giant's playthings. The howling gusts drown the strongest voice. To quote an old *Guide to Pilots*, 'the roar of the surge may be heard for 20 miles, the breakers rise to a height of 60 ft, and the broken sea on the North Shoal, which lies 12 miles northwest of Costa Head, is visible at Skail and Birsay'.

At Unst, a door in the lighthouse 195 ft above sea level has been broken open, while windows of the lighthouse at Dunnet Head, on the summit of a 300-ft cliff at the sw entrance to Pentland Firth, have been broken repeatedly by stones flung aloft by the waves.

Fair Isle lies halfway between Shetland and Orkney. Foula, 30 miles to the westward, has the highest cliffs in the British Isles, nearly 1,300 ft. The wildest cliff scenery on the mainland is in the parish of Northmavine, lying within the isthmus of Mavis Grind, so narrow that in places a stone can be thrown from the Atlantic into the North Sea and vice versa. In the south is Dunrossness—the ness of the dinning roost, with the majestic Sumburgh Head a prominent landmark.

The full fury of the ocean is unleashed when the tidal currents cross the path of the waves, or are in direct opposition. The Sumburgh Roost runs at seven knots at springs, four knots at neaps, westbound vessels having the advantage of the stream for seven and a half hours. During nor'easterly winds the roost is quiescent, but when the wind-driven waves roll in from any other quarter they meet the tidal currents either streaming shoreward on the flood or seaward on the ebb. This contending of the waters covers an area about three miles in width, a maelstrom of confused, tumbling seas as long as the roost is breaking and cresting heavily off the Head; once the strength of the tide is spent and it can no longer run down the seas, a heavy surf rolls in against the coast and rises to great heights on the cliffs. Northwards is the Skaw Roost, and between islands the tide runs fiercely. Boats usually 'cut the string' at slack tides, as crossing these tideways is called.

At opposite ends of the Pentland Firth, the Bore of Duncansby and the Merry Men of Mey are encountered. Even in the finest weather 'it is difficult to see what may be going on in the distance and the transition from smooth water to a broken sea is so sudden that no time is given for making arrangements' states the 1875 *Pilots' Guide*, which advises ships to batten down and secure hatches prior to entering the Firth.

Both these roosts are caused by the meeting of swells from the open ocean and opposing tidal streams, so that at the east end the Bore of Duncansby is to be feared with easterly swells and a flood tide; to the westward, the Merry Men of Mey with the ebb tides and a westerly swell.

The difference in the times of high water, according to whether it passes to the north or south of the islands, is responsible for the roosts, together with immense volumes of water. The flood is forced eastward from the Atlantic between Shetland and Orkney and Scotland into the North Sea and the ebb returns through the same narrow passages. At certain stages of the tide these waters are dotted with dangerous eddies 'with strange upward domings, sinister pits or depressions . . . even in calm weather boats are warned to avoid the eddies of Pentland Firth known as The Swilkie, and with an ebb tide and a northwest wind the heavy breaking seas of the Swilkie are a menace.'

Men who served in the Royal Navy in the two world wars will have vivid memories of the tremendous seas encountered at times in Pentland Firth, seas in which battleships and cruisers were swept from end to end, even losing bridges and upperworks and being forced to return to Scapa Flow. How much more terrifying were such waves seen from an open boat in the days of which I write.

Shetland was colonised in the ninth century by Norsemen fleeing from the tyranny of Harald Haarfagre, who pursued the fugitives and made Shetland and Orkney a Jarldom of Norway, the islands remaining under Norse or Danish rule for nearly 600 years. It is not surprising, therefore, that their boats have a marked affinity to those in Norway and Denmark.

In the 1460s a marriage was arranged between Princess Margaret of Denmark and James III of Scotland, who insisted on a dowry of 60,000 florins. But her father, the King, could barely raise a sixth of this immense sum and gave the islands as security for the balance. The pledge was never redeemed and the islands came under Scottish rule, exchanging reasonably good government for bad. The crofters were oppressed by the lairds, all fish caught had to be handed over for a miserable pittance, with no alternative employment except going to sea in a merchant ship. If a lad did so he was even forbidden to return, his parents were fined heavily and often evicted from their crofts. Poverty forced many a family to emigrate, and it was not until 1889 that the Crofters Commission secured the rights of those still remaining.

Owing to the scarcity of suitable timber all boats, as well as fishing gear and other commodities, were mostly obtained from Norway, and for the following details of purchases and prices in the first half of the eighteenth century, I am indebted to the late R. Stuart Bruce who allowed me to quote from documents in his possession.

An order was sent by Thomas Gifford of Busta, Chamberlain of the Shetland Isles, to Robert Barclay of Bergen on 30 April 1731. The currency is the Rix dollar, worth about 5s.

Twelve great lasts of salt cost Rd 720, about £180, 20 barrels of Ground lines and four of Tom lines—snoods—£123 10s, 8,000 ling and 30,000 haddock hooks £25. Six 'pises hemp linin for boats sails' £18. One 'long hundred' planks, a full

Page 35   (*above*) Shetland fourern, *c* 1895. Note high-peaked lugsail and long tiller; (*below*) scaffies leaving Wick. In centre, under sail is *Chevalier*, WK 865, mizzen lug not set; in foreground, a one-masted scaffie. Note wide transom of small boat in tow

Page 36 Crail harbour. Note lobster cages on quay, masts lowered on fifies in background, slates on oars in ML 478, timber heads up to gunwale and straight stems and sterns

inch thick and 16 ft long, cost £25, and half a hundred 'sawen in two' £12 10s for the boat builders, much being supplied already cut to shape.

Another request was for 'a Rop about 48 fadom long and 4 ench thick for a boat's cable', to cost £5. Orders for household goods included six firkins of soap £12 10s, hats, broad linen, starch, hair cloth, loaf sugar, barrels of flour, rye-meal, barley, biscuit, vinegar, raisins, currents, figs, almonds, pepper, prunes, white ginger, honey, nutmegs, mustard seed, cinnamon, cloves, blue powder, rice, thread and other items; many no doubt for the consumption of Gifford's family, as they were far out of the reach of his crofters. Liquid refreshment was not overlooked as 30 barrels and 30 ankers of gin cost £175, the second largest individual item, brandy £26 5s, claret £12 10s for a hogshead, an anker of Canary and another of 'Cherie' (? sherry) £11 15s.

The total bill amounted to 3,143.8 Rix dollars, say £785, and the goods were to be shipped in the *Margt Rot Scollay*.

On 16 June a further order was sent for three lasts of salt £45, forty fir planks, each 22 ft long and 2 in thick, £15, 100 deals 1 in thick and 16 ft long, £25, and 'as many wrack pip staves as the veshell can tak in wt barrel houps' £25.

Gifford wrote to Amsterdam on 8 March 1733, for '3 or 400 lbs of Iron Ketles'. These were long, shallow oval kettles for boiling fish in the fishing lodges, rude huts known as 'skios'. The kettle stood on three short legs and, when no longer good for use ashore, these legs were knocked out and the kettle was taken to sea to hold the peat fire used for cooking purposes.

Before an Act of Parliament in 1756 gave all British subjects a right to fish in the high seas, every Shetland boat claimed a particular part of the sea, determined by certain landmarks, and this area was considered as much the property of the fishermen as the lands they rented. These 'roads' were registered in the Sheriff Court books and extended to an undefined distance seawards. Any encroachment by another boat led to the calling of the offending parties by all manner of names and Mr Bruce

C

had a complaint before the Sheriff Court at Lerwick, dated 1744.

Some idea of purchasing power in the mid-eighteenth century can be gained from an account of 1757 which John Bruce, Steward of Symbister and an ancestor of R. Stuart Bruce, tendered to Captain Thurot of the French 60-gun ship *Marshal Belleisle* which came into Symbister Voe on 10 October in urgent need of food and clothing for the crew. Although the Frenchman wrote politely, he left no doubt as to what he would do if his request was refused. His letter read:

> Sir, I have occasion for some beeves, sheep, bread, meal and other trifles which I shall be obliged to you and your people to supply me with. If you do it friendly, I shall pay you the price you expect, but if you refuse, you can't take it ill that I furnish myself according to the Rules of Warr. . . .

He was promptly supplied with four good oxen at £5 each, 12 sheep at 6s each, 440 lb of good butter at 5d per lb, six barrels of potatoes at 10s a barrel, 216 pairs of coarse stockings at 8d a pair, 16 firkins of flour at 13s per firkin, a bag of bread 24s, 22 pairs of 'mittons' 14s 6d, and various sundries amounting in all to £70 5s 2d, plus a charge for pilotage of £10 10s.

In return, Stewart received two hogsheads of claret, value £5, and bills for the balance, but these were never met as Thurot was killed in action in 1760. In view of the risk, it is hardly likely that the goods were under-priced.

On 20 July 1733 an order was sent to Bergen by James Wallace: 'buy thirty four-oared yoals, but no six-oared boats . . . to be shipped in the sloop *Mary* of Yorry'.

In 1774 a six-oared boat—a sixern—complete with mast, sail and oars, cost about £6 and measured 18 ft on the keel, and 24 to 25 ft overall. The ordinary complement of lines was 120 'bughts', each 55 fathoms long, with hooks at intervals of four fathoms, or 14 hooks on each bught. The whole length mounted with about 1,600 hooks, was 6,600 fathoms. Each bught, or ground line, cost 1s 8d, or £10 for all the lines, making the total cost of a sixern, ready for sea, with a haddock line, around £18.

The four-oared boats—fourerns—fished with about 1,000 fathoms of line and, as a rule, the fish were sold by 'tale' at threepence each for those 28 in and over in length; if under, two were given for one and three for two, according to size. A dozen haddock fetched 1d or 4s to 5s a cwt, and herring and piltocks, 1s per score.

The Shetland fishermen were unsurpassed in the handling of open boats, thought little of pulling long distances, and frequently rowed to and from fishing grounds 20, 30 or 40 miles seaward. It can readily be understood what danger faced them out in those lonely northern seas. Fog descending or a gale springing up brought a risk that the islands might be missed and the boats carried out into the Atlantic if the men were fishing off the coast of Norway. Many of the old men had a wonderful sixth sense and could steer for the land in dense fog by following the 'moder-di', the current running towards the land and making slight undulations on the smooth surface of the sea. In a breeze, the shore-going waves could be discerned even better, although they might be setting in a contrary direction to the main run of the tide.

An aged fisherman told John Smith how, as a lad, he had gone on his first fishing trip and, when far from land, thick fog had rolled up and he had thought he would never see his mother and home again. A bearded old stalwart told him not to worry but to kneel down beside him in the bows and mark what he was told. Peering down over the stem, he pointed out the mystic current which could bring them to land and, sure enough, after some hours the sound of breakers against the cliffs was heard and soon harbour was made.

The 'haaf', or deep-sea fishing, generally began about 'Beltane' Day, 1 May, and continued until Lammas Day, 1 August, but these days were by no means arbitary. The sixerns fished from stations conveniently situated to the grounds, the men living in rough and tumble 'lodges'. The principal fish caught were cod and saith, taken on hand lines, and tusk and ling on long lines.

In the early part of the nineteenth century the ground lines were 50 fathoms long with 15 hooks to a line, equally spaced. The snoods—'toms'—were about 4 ft long and made from the same kind of line, but with one thread taken out so that the 'tom' would part before the line, should it get caught up. The hooks were baited with 'piltocks' cut into three pieces, though haddock was the best bait if it could be obtained. Small ling and halibut were also used; the latter, not a saleable fish until the 1860s, were laid slate fashion over the catch in the 'shot' room, forming a roof over which the seas washed when a big one was taken inboard. On reaching land, the halibut were flung down on the ground and used as 'linns' over which the men hauled their boats up into the 'nausts'. Small kegs, or sheepskin buoys with poles attached, marked the end of every forty lines.

The boats at Skerries, near Whalsay, each carried 40 lines of 50 fathoms which were baited at sea, joined together and sunk by two stones called 'cappies', each weighing about 16 lb. These marked the two ends of the ground line, and smaller stones—'fenders'—of about 4 lb weight were attached at the end of every four, or even two lines. When 40 lines were in use they extended for a distance of two and a quarter miles. After about an hour one man hauled—'hailed'—the lines, another took off the fish and rebaited the hooks, while the remaining four men rowed the boat.

The men received 4s per cwt for wet fish, although sometimes 5s 6d was given to the young men who had no land. A boat's catch in the season—1 June to 12 August—varied from 60 to 140 cwt. At Skerries, in the parish of Northmavine, it went from 60 to 200 cwt of ling, cod and tusk. The profits of a man at the ling fishing amounted to £3 to £5, in addition to certain privileges. Mr Irvine of North Yell allowed a free fisherman a boat, lines and hooks and sometimes meal for bread when at sea, the allowance being from 16 to 64 lb, depending upon the difficulty of obtaining men to complete the boat crew. This was over and above the payment for wet fish.

In Fetlar, a boat cost £15 fit for sea, the fishing gear was 120 lines at 3s, or £18, 'toms' and hooks £3 15s, four buoys 3s each, water cask 4s, compass 5s, sea knives 5s, creels and boat hooks 3s, a total expenditure of £38 4s before any fishing could commence. The men paid rent in fish-oil, butter and a kind of coarse cloth called 'wadmal'.

Despite the sea-keeping abilities of the sixern and the skill of the crews, fearful disasters occurred during the fierce summer gales, one of the worst being the storm of 16 July 1832 when 17 sixerns and 195 men were lost.

When cured ashore, the fish were first split from head to tail, well washed to remove all blood, and a piece of the backbone cut away. After draining, the cod were laid in vats and covered with salt, Spanish for preference, with heavy weights on top to keep the fish under the pickle. Next, they were taken out of the vat, drained, washed and bleached by exposure to sun and air, on the beach or rocks, the process being completed when the 'bloom' or whitish appearance came. Approximately 30 cod made 1 cwt of dried fish which found a ready sale in Spain and other Catholic countries. (Picture, p 18.)

In the 1870s each man in a sixern had 12 'strings', each with 10 hooks on 'toms' 18 in long and three fathoms apart, baited with any suitable small fish, chiefly young coalfish.

For an account of the last days of the haaf fishing I was fortunate enough to get into touch with John Smith, boatbuilder, who wrote me many long and interesting letters, finally sending all his notes, hoping they might be of interest to posterity—a wish which can now be fulfilled. This first-hand information is invaluable and I use his own words and spelling.

As a boy I first went to sea two months after my 14th birthday and in the merchant service wages was so little that it was hardly worth while, so there was nothing for it but fishing as at that time fishing was paying well in sail. . . . When sail went west I left fishing and went in wholesale for carpentery. . . . When a young man and boy while these old haaf men lived, nothing gave me more pleasure than to go in to the old haaf man's home and get him to tell stories of wild days and fine days at the fishing in these open boats. I have in my possession some notes which in itself might make a little book and good reading to those who care about what our forefathers did and how they lived ... if it sinks into the past it will be lost for ever. Their mode of fishing is told as it was told to me by these old men so is first hand ... they were the main stay of Shetland in the summer months, going as far as the top of the highest hill in Shetland like a cap on the water in a fine day when there was no wind six men rowed these boats too and from these grounds twice a week with upwards of two to three tons of fish on board out on Monday at back of twelve o'clock back on Wednesday afternoon have a sleep off early on Thursday morning and back on Saturday afternoon for the week-end till the month of August when their lines were put on shore and a net a man taken on board and off they went to fish herrings.

I thought I would outline in pencil a sixareen where I could name the different sections and rooms as called by the old haaf men, it is a pity but people of not so far back did not seem to understand what they were looseing. . . . The haaf fishing was an epoch which bred men peculiarly adapted to such an arduous calling. It would be a thousand pities if they and their trim crafts were allowed to sink into oblivion.

Sentiments which strongly appeal to me. I asked for the correct spelling of many terms, but it seemed that different parishes used variations of the old Norse names.

I don't think there is any correct way of spelling the word sixareen as in days gone by I heard a very old man call it a saxareen. . . . I think every place had its own way of saying the word as you will hear it called to this day especially in Whalsay they pronounce it sax-areen, some call it a sixern meaning six oared which I think is very much Norse. Some call it a sixtreen so I think it is very much amalagated, so I think the word sixern would be nearest to right.

Sixern is the term I use, but the old notes sometimes have sixareen. Now to turn to those fascinating stories.

Before proceeding to what was known as the 'deep water', the fishermen had to procure bait in an inshore fishing known locally as the eella. For this they used a smaller type of boat of from 9 to 11 ft of keel and somewhere from 15 to 17 ft overall length. The stems were curved with a long rake on each and a beam of from 5 to 5½ ft and a depth midships of 20 to 22 in. An old boat-builder said the rule was 2¼ in per foot of keel. Those boats were of narrower beam than the boats of the present day and not so deep . . . somewhat shallow in the waist these eella boats were fairly high in the ends and had a big shear which gave them a sea-fendy bow and when pulled head on to the wind could, like her bigger sister, the sixareen, live in a strong gale. They were good rowing boats, usually carrying four oars . . . all round boats and served as tenders to the sixareens, either at home or at the fishing stations. . . . Many of them came over from Norway and were improved on to suit the requirements of the haaf fishermen, being made deeper by the addition of a top strake . . . the boats from Norway were built with three boards a side and were very cheap, much cheaper than they could be built in Shetland. Many of them came over in board or unassembled and were put together by the local carpenters. I was told by a very old man that in his youth those boats cost about £2 10s ready for sea.

The eella boats were to procure bait for their cod and ling lines. The fish usually sought after was the piltock or young saith, when smaller they were called sillock. . . . There was an abundance of such fish round the Shetland coast in the haaf days. This fishing was done by rod and fly. The latter was at that time made from horse hair, the horse, of course, being the Shetland pony owned by the fisherman who were also by way of being pony breeders and did considerable business with buyers from the mainland of Scotland . . . when engaged working their crofts found the labour of the pony of valuable service.

The long hairs from the tails were taken and twisted by a homemade instrument called a spinney, made from a piece of cured peat. Having cut the peat round, the fishermen would then make a wooden pin with a notch in one end, the other being stuck in the centre of the spinney which was six to seven inches in diameter. The notch was to take the ends of the hairs he intended to spin for his fly. About four hairs were drawn from the bunch and knotted at the ends, the hairs were then divided equally and one end was inserted in the notch and the other held in the left hand while the spinney was struck with the right hand and spun round till the hairs were twisted sufficiently. The spinney was then caught between the knees and the twisted hairs taken from the notch and laid to the end held in the hand, both lengths were then twisted together. When enough of these lengths of hair had been twisted the fishermen set about making his fly for the piltock. Each length was knotted to the other, six or seven lengths being

the usual quantity. At the knots ends about two and a half inches
were left for the hooks which were dressed or 'busked' with pig
bristles or feathers. This process was also performed in making
lines for the haaf fishing, but more hairs would be used for greater
strength. The old fishermen always made sure they had a good
supply of flies for the summer. The men would start off for the
smaller isles or anywhere round the shore where they knew piltock were in abundance and fish with rod and fly till they had
sufficient bait for several settings of their haaf lines. Another bait
much favoured was eel bait and many old men unable to carry
on with the haaf would prosecute the eel fishing and sell their
catches to the deep-water men. This kind of fishing was known
locally as 'the eel tows' . . . nothing could beat the eel bait as it
was tough and did not come off the hooks easily.

Another form of small fishing in which the smaller boats were
often engaged in the off season of the haaf was pock fishing, the
term being purely local. I am of the opinion it means 'pocket'
fishing as the net arrangement resembled a pocket into which the
sillocks were caught. The net was suspended from an iron rim
about 18 ft in circumference and the net had very small meshes.
When this net was let down into the water some offal or anything
likely to attract the fish was thrown into it and hundreds of sillock
would thereby be trapped. There was a hinge arrangement on the
rim that opened the net when it rested on the bottom and it lay
flat under the hundreds of sillocks that gathered above it. It was
attached to a long pole or one of the boat's oars. . . . At one of the
joints of the iron rim was a small hoop that slid in on one of the
ends and by a rather ingenious arrangement prevented the pock
to close when being hauled up from the sea bottom. When the net
was gone alongside the boat two men caught the rim and one side
was rested on the gunwale, the sliding hoop was knocked off and
the mouth of the net closed, then lifted on board. . . .

Fish oil was valuable, the sillock livers were put into small
barrels or kegs, the oil being the only means of illumination
during the long winter nights, except when the big peat fire
was blazing on the open hearth. What was not required for
domestic use was sold to the local merchants, the price paid
being about half-a-crown per gallon. A very primitive kind of
lamp was used, locally known as a 'colley'.

The lairds or landowners held sway in the islands and often

owned the sixareens . . . and being owners of all means of produc-
tion they assumed that they owned the sea as well. To relate a
story told me by the grandson of the hero. In a certain part of
Shetland dwelt a laird whose orders were that no boats from
neighbouring voes were to be allowed to take fish from the voe
that was situated in his property. At another fishing village about
three miles from this laird's domain there lived a hard-cased haaf
skipper who feared no man. As the piltock and sillocks had deserted the vicinity of the latter he decided to go to the forbidden
voe as there was an abundance of fish to be had with little or no
trouble. He was warned by his crew that there was little use of
going owing to the prohibition of the laird. He passed off this
warning with a slight remark, gave the necessary order to make
ready and leave the rest to him. In due course they arrived at the
forbidden voe and made fast their boat at a small jetty . . . they
had well begun when the irate laird appeared, livid with indigna-
tion at such an imposition. He kicked up a terrible din in order to
frighten the fish away, besides threatening the fishermen with the
terror of the law, which he imagined existed for his especial
benefit. This went on for some time, then the skipper thought it
was time to interfere. Stepping up to the laird he picked him up
with as little difficulty as he might have picked up a bag of straw
and with one good heave pitched him into the jaws of the pock
net. Then he gave orders for the net to be lifted and it was the
sight of a lifetime to see a bedraggled and much humiliated laird
being pock fished out of the water gasping and gurgling. As soon
as he was landed on the jetty the skipper picked him up and gave
him a good shaking, telling him in unmistakable language that
the next time he came to interfere with honest men and their
fishing he would be thrown into the sea and left to drown like a
dog. There is no record that he ever tried to stop fishing in 'his'
voe again.

To return to the eella boats . . . many were built by local carpenters from imported wood or driftwood found along the shores,
which was usually cut by the men themselves who made pits at
the beaches and they would toil assiduously with the big double-
handed saw till the logs were reduced to a size suitable for boat
building. There was generally a spirit of co-operation among the
men about driftwood and they usually worked on a fifty-fifty
basis. The wood intended for boat building was thrown into the
sea again with rough weather when the seas would be pretty
heavy and if the wood turned over from one side to the other it

was condemned as unfit for boat building. This was in accordance with an old saying that a boat built of such wood would be unseaworthy, in which no man could trust his life.

As a body, fishermen are notoriously superstititious and Shetland haaf fishers could not be expected to lack their share of what many men even in these enlightened days are not guiltless of. There was a superstition regarding the knots in the wood. There were 'windy' knots, 'fishy' knots denoted vast catches, 'windy' knots stormy weather, 'misform' knots showed a boat was doomed to be cast away and it was believed that whatever kind of knots were in the wood of which a boat was built that particular brand of fortune or misfortune would attend the owner when fishing or using her in any way.

So rooted were these beliefs that when a consignment was ordered from Norway, one of the wise old men went across to select and discard any wood with knots of ill-omen. A boat built of 'she-wood' sailed faster by night than by day, 'she-oak', or chestnut, being lighter than white oak. Making a new great line was always started on an outgoing tide, but barking nets during an incoming one, and never on a Friday.

John Smith goes on:

The old time carpenter (or boat builder) used wooden pins in his boat building to fasten the outside to the 'bands' or frames. . . . The carpenter would look for the best piece of white fir he could find, split it up in lengths to get the grain as straight as possible. When he had got enough split he tied the lengths in bundles and hung these near the fire for some time to ensure that when he made his wooden pins they would be well seasoned. Those little boats were not built from any drawing or plan but just by the look of the builder's eye. When the keel and stems were made they were placed on a plank fastened to the floor of the building shed, a taut line was stretched from the aft stem to the centre of the fore stem. Two plumb bobs were hung from this line and indicated the centre of the keel. For laying down the boards, an improvised plumb level was used as the carpenters of those days did not possess spirit levels. The plumb level was T-shaped and made of suitable thickness of timber, usually three-quarters of an inch. A plumb bob was then hung from the centre of the upright part of the plumb level, the cross piece resting on the upper (or last) row of boarding as it was built up from the bottom of the boat. The plumb bob hanging perfectly perpendicular kept the carpenter's work level. As a rule the Shetland-built boats had six boards, but the method of building was to put in the floor frames after the first three boards had been fixed. The method of levelling was rather slow without the spirit level, but perfectly correct. . . . Like their big sisters, the sixareens, they were usually fitted with square sails, as often they had to include fairly long trips to the neighbouring isles.

I have been told that not infrequently the local carpenters would take condemned sixareens, remove all the good timber from them and build little boats of nine or ten feet, usually for the men who owned the sixareens. This would mean a lot of adze work as the timber had to be reduced to the required thinness. The old-fashioned Shetland boat was clenched with diamond-shaped roves. I am afraid one would not find a boat in use nowadays that is made with those old-fashioned roves, and personally I think they could not be improved upon. They came from the makers in lengths or sticks of from a foot to eighteen inches long and for small boats were about half an inch in breadth. Holes were punched on the stick the distance between the length of each rove and the carpenter broke the roves off as required.

In the southern part of Shetland (the Sandwick district) a different type of boat was used for the saith fishing inshore, usually carrying three men. The Ness 'Jol' or 'Yole' was a narrow, shallow type of boat, very suitable for pulling in the dangerous tideways near Sumburgh and Fitful Heads and was peculiar to the parish of Dunrossness. It was very lightly built with only five pairs of ribs, which, following Viking practice, were not bolted to the keel, but only connected to it by means of the garboard strakes. Length overall was 23 ft, keel 15 ft, beam 5 ft 8 in, depth inside 1 ft 8 in. (See plans, p 48.)

One might have thought fishermen had enough of rowing in their way of life, but they loved regattas and pitting their skill against men from rival parishes. John Smith has this to say:

The yawl-type boat is not built in the north isles of Shetland, though from time to time a few have been bought and used there with much acceptance. . . . The yawl is a very swift craft on the oars and largely used for saith fishing . . . at rowing races in the north isles the yawl was so successful in winning against the other

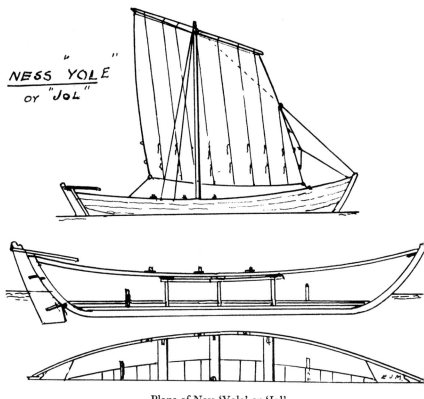

NESS YOLE or "JOL"

Plans of Ness 'Yole' or 'Jol'

Shetland boats that she was disqualified as not being in the same class of boats at all, being long and narrow she went through the water at much greater speed. . . . There are boats of almost the same type built in the Fair Isle.

How this statement brought back my own boyhood days. Many of the boats on the beach at Westgate-on-Sea were longer and narrower than those in neighbouring towns. One or two were exceptionally fast under oars or lugsail, but when they went to a regatta at Herne Bay, the locals refused to race against them, alleging they were built specially for racing, whereas in fact they were working boats, often spending a night at sea when sprat or herring fishing.

The Fair Isle 'skiffs' were very shallow, some being barely 18 in deep inside at the mast-taft, and they retained the square sail to the last, whereas John Smith writes of the yawls, 'I have never seen any of the boats with sails, I should think they are too narrow to do much sailing.'

The midship section of the skiff was flat with low gunwale and pronounced sheer. Keel length was around 16 ft, length overall 22 ft 9 in, inside depth amidships 1 ft 9 in, at stem head 2 ft 3 in, at stern 2 ft 1 in, extreme beam 6 ft. The mast was the same length as the keel with a 14 ft 6 in hoist of sail, the 11 ft 2 in yard being hooked nearly in the centre. The crew of three each pulled a pair of short oars, some 10 ft in length, the stroke being a very short, chopping one, and when cutting an eddy or string of tide the rate of striking sometimes reached 45 strokes a minute. These small boats were built for about 10s a foot length of keel, a twelve-footer, complete with lugsail, costing about £7.

In the latter days of the haaf fishing the 'fourereen' or 'fourern' pulling four oars was used. These did not go as far seaward as the sixerns, generally returning home every night.

Of the same build as the eella boats, the fourerns were used for the winter fishing for haddock, pay being four to five shillings per hundredweight by the local curers who sent them in ice to the south markets. In the summer they would be manned by three or four men, or perhaps three men and two boys, and would fish for cod and ling on the home ground, sometimes the mid-ground, about 14 to 20 miles from the shore. The men would row if the wind was not suitable for the square sail—an excellent sail for running, but not much good for tacking. These boats were built with oak frames and larch boards and were very sturdy craft. . . . As time went on the square sail was condemned for fishing purposes and a lug and jib took its place . . . the square sail needed most careful handling, especially during squally spells, or when the boat was being stayed. One man was selected to be 'sailsman' and he had to stay by the halyards all the time and the lives of the crew depended more on the sailsman than on the skipper or whoever was steering. This care had to be exercised much more when the sail was close-hauled as there was always the danger of it back-filling. When caught aback, as was often the case with squally and variable wind or passing land, the sailsman had to be quick to get the sail down, for had it stuck to the shrouds and mast the boat would be in danger of being upset. He was selected for his special abilities in alertness and watchfulness for squalls striking the water ahead . . . one might almost say one with eyes in the back of his head. His halyards were never properly fastened—he just took one or two turns round the 'clett' so that he had no hitches to undo when the sail had to be dowsed or lowered quickly and of course he held the end of the halyard all the time.

The mast was amidships; when the lugsail was introduced the mast was placed in the fore thwart, or as it is locally termed the 'taft' . . . it was found that the boat steered much steadier in a running sea.

As time went on, these boats were laid past and replaced with a few of the haaf sixareens, some being decked as haddock fishers. Eventually the haddock fishing for a time died and in some of the islands the younger men preferred the merchant service to the cold North Sea in open boats in the winter . . . many hard days and nights were put in at the fishing in the fourereens and getting bait for the lines. Many who had no labour at home to afford assistance would be obliged to spend long hours on the sandy beach dredging for cockles, often with his bare hands in the icy cold water. He had to depend on the ebb tide for cockle taking, and as he could not choose his own weather he was often invisible from the shore owing to a snow storm.

As can be well imagined, those fishermen in the small open boats in winter had many harrowing experiences. In December 1887 many boats left one afternoon for the fishing grounds. They had just well arrived there when all of a sudden a blinding snowstorm and a northerly gale swept down upon them. The best the fishermen could do was to keep their small crafts head to wind and heavy sea. In one boat there were only three men who couldn't manage to keep their boat's head to the wind, as one had to bail most of the time and the two couldn't manage owing to the force of the gale. Taking one of the ballast stones, they tied it to the end of the line used for letting down their fishing lines to the bottom. When working their lines they as a rule had three stones attached to this line, one at each end and one in the middle in case some of their lines fell on hard bottom. When this happened there was always the chance of the lines getting cut on the bottom by sharp stones. When this happened these stones were there to pull their boats to and the lines could be recovered.

In this case one stone was attached to the end of this line and thrown overboard and let down as a kind of sea anchor and this helped to keep the boat's head to the wind, with two men at the oars. Time and again the line was cut, but another stone was put on and let over and they were driven before the gale . . . at last through a kind of rift in the snow they sighted land . . . beaching their boat about five miles from their own homes.

The remaining boats, fully manned, could make a little headway, but were in constant danger of foundering owing to the heavy seas breaking over them and but for constant bailing this would undoubtedly have happened. Some other boats from the mainland of Shetland were able to run before the gale and got back safely. One boat was found at a neighbouring isle but there was no trace of her crew, it was thought that they had broken their oars and a heavy sea had struck the boat amidships, foundering her. Another boat reached the home island, but on coming to the beach turned completely over, just as the men had jumped clear, except one man who got entangled in some gear. When the others missed him they rushed back through the boiling surf and by their combined though desperate efforts righted the boat and found the man underneath. They got him safely ashore but he was suffering from a broken jaw. Another boat was brought home by one man through a rock-infested channel for a distance of between twelve and twenty miles, the man bailing with one hand and steering with the other; two of his crew were dead and the third unconscious from sheer exhaustion. Being driven before the gale and snow he knew not where, when suddenly the snow cleared and he found himself entering Lerwick harbour as if guided, as he fully believed, by a merciful Providence.

As a boy, I remember one terrible morning in the winter time when some boats had left for the haddock fishing ground. To begin with the morning was fine and tempted the men out and as the wind was light they left very early. They were well out when a cloud began to rise in the northern sky and in an incredible short time a gale and blinding snowstorm burst from that cloud. They lowered the sails and took to the oars as it was not possible to sail a boat owing to the thick snow obscuring all vision. They toiled steadily at the oars for several hours till a break in the snow showed them a headland where they lay in shelter until the storm abated.

On the morning of the 21st December, 1900, four boats were lost with twenty-two men, leaving fifteen widows and many other dependants. They had proceeded to the fishing grounds in the early morning and were working their lines when a nor'westerly gale swept over them with great violence. To the man on land it would have appeared that no open boat could live in such weather, but strange to say it was the smallest boats that survived. Those who came through said that had it not been for their action in crushing fish livers and putting them on the sea their boats would have been filled by the breaking sea. . . . When the gale broke they knew it was useless making for their home port as the wind was blowing off the land and they still had the square rig on their boats. They decided to run for the lee land and continued to put oil on troubled waters practically all the way while the sailsmen kept lowering and hoisting the sails to avoid being engulfed by oncoming seas. The land they made was the Outer Skerries where they got safe harbour. Two bigger boats, one a sixareen, did not return and two a little smaller shared the same fate, but the two smallest boats were saved.

I am afraid the art of handling a sail boat is a decaying one, the motor boat taking the place of sail. I am of the opinion, but doubtless being an admirer of sails I may be prejudiced, that a sail is much safer in a heavy running sea than an engine. But the sail must be handled properly, else any craft having a sail will become the coffin of her crew.

I remember being told by an old sail fisherman about a bad morning in winter time when a number of boats were at the fishing ground and fate seemed determined to bring the boat to grief that my friend was in. They had just finished hauling their lines when a heavy sea swept over the boat almost filling it. One of the crew jumped up and caught the yard of the sail and held it up and the boat moved ahead, two men caught a bucket and a line creel each and commenced bailing like fury. The oil from their fish was believed to have stopped the sea from breaking over them again, because had another sea swept over them the boat would surely have sunk as she had a good load of fish aboard. However, they got the water out and the mast and sail set and were homeward bound when another heavy sea swept past and ripped the rudder clean away. The sailsman instantly snatched an oar and pushed it towards the man in the stern who in a few seconds had it installed as an improvised rudder and steered the boat safely to land. . . . One skipper had a new boat first time out

Page 53 (*above*) A Burnmouth fisherman with 'scull' for lines, *c* 1882; (*below*) clench-built fifie *Iona* and salmon cobles at Burnmouth, *c* 1882. Note length of oars and bladders drying over scudding pole

Page 54 (*above*) *Gratitude*, a Whitby-registered coble has just come in on the beach, stern first. Note how the keel is lifted at the stern—the 'kilp', the single thole pins and the bold sheer at the bows; (*below*) Amble pilot coble. Note length of rudder and tiller

and she behaved so well that when asked what he thought of his boat his answer was that there might be as good a boat but certainly not a better.

Fishing in this way went on in open boats until the introduction of the motor, but in the course of time the square sail gave way to a high-peaked lugsail. The fourern fishermen generally 'sank the land' about 20 miles seaward, but the bigger sixerns often fished within sight of Norway. (Picture, p 35.)

I have been told by a very old man that as far back as they could remember, the sixareen, though the same form of hull, was shorter on the keel, ranging from 18 to 20 ft keel. As time went on they were enlarged and from 22 to 25 ft of keel was more common, but seldom, if ever, did they exceed 25 ft as they were difficult to handle at that size. The most popular size was 21 and 22 ft on the keel. As very few fishermen owned their own boats in those days, the bulk of the sixareens were owned by landowners who hired them out for the fishing season. Built by local carpenters, oak and larch were the principal kind of timber employed and they were trenailed to their frames by wooden pins. They were built as lightly as was consistent with what was required of them for the sake of easier handling and rowing, their frames being about 3 in moulded by 2½ in sided. In the very early haaf days they did not carry a large sail as they depended so much on the oars, the sail was only used if the wind was fair . . . later the sail was enlarged and a peak added which enabled the boat to lie closer to the wind when close-hauled. The idea of the old-time fishermen was that they reached the fishing ground quicker by rowing than tacking.

The mast was usually the length of the keel but about 130 years ago it was much shorter. The rigging was tarred hemp, two shrouds a side, the sail being perfectly square, the mast was right amidships. When tacking to windward, a great deal of work had to be done when the boat was put about, so it was little wonder that the men preferred rowing when they had a head wind. When putting the boat about the sail was lowered and taken forward round the mast and passed aft along the lee side and set again. There was not a great deal of ballast carried, but what the boat could comfortably do with as she was mostly rowed—stones from the beach which could be thrown overboard as the weight of fish taken increased. It was stowed just aft the mast and for'ard the mast.

D

The fishing lines were not kept in boxes or creels, but in a line 'meshie' woven like a net. It was spread out and the line coiled on it and wrapped closely up so that the owner could carry it on his shoulder when taking it to the boat. The six meshies, or 'packies' as they were called, were kept in the bow of the boat till the crew were ready to set (or shoot) their lines at the fishing ground, or reach the shore on their return. The divisions in a sixareen were mostly called 'rooms' and were as follows: the fore head, fore room, two ballast rooms, the owse (bailing) room, the 'shot' where the fish was kept, and lastly the cuddy where the skipper sat and steered. At the sides of the ballast rooms were two small fish lockers which acted as an overflow when the 'shot' could hold no more.

In the early haaf days Shetland fishermen were not allowed to leave the islands to seek fortune elsewhere if their families lived on the estates of the boat owners, whose word was law. If any young man left the islands, his parents would have been put out of their houses as all were obliged to stay and fish for the landlord. In many cases where young men did leave they could not return . . . so that kept the haaf fishing a going concern for much longer than it might have done. . . . It is thought that many of the fishermen who never returned to their homes were taken by the press-gang ships or by unscrupulous sailing masters who sold them into slavery. . . . Eventually times improved and there was a general exodus of young men from the islands who acquitted themselves well in the merchant service, both in sail and steam. Anyway the haaf fishing was a good background for those men who chose a more resounding career and many became captains of large ocean-going vessels.

The haaf sixareen was a cheap craft to build . . . something like £1 per foot of keel and that would include sail, rudder, six oars etc . . . a 28-footer cost from £20 to £22.

Like the warriors they were, the fishermen choosed their oars before doing battle with the mighty deep. When new oars were supplied their strength was tested across the knees of those sons of the deep who were only satisfied if their weapons neither snapped nor cracked. . . . An old haaf fisherman had been chided by a member of his crew that he wasn't pulling enough and there wasn't enough propulsion coming from his side of the boat. He replied that he was pulling all that the oar would stand and to prove his words he began to pull harder with the result that the oar snapped like a carrot. He lifted the broken piece of the oar

that was in his hand and pushed it towards the man who had
chided him and ordered him to pass another oar. This silenced
the dissatisfied one, who evidently realised that it would be better
to leave a man of that strength well alone.

An old fisherman told me he always liked going to the deep
water as they always got something worth going for. He had
hauled lines in the deep water when they had to do so in the fore
head, the weather being so bad, four men pulling at the oars for
all they were worth and two hauling the lines. To illustrate how
averse the haaf fishermen were to sailing when a lot of tacking had
to be done: the skipper's son had been in the merchant service in
sail and being home had gone to the fishing for a trip or two.
They had hauled the lines but as it was a head wind for home the
crew were getting ready to row as usual. . . . The son expressed the
wish to put the sail up and tack to windward. The father replied
that if there was any tacking he would refuse to steer, but gave the
son a free hand. The sail was hoisted, the son taking charge; the
old men grumbled that it would only be a waste of time, caring
apparently nothing about the easier journey. . . . But the son had
too much experience of square-rig ships to be annoyed . . . he
tacked the sixareen home, close-hauled, tack for tack. They were
home hours before the other sixareens that were rowing and this
was really the introduction of tacking with the square sail as it
became general after that.

All Shetland oars were square in the loom and could not be
feathered. Pieces of hard wood—the 'sklettes'—were nailed on
the loom on the part sliding on the 'rowth' and on the part
pressing against the 'kabe'—the flat wooden thole pin fitted
into the rowth. 'Humble baands'—grommets of cowhide,
whale sinew or rope—passed through a hole in the rowth, round
the loom of the oar and the kabe, thus giving sufficient play to
enable the oar to slide aft, preparatory to a fresh stroke being
taken. To make certain that I understood the peculiar shape of
the oar, John Smith sent me a beautiful model enclosed in a
thick block of wood, augered out, a treasured possession which
is before me as I write.

If the weather was not too rough, the men cleaned the fish on
the passage home. On coming ashore to the fishing station the
catch was weighed and checked by the factor and if time per-

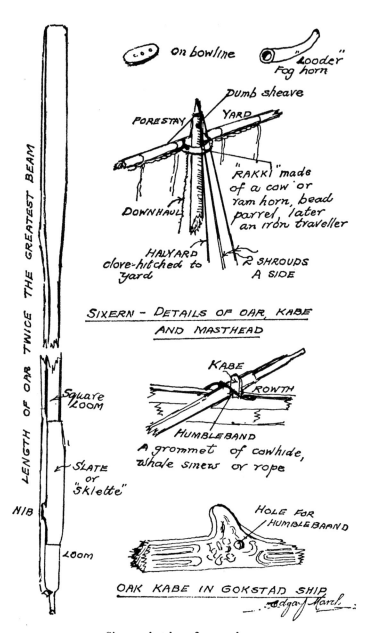

"on bowline"

"Looder" Fog horn

Dumb sheave

PORESTAY   YARD

"RAKKI" made of a cow or ram horn, bead parrel, later an iron traveller

DOWNHAUL

HALYARD clove-hitched to yard

2 SHROUDS A SIDE

SIXERN - DETAILS OF OAR, KABE AND MASTHEAD

KABE

ROWTH

HUMBLEBAND
A grommet of cowhide, whale sinew or rope

HOLE FOR HUMBLEBAND

OAK KABE IN GOKSTAD SHIP
Edgar March.

LENGTH OF OAR TWICE THE GREATEST BEAM

Square LOOM

SLATE or "Sklette"

NIB

LOOM

Sixern: sketches of oar and gear

mitted the men had a few hours rest. When the weather was very bad they would fraternise and while away the time by visiting the various lodges and spinning yarns. A weather glass was unknown—'these old chaps just had to use their own ideas of the weather that was coming or what was not coming. When they thought of putting to sea, all the skippers would gather together and go up to the nearest hilltop and either return with a good or bad report. No weather report in those days but their own.'

Before leaving his home, a man prepared provisions to last him a week: oat cakes, scones, sugar, butter, a handful of tea and a mug. These were often pooled and kept in a watertight box. Fresh water was carried in a keg. Two trips were usually made in a week, weather permitting. The men liked to reach the ground before sunset; setting the lines took from two to two and a half hours—the men baiting the hooks as the line was thrown overboard. They then rested for about an hour or took a morsel of food before hauling. If the catch was good they made for home. If not, they rebaited the hooks and tried again. The carrying capacity of a sixern was about three tons.

To illustrate how numerous were the fish round the coast in the haaf days. A sixareen was hauling her lines and taking home a lucky catch, the crew beginning to form the opinion that their boat would not take it. One of the men happened to spy a boat in the distance which appeared to be floating at random. This aroused curiosity and the day being fine the unhauled lines were buoyed and the men rowed over to the boat—a ship's boat entirely empty but undamaged. . . . The men filled her with the surplus fish which their own boat couldn't take . . . and that day landed two boats loads for one trip. . . . When the fishing was in full swing great competition went on as to what boat should be the best fished of the season . . . considered good if each man earned £15.

One man of each boat's crew was selected as cook, and he was obliged to cook on shore in the lodge as well as on board. The men's diet consisted of fish, and fish liver played a prominent part in their menu. A favourite dish was a preparation called 'liver muggies', which was the stomach of the ling washed clean and filled with liver, salt and pepper, and either boiled or roasted. Together with potatoes, this was a healthy and satisfying meal ... another was called 'fish and gree' and consisted of boiled ling, cod or saith, and cleaned livers boiled and the oil skimmed away, then poured over the fish and seasoned to taste. Superior people may twist their faces at these diets but let them sample the same and they will change their opinions.

The haaf fishermen usually kept two and two together when fishing. This would be for companionship and in case one got into difficulties. Either of these boats was what was called 'ranksman' to the other and indicated a friendliness among the men characteristic of those days ... akin to that of one big family. Being confined within the narrow limits of a small boat for days and weeks, sharing fortune and misfortune, tended to weld a bond of friendship very rarely found in these days of rush and commercialism.

Now to turn to the handling of the sixern:

It can be said with much truth that the sixareen herself had a soul. She seemed to respond to every mood of her crew and entered into their victories and defeats, for the prosecution of the haaf fishing was an eternal fight with wind and tide and fatal casualties were very frequent.

The early sixerns, when hard driven to wind'ard under sail, were prone to split one or more planks, but in the beginning of the nineteenth century two short ribs 'da bettin baands'—the beating ribs—were put low down in the bows between the 'staamering' and the fore 'baand'.

The helmsman—the skipper—was the most experienced man in the boat, the next the sailsman who sat by the halyards. It was essential that the boat did not run too fast, or slide on to the crest of a following sea, lest she be driven under or broach-to. The sailsman sat with the sole of his foot on the garboard strake and could tell by the trembling and vibration of the plank if the sixern was running too fast. He would ease away on the halyard and pull the sail down with the downhaul, hoisting again when the moment of danger had passed. Careful attention was vital, because in the trough of a sea the sail would be partly becalmed, whereas on the crest it might be almost overpowered by the force of the wind. When running, a sixern appeared to fly through the water.

The square sail had two rows of reef points in the head, one row in the foot, the reason being that with a wet sail the water soon ran down the cloths and off at the foot, whereas with a double reef in the foot any spray flying into the sail ran down and kept the reefed part always wet and heavy. Sails were usually white, rarely barked, and when making a new sail $1\frac{1}{2}$ yd of cotton were allowed for each foot of keel.

In the early sixerns a 'rakki' made of a cow or ram horn, or a bead parrel held the yard to the mast instead of the iron traveller used later. The bowline went through a hole in the stemhead just abaft the forestay hole and led aft, usually to the 'fore taft' where it was hauled taut and made fast. The sheet, when a lugsail was carried, was fastened to the clew, led down through a hole in the gunwale, back through a cringle on a short pendant and the end held in the hand of the steersman. When the boat was on a close board, the halyard was shifted further forward on the yard in order to peak the sail a little more, but off the wind the halyard was made fast about the centre of the spar.

It was an unforgivable sin to have a sheet either fast or foul, and all too often a man's first mistake was his last; he dared not even take a hard turn round his fist. A skipper often sat with the tiller against his weather cheek, steering with the pressure of his head against it, and both hands on the sheet.

Another story was told of a boat running with a bad day before a heavy sea and a strong wind. The sail was going up and down . . . as the sailsman thought fit. The sailsman for the skipper's liking held the sail a bit too long so the skipper said, 'Jemmie, did you not give her a bit too much that time?' Jemmie answered the skipper who was no mean chap at carrying sail, 'Well Tommie, mind your business and I will mind mine, it is her heels that must save her.' The skipper's rebuke must have touched the old sailsman who always had a man sitting by to give him a pull in bad weather. Of course the skipper and sailsman went hand in hand when running for their lives. The skipper always pointed the boat where the sea had broken ahead and if a big breaking sea appeared astern the helm was put down a little to allow the boat to come up a little so as to take the sea across the stern. They tried as far as possible to cheat the sea from coming in fore and aft the boat if there was fish in the after room or 'shot', as the fish room was called. The skipper would take the sea, if he could not avoid it, over the fish room, then most of the water would go out over the other side. When the sea had broke over the boat up went the sail at once and drew her out of it. . . . In bad weather, when hauling their lines sometimes it was impossible to get them in over the lineboard side—the side they usually hauled their lines over. They would then take their lines in over the bow, four men on the oars and two on the lines pulling as much as the line would stand, toiling for hours.

Before I bring my pen to a stop I might relate a few of the stories of the wild days and accidents told me when a boy by some of the old haaf men. I thought a night well spent sitting listening to the tales they had to tell. One said, 'We were running in from deep water with a heavy sea and a strong following wind . . . as was our wont we headed and gutted our fish and threw the livers overboard which helped to smooth the breaking sea. Our ranksman was running not very far ahead when all at once our lookout man said he did not see the boat running ahead, so a good lookout was kept (all the crew always sat facing forward). On the top of a sea the lookout man sang out that he saw the boat bottom up and some men on the bottom of it. Our skipper headed for the upturned boat and told the sailsman to take the sail down when coming down to them and told the crew to man the oars . . . down came the sail, out went the six oars and the boat was allowed to come close to the lee side—there was just five men to be seen. . . . I looked around for the other man and saw him floating with a ling under each arm. I at once got up and pushed my oar to arm's length towards the man who got hold of the oar and I pulled him right into our boat's side where willing hands pulled him on board. This man happened to be the skipper, meanwhile the other five had jumped from one boat to the other. We gave our boat sail again and arrived safe at the beach.'

Some may think it bad seamanship; but not so, chiefly the cause of a capsize was this. Some men had a habit of going to the haaf with very little ballast as it was rare that they did not get plenty of fish for ballast, but in this case they had not got very much. The boat being light when she came on the top of a big sea, the rudder lost control of the boat and over she went.

Another story . . . Skipper Williamson and his ranksman was running in a gale and heavy sea for the shore . . . the lookout said he did not see the boat ahead of them, some of the men thought it was some 'thicker' in the haze and they would see her if it cleared a bit. This did not satisfy the skipper who told another man to go on lookout also. They had not run very far when the boat was seen. The skipper said 'look if you see all the crew'. The men said they could see them all but what good was that they could do nothing in such a sea, the boat was bottom up. They could not row under oars if the sail was taken down. Williamson replied, 'Well, I am going to take those men home or go with them for I could not come home and tell their relatives that I had passed them on their boat. So just do as I tell you and we will get them with the help of Providence.'

By now they were coming close to the upturned boat and could see the crew signal them for help, so Williamson said, 'Stand by, look out for the sail, and down it when I say.' The upturned boat was floating broadside to the sea. The skipper stood on till nearing one end of the boat, then gave the order 'Lower away'. Down came the sail at once and down went the helm and the boat passed slowly along the lee side of the upturned boat and gave the men on the bottom time to jump for their lives . . . you could have put a biscuit between the boats . . . the sea seemed to go flat while the crew were picked off. No sooner were they on board, only a matter of seconds, when up went the helm, up went the sail and away went the boat, speeding on to safety and home to friends, wives and children.

Just one more story about a day that will always be remembered, as told me by one who in his early days was out in that awful storm of 1881, that took toll of many of our hardy fishermen and left many widows and fatherless children. This is in his own words. 'I being very young and had little experience, went to sea on that morning. The wind was light, but a heavy swell was rolling in from the north-west. The little wind we had was fair for the ground so we had to man the oars to help the boat along. Altho' very young I did not like the sea but said nothing as all the other men were experienced haafmen. However we toiled on till coming down to sunset when we got to the fishing ground. We started to set our lines the evening still being fine, no more wind than it had been all day long. We finished shooting our lines and

the time given for the lines to fish was while we boiled a kettel of
tea. You may ask where we brewed tea in an open boat. Well,
each boat had an old kettel which was known as an anchor kettel,
it had three toes it stood on which were knocked in to give the air
an access to the fire in the kettel to keep it alight. In this kettel
peats were put and a fire was made. A tea kettel was put on and
the tea brewed when all hands had a jug of tea and some bread
from the bread box kept in the fore room. Then pipes were lighted
each man had a smoke, then oilskins downed and the hauling of
the lines back began.

We had not hauled it very long when it started to lift a bank in
the north-west sky; still no wind but the sea rolled in as heavy as
ever. We keep at the oars and the hauling for a very short time
when the gale burst on us with hoorican force, takeing the sea in a
coldron. It took us all our time to keep the boat's head to the sea.
Some one remarked, 'Cut the lines and let's get away from here'
but the skipper said, 'No men, no line will be cut tonight, we keep
the boat's head to the sea with the lines and oars till the daylight
comes'. I may say at that time of the year the night is very short,
so we swung on and kept gathering in our lines as wind and sea
would allow . . . we had the smallest boat out that night, only
being nineteen feet on the keel, with an overall length of about
twenty-nine or thirty feet.

The daylight had well come when we got all our lines, which I
think was the means of us saving our lives for in such a wind and
sea and darkness no one could see where they were going. Many
boats had not shot any lines or a very few so they were at the
mercy of the elements, but the daylight had come up all over the
sea when we got the mast and sail on our boat, every reef tied in
and the balance reef also . . . the reef down the after leech of the
sail to equalise it on every side of the mast which made the boat
easier to steer. We run away, our little boat behaving well in such
awful weather . . . the skipper was a man of great nerve, we ran on
and on making fairly good weather of it till coming near land
when we passed a boat floating bottom up, but no life in it. No
man spoke, only I heard a faint murmur from the skipper, then
all went on as usual, every man attending to his job. We were
now coming into the 'strings', that is the tide rips running west
which was making the sea very steep. A large sea made on our
weather quarter when the skipper could not avoid it, he put down
the helm and the great sea broke over the stern, taking about five
hundredweight of fish overboard. I looked aft and all I could see

of our skipper was his head through the white foam. . . . Up went the sail and drew the boat ahead and what water came on board was soon put out by the pump and bailer. That was the only big sea we got on the whole run from the ground to the shore where we arrived all safe, but what we saw on our arrival can better be imagined than described. That day and night put an end or nearly so to the haaf-going days from the station I was fishing from, as fishing was only tried for two seasons after. The big decked boats and herring fishing then came in full swing, but a few sixareens tried fishing nearer home from a station at their own homes. Only a few of the older men, who very soon would be giving up fishing altogether.

One sixern, *Waterwitch*, came safely through that fearful storm which struck the haaf men on the ground on the edge of soundings 40 miles NW of Shetland, claiming 10 sixerns and 58 men. Fortunately John Smith took off her lines and he sent me his original drawings together with some of her history:

> The *Waterwitch* was a boat 21 ft on the keel, 9 ft beam 3 ft deep, 30 ft overall, skippered by Robert Henderson and fished from Gloup Voe, North Yell, her remains lye about two or three minutes walk from where I stay. Robert Henderson's father skippered her before young Robert took over. In her hay-day she carried many tons of fish from the deep water . . . and went line fishing from early June till the end of August when, like many of her class, her lines were put on shore and six nets, a net per man, was put on board and went herring fishing till the coming of the decked boats. . . . In 1881 all the boats were at the far haaf, she being among them when a heavy gale from the NW came down on them. The *Waterwitch* like more of the less fortunates started for the shore. In making the land she came to the west of the Holm of Gloup which lyes in the entrance to Gloup Voe. They had hit less than half a mile west of the proper entrance to Gloup. In Robert's own words he said, 'It was impossible to tack round the Holm against such a sea as was running so they decided to go through the wester mouth they had come to, altho there was a dangerious rock in the entrance. None of the crew had ever been through that entrance before but young Robert, so his father said, 'You'll take the helm and try and guide her through the narrow passage between the rock and the shore'. He took the helm and guided her through by the land marks. When she entered the narrow mouth he said a big sea came rolling in after them, she took the back of

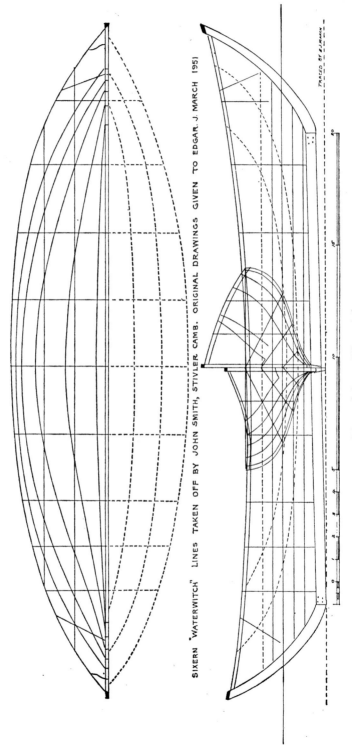

SIXERN "WATERWITCH" LINES TAKEN OFF BY JOHN SMITH, STIVLER, CAMB. ORIGINAL DRAWINGS GIVEN TO EDGAR. J. MARCH 1951

TRACED BY E.J.MARCH

Lines of sixern *Waterwitch*

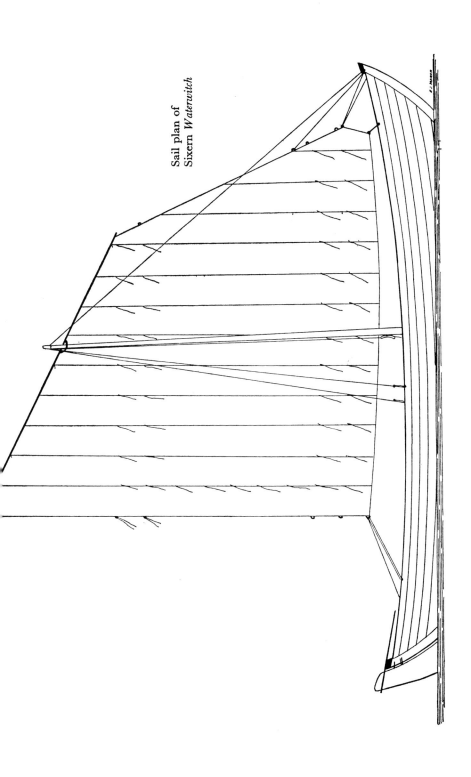

Sail plan of
Sixern *Waterwitch*

the sea with the help of the man at the 'tows' or halards, and
without takeing a drop of water, said Robert, she run right into
smooth water in the mouth of Gloup Voe.

I do not know how long she went to sea after the disaster of
1881 when six boats was lost from Gloup. In all 10 boats were lost
from different voes making sixty men altogether gone that day. . . .
I don't know how long she went ling fishing as they only went
from Gloup two years after 1881. . . . After her fishing days she
was bought by a merchant, taken on shore and in between every
band there was put a timber up past her bilge and floored over
all and turned into a lighter, or 'flitboat', bringing goods from the
steamer that ran among the islands. After serving as a lighter for
many years she eventually got past repair and was sold for £3 to a
crofter who had her drawn up and turned for a roof of a house to
house young sheep under in the wintertime, and there she lies
after a long and useful life falling to pieces. (letter 28.8.51)

Some years ago I tried my best to take off her lines . . . and I
believe is the only lines as far as I know in Shetland. . . . The
Waterwitch is sinking fast, her rusty nails not being able to keep
her in shape any longer and will soon be among the has-beens. . . .
Robert Henderson was a fine seaman and a grand helmsman who
had many a koorse day at da haaf.

These wonderful, graphic notes, written by a man who had
little schooling, record a way of life and traditions going back to
Viking days, now fast fading into the mists of the past. How
fortunate that John Smith recorded these facts and gave me the
privilege of having his notes. His letters were always so informa-
tive that I have altered nothing except a rare rephrasing to
ensure clarity, and some punctuation.

The arrival of the lines of Waterwitch fired my enthusiasm and
I asked for sizes of scantlings. His letters, sent by air mail,
emphasised the astonishing changes in his lifetime.

I give the construction in his own words:

The keel baton would be before making 8 in by 3½ in-sided . . .
finished off at the bottom with a taper down to the bottom about
2 in in the face. The centre of the keel was curved out till about
5 ft from the ends and the garbord riveted along the curve with
roved nails. The stems were made from 3-in oak and rabbited up
to the waterline where the boards were fitted in above that. The

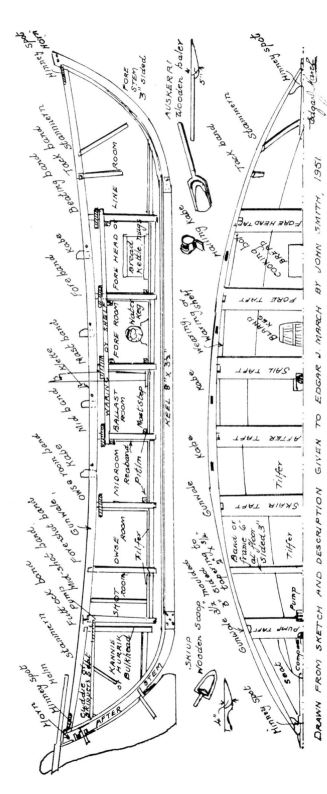

Sixern: sheer section and plan

DRAWN FROM SKETCH AND DESCRIPTION GIVEN TO EDGAR J. MARCH BY JOHN SMITH, 1951

Labels (upper drawing):

Himlee spot
Humlee spot
Tack Band Steamer
Beating Band
Fore Kabe
Mid Band
Mast Band
Fore Gunwale Kabe
Fore steamer band
Fore steamer band
Fish Hook Band
Pump steamer
Himlee spot
Horse Helm

LINE ROOM
FORE HEAD of SHELF
Bread Kettle mugs
FORE ROOM
Water Keg
WARLIN by SHELF
BALLAST ROOM
Reaband
Mast Step
MIDROOM
OWSE ROOM
SHOT ROOM
Tiller
Tiller
Kannie Murrik or Bulkhead
Skyddie Shott
STEM
AFTER

FORE STEM 3" sided
AUSKERRI Wooden Baler 5"
Tack board
Kabe
Hailing Kabe
Kabe
wearing of wearing shelf
Gunwale Kabe
'SKIUP' Wooden Scoop moulded to 3½" sideing 3¼" topering "B"
Gunwale
KEEL 8" x 3½"
Pitlin

Labels (lower drawing):

Himlee spot
Tack Steamer
Tigall Kane
Himlee spot
FORE HEAD TAFT
Cooking Boat
BREAD
FORE TAFT
Blarnd Keg
SAIL TAFT
AFTER TAFT
Tiller
SKAIR TAFT
Tiller
Band or frame 6" sided at foot sided 3"
Gunwale
PUMP TAFT
Pump
seat
compass
Himlee spot

boards were just beveled and nailed on the flat stem as it was thought that there was no need for a rabbit farther up. In different places there was different ways of doing it; some never rabbited farther than the end of the keels . . . The stem is beveled away to about slightly over an inch in the face and a raised bevel put on the inside to prevent the nail coming through, this shows above the rabbit. I hope you will understand.

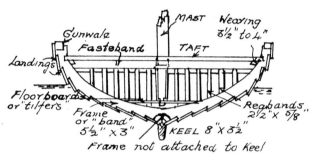

MIDSHIP SECTION - SIXERN

Sixern: midship section

The skin was from ¾ of an inch to 13/16 as near as can be guesed. Gunwalls were 3½ moulded to 3 in-sided and taper down to 2 in moulded at the ends to about ¾-sided at the ends. Next come the hinney spot that join the ends of the gunwalls at the ends. They were made of larch or oak about 1¾ to 2 in according to the size of the boat.

Next come the bands or frames, bands being used in Shetland, meaning binding together. These bands started at the keel with a depth of about 6 in tapering to the gunwall which was notched into the back of the band or timber at the top, with a through bolt at the head of the timber, with a moulded depth of 5½ or there by, sided by 3 in or a little over according to measurements. I do not think it was ever a standard size. All the timbers went right round from gunwall to gunwall, except one called a futtock where a bulks head was nailed on which divided the skipper's seat from the fish room or shot as the old haaf men called it.

The sixareen was divided into several rooms as it was called not by pertisions or bulk but by little strips of wood 2½ in by ⅝ ins or there by, spaced about 3 in. apart to prevent fish surging from end

Page 71   (*above*) Coble under repair by Mr Ritson, Snr, at Blyth, Nov 1939. Note shape of stern timbers and tumble-home on side frames

(*Right*) repairs completed; note 'inwyver' fastened to frames, and mast step

Page 72 (*Left*) Repairing nets at Scarborough

(*Below*) Salting the catch

to end of the boat. These little ribs were called reabands and the tops of which came up under the thart, taft, or seats. These rea-bands were nailed to what was called a fasteband, a piece of deal going from one side of the boat to the other and fastened to bands at the ends. This fasteband was made from $3 \times 2\frac{1}{2}$ and was held up by a piece of board the same thickness of the boat's skin. It went fore and aft along the boat's side from the fore band to the fore shot band. This would be $3\frac{1}{2}$ to 4 in moulded in between the timber heads. A bottom was put in; this was known as the scobe, it held knives used for cutting bait, or a man or two might have thrown in their pipe, it was handy little lockers for anything. The tharts or seats, which was known by these old men as tafts, were from $6\frac{1}{2}$ to 7 in down from inside of the gunwalls and was about $7\frac{1}{2}$ to 8 in $\times$ $1\frac{1}{4}$ to $1\frac{1}{2}$ in thick. The tharts was not kneed as in a ship's lifeboat, the fastebands acting to bind the boat together as the men could lift out any thart they wanted.

There were flooring made of the same thickness as the boat's skin to fit in between the bands when running or sailing in bad weather when water had to be put out. The flooring or tilfers as they were called, were lifted out of the owse room or bailing room for the dureation of the water throwing. There was also a hand pump fixed on the forad side of the futtock bulk head that could throw a lot of water. This pump went right down along the bulk head to the keel in the shot or fish room. The fish room was floored with very narrow flooring which kept any offal from getting to the pump and chocking it. In bad weather a big wooden shovel was used that could throw out an immense quantity of water, more than a big bucket with more ease.

There was one taft on every cross band and all was fitted to lift out. There was none of them kneed in except the aftermost which was a futtock and a bulk head across with the pump which was square on the fore side of the bulk head, the boat being held together by cross beams called fastebands on the main bands from the fore taft to the band on the fore side of the shot. How a taft is fitted on the timber head; a notch out of the middel of the end, the wearing nailed along the face of the main timbers to rest the end of the taft on which is called the lug of the taft.

For the oars I have made you a minature oar which will explain much better than any drawing I can make. The little nib on the top of the slate is if you left your oar to give a help with anything it would hang in the humbleband, which was the name of the piece of cow's hide used for the purpose. The length of the oar

E

was twice the beam of the boat. When rowing, the men pressed their feet against the pitlins.

The sixern had eight cabes, six from the fore taft and aft and one in the middle of the fore head for a couple of men to shift forad too, which made it much easier to turn the boat's head winward when working lines in a strong wind.

The mast was the length of her keel and the size of spar from 5 to 6 in at taft, the thickest part according to the size of the boat, tapering to upwards of 3 in at top. The yard would be 3 to $3\frac{1}{2}$ in diam, tapering slightly to the ends, most towards the lea earing.

As these letters had no comma or stop of any kind from beginning to end, I have added some punctuation. In reply to further questions, I received more information:

The length of a Shetland boat's oar was twice the beam at the broadest part and shortened as it came aft some few inches . . . you ask was steam used in bending the boards. Sometimes if the hausens were stiff they would be put in a box but the gunwalls were always steamed. The timbers were of grown oak when it could be got but was always notched on the 'lands', the overlap on the boards is as a rule one inch and the Shetland name for them was 'landings'. The landings when put together had a piece of flannel soacked in fir tar laid between them to insure tightness, the bands when put in were fixed in with treenails made of well-dried fir. After some years the boat was disbanded, the treenails were bored out and the bands lifted out and an overhaul made under them and if found fresh were retarred and put back. If not, the bad either in band or board was replaced. In a sixareen or fourern, from the waterline and up, there was a mould called in Norse 'a streak hovel'. This is something like the iron of a little plane which was about $3\frac{1}{2}$ in long, but it is not used now except on the top of the top strake, good for painting a bend along. The blade of the little plane would be $\frac{5}{8}$ of an inch broad; on the board it made two light groves and the centre was hollowed out. The mould showed on the outside and in from the waterline upwards.

In one of his letters to me, Mr R. Stuart Bruce wrote that he once asked an old man if he ever thought of building a fourern from lines and received the indignant reply 'Na, na, I hae her a' in mee heid. I dunno need lines.'

In 1937 Mr Bruce measured the Whalsay sixern *Haigrie-*

Heron—when she was hauled up for repair. No longer used for the fishing, she was employed as a 'flit-boat', taking goods ashore from the local steamer. Her dimensions were:

Height from ground to top of fore horn (stemhead)   5 ft 9 in
    „   „   „   „   „   „   afterhorn   5 ft
Length overall 30 ft, keel 21 ft, extreme breadth over gunwales 9 ft, depth inside at mast thwart 3 ft 2 in

The old boats were coated with Archangel tar; paint was not used until about 1870.

These authentic accounts from John Smith, a boat-builder for over 40 years, and R. Stuart Bruce, have preserved for all time the story of the haaf fishing and the boats which trace their ancestry back to Viking days.

In 1872 the number of boats registered at Lerwick numbered 1,613, 701 of which were propelled by oars only.

CHAPTER THREE

THE ORKNEY ISLANDS AND THE EAST COAST OF SCOTLAND

FISHING in the Orkneys was never on such an extensive scale as in the Shetlands, the crofters being mainly engaged in farming, with fishing a secondary occupation. Rapid tides and frequent bad weather presented serious difficulties and poverty precluded much expenditure on boats and gear.

In the northern isles, line fishing for cod, ling and saithe predominated, whereas in the south herring were the principal catch; the biggest takes being off the south-east coast between Stronsa and the Pentland Skerries, with Scapa Flow a good ground for both herring and certain kinds of line fish. In Kirkwall Bay, huge quantities of young coal fish or sillocks were caught by 'sweep-net', the local name for the sean or seine net, and were used for food and bait.

The French wars were largely responsible for the rise of the cod fishing, owing to vessels working on the Dogger Bank being constantly boarded by men from privateers. Westray and Eday soon became important curing stations with upwards of 100 boats engaged, but catches fluctuated wildly. During the 1850s and 60s they averaged upwards of 800 tons, falling sharply in the next decades before practically ceasing. At one time the crofters of Walls landed up to 40,000 cod in a season. 'Clip' fish were first salted, then dried, 'stock' dried without being salted; both found a ready sale in Spain.

The fishing began early in the year as the cod shoals came in from Arctic waters to spawn; ling, saithe or coalfish and tusk were also caught. Saithe, abundant round the Orkneys and the enemies of all fish, were known under various names, a few being blackjack, black pollack, coal whiting, cuddy, lythe, ley pollack and podleys. The fry, called sillocks, up to about a year old were 9 to 10 in long. They were then called cuth or cuddies, being at their best in June and July; and when grown they were known as lythes, at times running up to 25 lb weight.

The ling season began about the third week in May and lasted until the middle of August, the fish being caught on great lines, the hooks baited with herring or haddock, preferably live. In 1867 a monster, 4 ft 10 in long and weighing 46 lb, was caught. Tusk, or torsk, is a kind of cod, not a good-looking fish but suitable for curing and averaging about 7 lb in weight.

On New Year's Day, 1910, two Stromness fishermen caught a 13-stone halibut, 6 ft 6 in long, 3 ft 6 in wide, when it made a rush at a hooked cod. Getting this enormous fish inboard nearly capsized the boat and then it thrashed about so furiously that two planks were broken below the waterline.

Seldom exceeding 20 ft length of keel, the smaller boats cost about £23, carried a crew of three, and set some 1,400 fathoms of line. As in the Shetlands, the crofters used their boats extensively for communication between the numerous islands and rarely went great distances to sea, 20 miles being about the limit.

The herring fishery started about the end of the Napoleonic wars, David Drever of Huip being largely instrumental in encouraging the fishermen. With financial aid from merchants and others, a thriving industry eventually arose, employing upwards of 400 boats in less than 20 years, South Ronaldshay and Burray having 245 in 1838. After the early 1880s, the herring fishing began to fail, prices falling to as low as 12s a cran, or five a penny.

Before 1815 lobster fishing was probably the principal, if not the only one worked extensively. In the early days the lobsters were sent south in welled smacks, later by steamer to Aberdeen and thence by rail to Billingsgate, packed with seaweed in

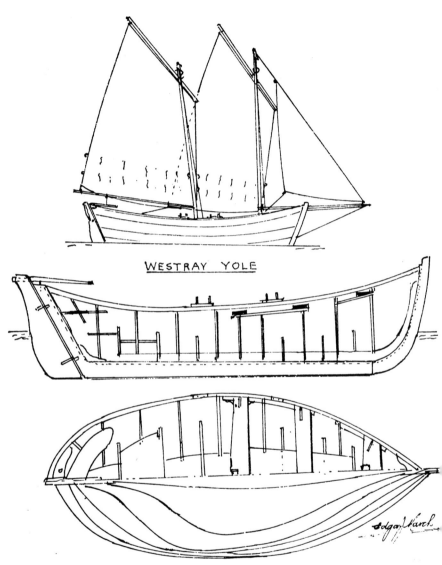

WESTRAY YOLE

Westray yole: sheer section and plan

boxes. Valued at twopence prior to 1808, then threepence, the lobster fishing brought in about £1,000 a year, rising to double that in the middle of the nineteenth century.

In the Northern Isles the smaller boats, owned by one fisherman or by partners, were known as the North Isles yawl, or Westray jol or yole. They were double-ended, clench built of Norwegian pine fastened with galvanised iron nails to oak frames, and of greater beam, fuller sterned and more robust construction than the Shetland boats. The rig was two standing lugs, one or both fitted with a boom, the clew of the mainsail was extended by a traveller, and a jib set on a reeving bowsprit, the outhaul leading under a cleat well down the stem before going inboard over the gunwale. Two pairs of oars were worked between double thole pins instead of against the single 'kabes' used farther north.

The South Isles yoles were similar in construction, but rigged with two spritsails instead of standing lugs; the snotter supporting the heel of the sprit was known as a 'shangie'. A fair average size in the 1880s was length overall 19 ft, keel 14 ft, beam 7 ft 9 in, depth amidships 2 ft 8 in, aft 3 ft 6 in. In 1872 the number of first-class boats was only 58, with 1,157 second class.

SCOTLAND

Open boats, light enough to be beached easily, were essential on a coast with few natural harbours other than the mouths of rivers—conditions common down the east coast of Scotland until well into the nineteenth century when government grants were given for the construction of harbours, following the terrible disasters of August 1848. Before intensive trawling developed, fish teemed in the waters close inshore and it was seldom necessary to go far out to sea—one to three hours to the grounds, fish and return after a few hours.

Along the shores of Caithness and in Moray Firth the boats were similar to the North Isles yole. In boats under 15 ft keel, the original rig was two spritsails and a jib; over 15 ft, two standing lugs. Both had great beam in proportion to length, and a very full stern. (Picture, p 35.)

Every creek had its fishing village, but space does not permit full descriptions of the numerous communities who earned a hard living from the sea, along lonely shores wide open to easterly gales. As times improved and larger decked boats were introduced, the men moved to more populated centres and houses became derelict. In others where harbours or even only breakwaters were built the fishing continued, the principal centre in Caithness being Wick. Lack of communications meant poor facilities for the disposal of catches, the finest cod being sold at 8d each, half the price obtained at ports with rail connections.

Wild, rocky coasts, in places high and precipitous, meant that the fishermen had to climb down by winding paths to get to their boats, which were often hung up by ropes to hooks in the cliff face, well out of reach of normal seas but liable to sustain serious damage in exceptional gales. At Lybster, a harbour was built about 1830 and hundreds of men fished from a tiny sheltered basin with a narrow entrance, a death-trap in bad weather, and accommodating only a few score boats.

Helmsdale was a great fishing station in Sutherland for over half a century when crofters, burned out of their homes to make way for sheep in the great clearances, had their homes there. Where the land was more fertile, the men often preferred to cultivate their farms or crofts, going to sea only during the herring season. Where the shores were flat and boats had to lie offshore, the women generally brought in the catches and gear, even carrying the men at times. Hefty wenches thought little of humping creels with a hundredweight of fish on their backs. The lads married young, and to build a 'but and ben' cost about £20, the profit of perhaps two years' fishing. A boat and gear cost around £20 at the end of the eighteenth century. Frequently large shoals of herring came close inshore, but prices realised were low, averaging 10s a cran.

Despite the hard life, many of the men were of magnificent

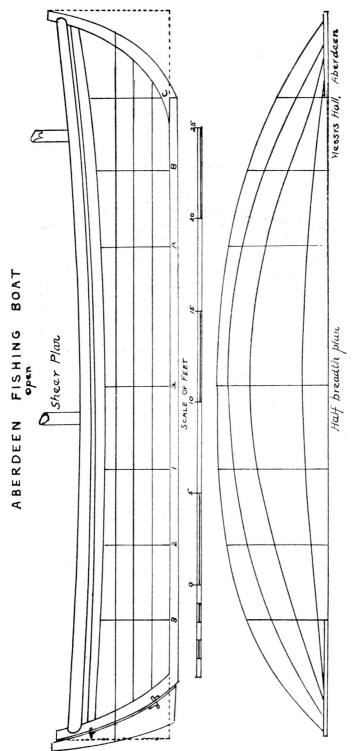

ABERDEEN FISHING BOAT

open

Sheer Plan

SCALE OF FEET

Half breadth plan

Messrs Hall, Aberdeen

Aberdeen scaffie: sheer and half-breadth plans

physique, the women comely if early photographs in my possession are anything to go by. Large families were the rule, the
boys going to sea after the briefest of schooling, the girls at an
early age learning to bait the lines, gather heather and furze for
fuel, and generally to make themselves useful.

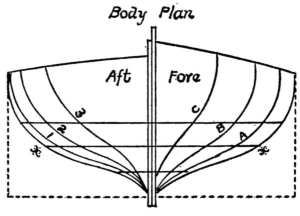

Body plan of Aberdeen scaffie

At Buckie, each man had a line with about 120 hooks, a
boy's line 60. In the small boats the lines had from 600 to 900
hooks, a fathom apart, a crew of four, who could then expect to
catch up to seven score of haddock each, receiving 10d a dozen.

In Aberdeenshire in the early nineteenth century, a 17-ft
boat could be built for £7, a 25-footer for £15, and the cost of a
set of lines was about 50s. Limpets were a favourite bait but in
places where mussels were scarce a 9-ton cargo could be obtained from Inverness for 50s a ton. Haddock were cured locally
and fetched about 9s a hundred, cod 4d to 6d each.

In 1848 a clench-built open boat 39 ft 9 in overall, keel 32 ft
6 in, beam 12 ft 6 in cost £65 ready for sea. Rigged with two
lugs, she had a capacity of 20 tons, carried two tons of ballast
and was manned by a crew of five.

Round the Firth of Forth the 'fifies' were used both for line
fishing and drifting for herring. The fishermen liked to shoot

their lines on a lee tide, either under sail or oar, and haul in on
the early weather tide, working the oars to keep the boat broadside to the tide, thus lifting her up to the lines, which might
otherwise break if there were many fish on the hooks. The
usual length of the lines was 500 fathoms for deep-sea work,
with 700 to 800 hooks on each line, and seven to eight lines to a
boat. The boats from Newhaven and Leith had to go some 60
miles down the Firth to the grounds and were generally away
from home for a couple of days, the boats having no shelter
whatever for the crew. (Picture, p 36.)

Deep-sea fishing began around the beginning of October in
about 30 fathoms of water, near the Mar Bank, drawing in from
17 to 22 fathoms off the Isle of May as Christmas approached.
Inshore, the smaller yawls were used up to June when the ten-
week herring season started. The design of the boats had
changed but little for centuries; the men refused to consider
decks, holding that they would impede the use of oars and make
the boat top-heavy with a big catch aboard, and fishing with
lines was easier. Fifies had straight, scaffies curved sterns.

In 1790 three haddock cost 7s 6d in Edinburgh market, in
1865 prime fish were 9d each, smoked Finnan haddock 6d a lb.
Cod at Newhaven in 1790 were 5s to 7s each, 75 years later 3d
to 4d each, line caught.

Kircaldy men fished for haddock with lines of 600 fathoms
each, using eight to a boat, but from St Monance and Cellar-
dyke the fishermen used 300-fathom lines, fishing for skate and
halibut on the Mar Bank in depths of 20 to 30 fathoms.

The open, double-ended boats averaged about 36 ft in
length, 13 ft 3 in beam, depth 4 ft 3 in, with a carrying capacity
of about 17 tons, clench-built and copper-fastened. Fitted with
two masts and lugsails, they cost £80 to £85 ready for sea.

The lines—'taes'—were laid clear for running in shallow
baskets called 'sculls'. Before intensive trawling ruined the inshore fishing grounds the men might expect to find from 700 to
750 fish on a line, with haddock weighing 5 to 6 lb. These fish
were split open and smoked over oak shavings, or better still,

peat fires which gave that special flavour to Finnan haddocks, so called because this cure was first introduced at Findon, a village between Stonehaven and Aberdeen. In 1865 the price of haddock for curing was 12s a hundred. Down to fairly recent times the taste was delicious; as different as chalk from cheese compared with much of the dyed, soaked-in-brine stuff sold today. (Picture, p 53.)

In the 1870s the long lines for haddock carried 800 to 1,000 hooks, each on a snood 14 in long and 2½ fathoms apart, the bait being mussels or lugworms. The fish being found not far from land, the smaller boats could be used. Fresh fish were taken to Edinburgh by fishwives who walked in with a heavy creel on their backs, sold it and then tramped home again, a very hard day's work. The Dunbar women walked 27 miles to market with creels weighing up to 200 lb, a journey done on occasion in the amazing time of five hours. From Ross and Burnmouth fish was sent by horse cart to Edinburgh every day.

The cod, or 'great lines', were similar to those used for haddock, but were worked at greater distances from land and had only six score hooks to a line, on snoods 5 ft long at intervals of 2½ fathoms. Small haddock or herring were used as bait, and cod, ling, skate and halibut, with choice turbot, were the usual catch. Cod are very fond of herring spawn and the fishermen used to drop a greased lead on arrival on a likely ground; if they found spawn on it, cod was sure to be plentiful.

The number of lines varied according to the size of the crew, each man having one, but all were fastened into a 'string' when shot. Fishing began about daybreak. First a cork buoy with flag and staff was dropped overboard, held by a heavy stone or small anchor; then the line was laid out as the boat was rowed or sailed along, the end being marked by another buoy. After a suitable interval the boat returned to the first buoy, the line was picked up, the fish taken off the hooks and dropped into the boat. This long-line season lasted from April to July when the herring fishing started.

Many Forth men went to the Wick cod fishing in February

and March, eight men making up the crew, each providing one line of 160 hooks, all tied together to make a length of up to four miles with some 1,280 hooks in all. The men's contract ended on 15 March, when the fish began to shoot their roe to be on the move directly after and so useless for sale.

The fish were cleaned, split, slightly salted and packed in barrels, each holding 20 to 24 cod, which sold at Aberdeen from 40s to 55s a barrel. Sounds and heads were used for manure; livers and roes were packed in separate barrels for southern markets. Cod and ling roes, weighing 2 to 5 lb each, were worth two to three pence apiece. Cod-liver oil was most abundant when the eggs were forming, least when ripening and, as well as being used as a sovereign remedy, the men worked it into leather, making the hides even more supple than did whale oil—these made up into excellent, soft sea-boots. It also served as a better kind of lamp oil.

Some idea of the extent of this line fishing from open boats can be realised from a study of the returns for 1878. At Anstruther 130,375 fish were taken, Fraserburgh 192,639, the Orkneys 326,663 and 1,554,008 in the Shetlands.

Halibut grew to enormous size. In February 1877 one landed at Wick was 7 ft 1 in long, and weighed 231 lb; it had been caught on a cod great line on which were hooked several smaller halibut and many large cod, from 16 to 36 lb in weight, and a number of skate. All were sent to English markets, there being no local sale for such huge fish. In May 1879 another landed at the same port measured 5 ft 10 in long, 2 ft 10 in wide, and 7 in thick through the centre, the roe alone weighing 18 lb.

These were by no means record fish, one sold in Edinburgh in April 1828 was 7 ft 6 in long, 3 ft wide and turned the scale at 320 lb, a monster to have on a hook. Another was stranded on the shore at Newbiggin in May 1873 after pursuing a shoal into shallow water; weight 294 lb, length 6 ft 9 in, width 3 ft 7 in.

Skate, another flat fish, also run to large size, but in the old days there was little sale for them in England, the best being exported to France and Holland where they were considered a delicacy, indifferent specimens being used for bait or manure.

Haddocks are a more handsome fish than cod although belonging to the same family, the upper jaw being larger than the lower, and the tail forked. The fish spawn in February and March, soon recovering, especially if they are able to feed on herring fry. The young are 6 in long by September and the fish best for table from October to January, a medium-sized one being about 18 in long. In winter, the shoals go into deep water, choosing ground covered with weed. In February 1878, a Banff boat landed a haddock at Wick, 29 in long, 17 in girth, weight 10¾ lb.

To return to the fishing stations south of the Firth of Forth. Dunbar, once one of the most prosperous, rapidly declined, legend saying the reason was that the fishing was frequently carried out on Sundays. As far back as 1830 open boats from this area sailed to Caithness for the summer fishing.

Along the coast of Berwick were many villages at the mouth of burns, Eyemouth having a history dating back for centuries. It is known that in 1298 the monks of Coldingham obtained the right to fish in neighbouring waters. Catches of white fish were sold in the countryside by hawkers known as 'cadgers', but prosperity really came with the opening of the railway in 1846, when herring curing yards were established.

Disaster struck this area on Friday, 14 October 1881, when 45 boats, manned by 279 men and boys, put to sea in ideal conditions and shot their lines about eight miles seaward. At midday ominous clouds began to gather, the wind struck with hurricane force and only 26 boats succeeded in reaching shelter, many having lost men overboard. Eyemouth mourned 129, Burnmouth 23 and other villages made up the appalling total of 189 drowned within sight of home.

Ross and Burnmouth crouch on narrow strands at the foot of precipitous cliffs, the houses lashed by the seas in easterly gales, but despite the hardships the population was healthy and long lived. The Rev G. Knight records a boat crew of four having a combined age of 301 years.

All these villages lie exposed to the full force of onshore winds, although the dangerous rocky approaches afforded some protection before the building of small harbours, but heavy seas often damaged the breakwaters, necessitating expensive repairs.

Mussels were the favourite bait, but supplies eventually had to be obtained from Ireland, coming by steamer to Glasgow, then by rail to Eyemouth, at a cost of £2 12s a ton, rail freight amounting to 22s 6d. The quantities required were enormous, in February 1879 boats from Burnmouth, Coldingham and Eyemouth used 61 tons in one week; cost £160, fish landed 25,260 stone of haddock, with a quantity of whiting and cod, average price 1s 8d a stone, the total earnings being around £2,500.

The boats had a keel length of 25 to 30 ft and cost, complete with herring nets, about £80. The old men who caught lobsters or netted salmon used 22-ft flat-bottomed 'cobles' with transom sterns, selling to dealers in Berwick. Ice was first used for packing in 1788 (Picture, p 53.)

Early in the 1870s the open boats at Burnmouth earned from £60 to £160 herring fishing, whereas at Coldingham, where decked boats were in use, the yields were from £100 to £550 a boat. Such economic factors could not be ignored and by the next decade decked fifies were becoming common.

George Cowan of Eyemouth stated in 1883 that some of their boats landed every day 10 to 15 cwt of fish caught on lines.

The men wore hand-knitted guernseys, heavy trousers tucked into leather seaboots, and blue bonnets with a tassel on top, but scores of photographs in my collection show an amazing variety of headgear—cheese-cutter caps of extraordinary shapes, seal-skin caps, tall conical hats with fairly wide brims, to name a few. At one time very tall silk hats tilted back—a 'rakie step'— were de rigueur for wear ashore. Although the majority of the men were strict Sabbatarians whisky drinking was common, especially if 'rapin' the nets'. Then the fiery spirit was sprinkled on the meshes—no doubt only a token offering—before the men did their drinking for luck.

Recently I had some delightful letters from John Hall who had read and enjoyed my book *Sailing Drifters*. In one he wrties:

> A native of Berwick-on-Tweed, I still have memories of the past and like to dwell upon the period 70 years ago when as a boy I spent the happiest years of my life amidst the scenes you describe. . . . Only three weeks ago I called upon one of the last of the old brigade, aged 84, who had experience of herring fishing at many stations and who also worked at the line fishing until he retired not long ago. He looked fit and well in his old house, with the old, clean traditional blue jersey and lovely white hair. He talked of the days when the family took a major part in the necessary operation of baiting lines which all took place in the living room, mussels in one corner, lines and hooks in another. It was all part of the day's work and it was all taken as a matter of course. The men were usually up at daybreak making a critical survey of the sea, if it was doubtful regarding safety if one said 'we will go' all the rest followed in the open boats known as cobles, each manned by four men. Many times the lifeboat had to stand by on the homeward journey to see that they got safely back. . . . I remember a boat named *Iona* sailing out with the Berwick fleet . . . definitely clinker built. . . .
>
> With reference to the East Coast disaster in 1881, my grandfather was a part-time fisherman but was not at sea on that day, both he and my parents have told me about it. After the storm my grandfather went to the sea front and saw a boat called the *Wave* bottom up. It was afterwards put into service and I had the pleasure of seeing her put to sea on many occasions. It is local knowledge that on that day an Eyemouth boat called *Aerial Gazelle* put to sea with a condemned sail. When the storm broke she headed out to sea, was able to ride it out and her appearance caused great excitement ashore when she headed for port, but it only raised false hopes as she was the only one to come back after the storm had abated.

Mr Hall sent me an old album he picked up for a penny on a second-hand bookstall about forty years ago, and what a treasure house it is, especially as my attention was called to various items.

Page 89 (*above*) Mules in Scarborough harbour. Note the big herring 'plosher' in the second tier; (*below*) Whitby harbour. Note difference in shape of sterns of cobles and the big mule in the centre

Page 90 Hauling up cobles at Runswick. Note oars in foreground with 'washed lashed to cleg', crab pots and baskets

At weekends during the season St Ives boats berthed side by side all along the beach shown and on the foreshore where the salmon fishing coble is lying, so you can see what a pleasure it was to us youngsters to have such a congenial playground.

Of another view:

In the near foreground is the grassy slope very near to where I was born within sight of the river and sea. A kippering yard was within 20 yards of our house but no one seemed to care about the clouds of smoke or smell of fish, no wonder when we could go into the yard and buy four freshly cured kippers at the price of one penny and the best of fresh herring at three a penny. During the season we could sit on the grassy slopes and watch the boats coming in and speculate according to their depth in the water as to what size their catch might be. As the shepherd knows all his sheep apparently alike, so did we pick up some distinctive feature when the boats were some distance away and were able to distinguish them before arrival. . . . In these days of expensive swimming baths and hot water treatment it makes me think of the time when all the local lads spent much of their time in the water as shown and many became expert divers and strong siwmmers. As most of us had only trousers, shirts and jerseys during the school holidays it took only a minute to undress, a frequent occurence during the holidays. I would not have exchanged the thrills of the water front for any other form of amusement . . . sad to say that on my last visit to Berwick I did not see a youngster having a bathe.

A delightful photo card was of

semi-retired fishermen of sixty years ago having a friendly chat. I have yet to meet a more contented group of men who can equal them. These were men who never had luxuries of any kind. . . . I left school at the age of fourteen and started work at 3s per week as an apprentice joiner and continued in that occupation all my working life. At the age of twenty-two work was bad to get and no welfare state so I was compelled to leave all the scenes I loved and go inland where I felt like a fish out of water. I well remember leaving Berwick during the summer of 1910. It was a good year for the fishing, as I looked over the river at high tide it was full of herring boats coming in under sail. . . . I was sad at heart to be leaving all this, my natural environment, to go to the drab interior of a mining village, but it was either that or be unem-

F

ployed and I made up my mind to stick it out . . . at weekends I
longed for the sea breezes, the cry of the seabirds with their free-
dom and pictured the Sunday morning scene in the Tweed dock.
The summer mornings were full of sunshine then, scores of fishing
boats lying as if they as well as their crews were enjoying the week-
end leisure, their brown sails stowed and galley chimneys smoking
and the sound of the church bells ringing across the river, all was
at peace. . . . Before leaving Berwick it was the custom to walk
around the quayside on a Sunday morning and take stock of all
the craft moored there, and up to this day I always remember the
names of the Scottish boats whose crews were made up of sturdy,
quiet, independent men and never once can I remember any
harsh or undesirable conduct among them. No wonder that the
names of the boats typified the class of men. I often wondered
who chose the names such as *Integrity, Concord, Fidelity, Dauntless,
Kindly Light, Familys Pride, Good Tidings, Consolation.* How different
from the present affluent age.

Every page of this 21-page letter was beautifully written and
over the years I have received scores of similar letters in appre-
ciation of my efforts to preserve the memory of days now gone
for ever—a gratifying reward indeed.

The extent of inshore fishing and its value to the economic
life of the East Coast of Scotland can be realised from the
following returns:

Year	Boats	Men employed
1849	4,010	15,767
1881	6,851	15,242

THE NORTH-EAST COAST OF ENGLAND: NORTHUMBERLAND, DURHAM AND YORKSHIRE

SOUTH of the Tweed along the Northumberland coast to the vicinity of the Farne Islands, the sharp-sterned open boat—the 'keel boat'—predominated, a fine, powerful craft setting a single lofty lugsail with seven lines of reef points; occasionally a smaller mainmast and lugsail were carried. These boats were used principally in the herring fishery, but as the fish here were small and not suitable for curing, the catch was sold fresh in neighbouring towns and villages. The rocky coast was famed for lobsters and crabs taken in pots, work suitable for the old men using small cobles.

The great enemy of the line fishermen was the 'hag', or 'rapper eel', which attacked any hooked fish. Entering through the gills or mouth, they devoured the flesh leaving only the skin and bones. Abundant in summer they ran up to 10 to 12 in in length and were so rapacious that at times large halibut were completely eaten to a skeleton.

The typical boat was the coble, used for fishing, by pilots, salvagers and for pleasure, designed for launching off open beaches against heavy seas, capable of going to sea for long distances and, in the hands of men accustomed to their handling from boyhood, able to live in a gale.

It is reasonable to suppose that the coble owes its design to Viking influence, the broad, flat keel aft being similar to that in the Nydam boat. The proud stem and fine entry were no doubt due to later developments. The brightly coloured planks may go back to the days of King Harold, similar strakes—green, blue,

93

white, red and yellow—being depicted in the Bayeux Tapestry.

The name itself is of great antiquity. In 1480 the Brethren of Dunfermline had a 200-year grant confirmed to employ 'two cobils' and two nets at the fishery of the Aldstelle. A letter written during the reign of Elizabeth gives an extremely accurate account of the handling of a coble. It appeared in the 1838 Report.

> Truly yt may be sayd of these poor men, that they are lavish of theyr lives who will hazard twenty or forty myles into the seas in a small troughe so thinne that a glimse of the sunne may bee seene through yt, yet at eleven or twelve of the clocke in the morninge, when they come from the sea, they sell theire whole boaty's lading for 4s, or if they doe gette a crown they suppose to have chaffered fayre. Three commonly come in one boate, each of them having twoe oares, which they governe by drawinge one hande over the other. The boate ytself is built of wainscotte, for shape excels all modeles for shippinge, two men will easily carrye yt on lande betweene them, yet are they so secure in them at sea that some in a storme have lyved aboarde three dayes. Their greateste danger is nearest home, when the waves breake dangerouslye, but they, acquainted with these seas, espyinge a broken wave reddy to overtake them, suddenly oppose the prowe or sharpe ends of theyre boate unto yt, and mounting to the top, descende downe as it were unto a valley, hoveringe untill they espye a whole wave come rowlinge, which they observe commonly to be an odde one: whereupon mountinge with their cobble as it were a great furious horse, they rowe with might and mayne, and together with that wave drive themselves on lande.

Mention is made of a 'five-man coble' considerably larger and no doubt the original of the modern (1838) fishing boat called a 'five-man boat'. Describing the coast near Redcar:

> It was my fortune to see the cominge in of a five-man coble which in one night had taken above twenty-one score of greate fishe, of a yearde or an ell in length. Happie were that country yf a generall fishinge were entertained by building vessels and store of fish boates.

The 1838 Report states that Holy Island, $2\frac{1}{2}$ miles by $1\frac{1}{2}$, had a small village to the north of the ruins; population in 1831 was

836, with two-thirds of the fishermen licensed by Trinity House at Newcastle as pilots. About 60 cobles fished for cod, ling and haddock, the fish being mostly sent to London in smacks employed by fishmongers or salesmen who annually contracted to pay so much per score for all fish sent during the season; lobsters at 12s a score from December to April.

Cobles are generally employed on the coast from the Tweed to the Humber, sharp and wedge-shaped at bow, flat-bottomed towards the stern. One mast, stepped close forward, lug sail. Excellent sea boats, for their size carry a large sail, enabled to do so by length of the rudder which extends about 3 ft perpendicularly below line of boat's bottom. The usual length of a Holy Island coble is from 25 ft to 27 ft overall.

It was in such a boat that Grace Darling and her father rowed to the wreck of the steamer *Forfarshire*, lying about a mile from the lighthouse at Farne Island, and rescued nine lives.

The herring boats were of larger size, 30 to 36 ft long, about 11 ft broad and 4 ft 6 in to 5 ft deep, rigged with two lugsails, no deck and a sharp stern. An old engraving shows some making for the shore, their square-headed lugs set to run before the wind.

The herring fishing began off Holy Island about 20 July and terminated around the first week in September:

... many caught in the Fare-way, between Farn Islands and mainland, but the principal fishery is a little to the southward of the Staples, a cluster of small islands lying two to three miles to eastward of the Farns. Most are taken to Berwick to be cured and thence exported to London, Hull and Newcastle. The harbour is a small bay on south side of the island, between the castle and the ruins of the monastery. On the bar, about one mile distant from the town, is about 9 ft at low water springs. The flood at spring tides sets with a strong current in the channel between Is. and mainland ... no lighthouse, but a beacon on the Heugh, a hill between town and harbour, on which, in bad weather when pilots cannot get off, a flag is hoisted during time of tide that ships may safely enter.

The Staples and Farn Islands, with rocks and shoals between

them and Holy Is., render inshore navigation of coast of Northumberland from N. Sunderland point to mouth of Tweed very
intricate and hazardous, various settings of rapid tide run in
different sounds between the islands.

At Cullercoats a 'dand', or buoy, marked the place where
nets or lines were cast. It was made of an inflated bag of tanned
skin through which a light pole passed, with the ends of the
openings tightly tied with cord. The lower end had a lead
weight with a loop or ring to which the rope was bent, and a
piece of coloured bunting or cloth at the upper end.

> The wives and daughters search for bait, sand-worms, in
> muddy sand at the mouth of the Coble-dean, at head of N.
> Shields, gathering mussels on the Scalp, near Clifford's Fort, or
> limpets and dog-crabs among rocks near Tynemouth. They assist
> in baiting hooks . . . carry caught fish to N. Shields in large wicker
> baskets called 'creels' and sit in the market to sell them. When
> fish are scarce they often carry a load on their shoulders weighing
> between 3 and 4 stone, to Newcastle, ten miles away for a better
> market. Codlings, cod, ling, holibut (usually called turbot in
> Northumberland), haddock, and whiting. Herring in the season
> and colesay. The most valuable is the 'bret' or turbot proper of
> London market, mostly sold to bret smacks for conveyance to
> London.

The late Mr R. M. Hewett told me that the captains of their
welled cod smacks always had with them a 'turbot bag', a large
bag of silver entrusted to them for the purchase of choice fish
from the inshore fishermen.

When fishing for whiting, the men used sprats cut in small
pieces for bait:

> Three men with half-a-dozen lines, take 12 to 15 doz. in three
> hours on a summer evening inshore, six to eight miles out . . . best
> bait small dog crab—a 'pillan'—shell easily stripped off, if not
> obtainable ordinary dog crab used. Codling to east of Tynemouth,
> but haddock and cod seldom caught within seven miles of shore.

In 1831 Cullercoats had 89 houses, 145 families or 542 persons. Ten cobles were fishing in 1815, half a century later 38.
At Newbiggin 8 and 27.

When fishing for herring in these small cobles the mast was lowered when the fleet of nets were in the water; no lantern was hoisted, but a coal or charcoal fire was made in a small brazier standing in a flat iron pan in the bottom, serving a double purpose by giving out some heat and acting as a drift light. In the 1860s the line fishing began to suffer from the incursions of trawlers as well as the scarcity of mussels for bait.

Northumberland cobles differed from those farther south, having a long, straight forefoot with some 'cutaway' to make for easy beaching, and the keel lifted a few inches at the stern— the 'kilp'—to prevent broken water coming aboard when going through the breakers, stern first, to the landing wheels. (Picture, p 54.) To quote an old boatbuilder, 'pier cobels using moorings in harbour, at Hartlepool and Shields, sometimes have a deeper forefoot to give a good grip of the water forward when going to windward'. Minor differences were a circular instead of a square hole in the thwart to take the heel of the mast, which was held in position by an iron strap. A hardwood chock was put fore or aft of the mast in this strap or the half hole to give the necessary rake, there being only one mast step. The chock aft was the normal position, the housing was three-sided. Sails were tanned in boiled oil and red ochre, yards held to the mast by bead parrels, later by iron travellers.

In the 1840s Hodgson of Sunderland was building cobles 19 ft keel, 25 ft overall, beam 6 ft 4 in, moulded breadth 6 ft 2 in, extreme breadth 6 ft 4 in, depth 2 ft 3 in for £25. Rig: lug, jib and mizzen; half a ton of ballast, crew three.

From notes sent to my friend, the late C. J. Greene, by Hugh R. Viall I quote:

Information given by W. Pounder, Hartlepool, employed by J. H. Pounder & Co, Hartlepool. Due to bad times, Mr Pounder often works at Whitby when cobels are built there. Pounders of Hartlepool are noted boatbuilders (note difference) supplying Admiralty and Board of Trade and Trinity House craft. About two years ago (c 1932) two cobels were built by Pounders for Amble fishermen, Mr Cambridge, a noted Hartlepool coble builder, superintending the building, although nearly 80 years

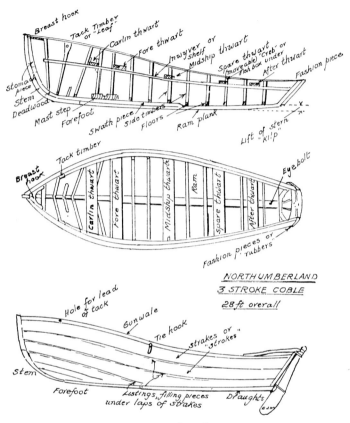

Northumberland 3-stroke coble

old. The only fault found was that about another 2 in of lift should have been given to the stern.

METHOD. 1. Ram is shaped and laid with its attendant 'swath' piece.

2. Stem is fitted with its deadwood at knee and 'stomach-piece' above, these forming the rabbit for the stroke ends.

3. 'Sandstrokes' are next fitted. (Name of these in a boat would be garboards.)

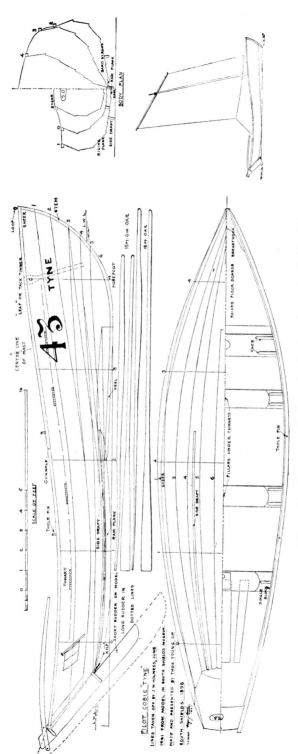

Pilot coble *Tyne*: lines, body and sail plans drawn by J. W. Holness

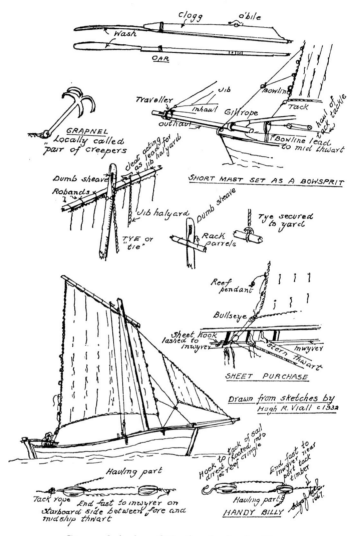

Gear and rigging of Northumberland coble

4. Other strokes are then built up to a set of scrieve marks. No frames are used at all in building. The shape of the planks gives the cobel its fine lines.

5. The stern, never called transom, is next fitted, being a horseshoe fashion-piece with planks fastened athwartships. The

art of cobel building and the high-water mark of efficiency in the builder is the fitting of the stern.

6. The floor timbers are next sawn to shape from templates and notched over the clinkered or clenched planks.

7. Side timbers are next shaped and fitted, being scarphed to the floors.

8. Gunwales are fitted and spiked through top stroke and timbers.

9. Breasthook is fitted at stem between gunwales.

10. Shelf called 'inwyver' is set and thwarts fixed across with knees to give support.

A conversation with Mr Cole, boatbuilder, Staithes, Sept. 1932: Old-type cobels were built with three top strakes, called 'strokes' locally, and bottom strakes. The planks next to the ram were called 'sandstrokes'. Modern trend is to have four top-strokes, while in a large motor cobel as many as seven strokes are worked in, unfortunately spoiling the bold line and tumble home of the true cobel, usual size 28 ft overall.

FORM. In Staithes, boats need to have no lift to the stern as they are beached or moored within the shelter of the breakwaters. All cobels are flat at stern, drawing only a matter of inches of water. Grip of the water is obtained by a very deep rudder projecting below the heel four feet and acting as a centre board.

It will be noticed that Mr Viall, a Whitley Bay man, spells coble 'cobel' as it is pronounced in Northumberland; in Yorkshire it is 'cobble'. (Pictures, p 71.)

Mr Robb Freeth of North Shields sent me information he had collected concerning costs. A coble built in 1912 by Cambridge of Hartlepool for J. Brunton. Ram plank 18 ft, 26 ft overall. Total cost £20, £1 refunded for each payment. A set of oars, 25s, is included in the total cost. She was named *Protector*.

It is interesting to compare this low price with that quoted for one 20 ft overall *c* 1960: £320 with sail and oars.

Many of the North Shields boats were used for racing on Sundays and had their bottoms blackleaded. *Protector* carried twenty-six 4-st sacks of sand, all put to windward in heavy weather.

Coble sail made by Richard Irvin & Sons in May 1917:

	£	s.	d.
31 yd 36 in cotton	2	16	10
8 lb bolt rope		12	
16 1½ thimbles		2	
20 fthm line for reef points		1	6
1¾ hr machining	1	1	
1½ hr handwork		18	
	5	11	4

Cobles would put to sea off an open beach in weather which kept other craft sheltering, as is graphically told by the late W. Pezzack, a Cornish fisherman in the 1870s.

The feat by a coble was from the pebble beach between the north and south entrances at Sunderland the year I was fishing in the North Sea (1872). It was blowing a gale from the east with a heavy sea, too bad for us to go to sea. There was a crowd on the beach and presently a crew had got a draw seine into a coble as there were numerous pollack chasing sprat just clear of the breakers. Four men made the crew and many helpers ran her down the steep beach on the back of a wave. The four men stuck to her till the water was above their knees, then they tumbled in and three pairs of paddles were out and the man aft was throwing out a buoy with the hauling line fast. With the way she had in launching she went up the hollow of the first breaker straight up on end, the men on the thwarts lying in one another's laps. We all thought she would turn end over end, but her lovely great fore-foot got through the crashing wave and split it off in the curve and not a bucket of water was shipped. She slid out of sight and up into the next in the same way, the men pulling like de-mons and the skipper watching the net run out after he had thrown the first few bights. They kept her almost head to wind, manoeuvring her to make a half circle with the net, finally reach-ing the breakers and came in stern first with the rope from the other end, running her vane of a stern up on the beach with the last breaker. The crew tumbled out and held on to her, others took a hand, and she was up safe and sound with only a few buckets over the side in the final scramble, not a drop over the bow. Then all hands manned the two ends of the seine and hauled it in. That finally came in with a huge wave, pollack, black Jack, sprats galore and all the detritus of a lee shore in a gale. They seemed to go out into sure disaster and at least a mess-up on return, but they took it as all in the day's work and except four pairs of wet legs all were happy and unexcited, and a good haul.

In 1872 Berwick had 599 fishing-boats under 15 tons on her register, North Shields 489, South Shields 44, Sunderland 103, West Hartlepool 172 and Middlesbrough 55.

YORKSHIRE

In the days of sail and oar, practically every village down the coast from the Tees to the Humber had its fishing cobles. In 1817 Redcar and Coatham had already become 'fashionable bathing resorts' and 20 years later Redcar had 'many fishing boats and great quantities of fish—cod, crabs, lobster, shrimps etc—are sent weekly to various parts of Yorkshire. The coast is very rocky and navigation dangerous but it has been proposed to make a harbour of refuge here . . . the fishermen notwithstanding their intimate knowledge of the rocks and shoals are sometimes wrecked within a short distance of their homes and about 15 years ago seven of them were lost in one night', wrote W. White in 1840.

I am indebted to Malcolm Hay of Whitby for much of my information. He wrote to me, quite out of the blue after having read my three books, 20 closely-written pages of foolscap concerning the old days:

> The Tees pilots used to work from Redcar in double-ended cobles, painted black and I have often heard my Father say he still remembers what a sight it was to see them racing off to get first alongside a ship wishing to enter the Tees . . . the harbour of refuge was never built. . . . The boats used here are double-ended, not true cobles, but of the whaler type, all of various sizes from about 18 to 25 ft or so, mostly motor. They are hauled up the beach on wheels, as are the boats at Marske, Saltburn and Skinnigrove, in the next three villages. . . . Saltburn was a smugglers village.

The next village, Staithes, was described in 1840 as:

... a large fishing village with about 400 men and boys employed. During the winter and spring seasons they go out to sea in small flat-bottomed boats or cobles, each carrying three men and so constructed to live in very tempestuous weather, but in summer they go out in large boats of from 10 to 20 tons burthen called 'five-men boats' or cobles.

They generally sail on Monday and if the weather permit continue at sea the whole week; on their return the fish intended to be cured is cut up and salted by the women and after passing through the brine it is spread out to dry on the beach, but the greater part is sent out fresh to distant markets, the curing trade having declined of late years. In the herring season this village generally sends 15 vessels to Yarmouth.

Staithes then had no harbour at all, but being situated on a creek was somewhat sheltered; breakwaters were built later.

Writing in October 1849 John Edmond, foreman to R. Skelton, boatbuilder of Scarborough, stated:

> Before the introduction of these yawls we had but two sorts of craft, the large five-man boats and the open cobles, which are still used for the long lines, commencing about October and ending in April or May. These cobles are 27 ft long, 7 to 7 ft 6 in wide and 2½ ft deep. They are built of wainscot ⅝ in thick in their bottoms and ½ in in their sides, floor timbers 1¾ in thick, 2¼ in deep, futtocks 1¼ in thick, 2½ in deep. Their bottoms in midships are quite flat, and have a rudder projecting 5 ft below. They are usually managed with one lugsail, but have a jib and mizzen for occasional use. Carry three men. Price of hull, £24. Total £32 exclusive of fishing tackle. The yawls carry one coble, value £22, on deck in the spring fishing . . . or until they suppose the weather will be so fine as to warrant them in taking two . . . total cost £310 includes a small boat value £7.

Regarding five-man boats he wrote:

> This boat, *York*, cost £550, including one small boat £13 . . . the two cobles carried on deck in spring fishing don't necessarily belong to the owners of the large boats, but the crew take their favourites, for which they pay 4s a week. These are 24 ft long and 6 ft 6 in broad.
>
> Price of hulls from the builder, this only includes rudder and tiller, and a few boards to divide the fish from the lines, £17,

three pairs of oars £2. Two masts, long and short, 12s, sail £2 10s, anchor, cable, rope and sundries £1. Total £23 2s.

The Filey fishermen use these small boats in fishing from the time the large boats lay up—23 Nov—to the time they fit out in February. They go off the beach in the morning and return in the evening, weather permitting.

John Edmond mentioned that the larger cobles used for the herring fishery 'are generally 32 ft overall . . . entirely without deck or gangways'. He said Mr Skelton had built only one five-man boat 'for the last 18 years . . . there seems to be a reaction at Filey in favour of the five-man boat . . . Staithes and Filey are the strongholds for them. . . .'

Wainscot was an Old German name for oak board. At Staithes, the cobles came in on to the beach stern first and were pulled ashore by hand, the oars being used as skids, the looms being made very heavy and big for that purpose. A photograph in my collection shows women in long white aprons and sun-bonnets helping the men, with younger girls hauling on a rope from the stern. Another photograph depicts many cobles lying in the creek, well sheltered from any winter storm.

Writing in 1954 Mr Hay says: 'At Runswick village situated on Runswick Bay, the last two true cobles were sold to Whitby a year or two ago, both motor craft . . . both at Staithes and Runswick cobles are hauled up over wooden skids by winches and not on wheels. (Picture, p 90.) At Sandsend there is a little fishing done in the summer, mainly salmoning . . . the last coble, only a small one, was sold away to Whitby about 1939. The boats here are small as they have to be dragged up the beach on rollers by manpower.'

Although at the time of the monastery at Whitby the fishing must have been of considerable importance (Leland describes it as 'a great fisher town'), in 1816 it had only nine fishermen and three fishmongers. This figure was probably on the low side due to the Napoleonic wars having just ended, a time when the press-gangs made it unhealthy for any seaman to hang about; also service in the privateers and transports paid better than fishing. Shipbuilding was booming and 'the fishery' was seeking the whale in Greenland waters. But the coming of steam and the decline of the sailing coaster forced many a shipyard to close, and Whitby reverted to a fishing port. At high water the river Esk above bridge made a spacious harbour; at the ebb, except in mid-channel, it dried out. Below bridge, no vessel could ride in safety in onshore gales. The 1838 Report says: 'In gales from the eastward Whitby is one of the most dangerous harbours that a vessel can attempt to take between Yarmouth Roads and the Firth of Forth. As the flood sets strong to the southward across the entrance, vessels attempting to enter with a gale from the NE are liable to be driven on rocks and wrecked at the foot of the cliff beyond the east pier.' (Picture, p 89.)

In the great gale of February 1861 70 vessels went ashore near Hartlepool, 10 being lost with all hands. The beaches all along the coast were strewn with wreckage and drowned men; a ship at Redcar, a brig at Staithes and three vessels at Robin Hood's Bay. At Sandsend, Will Dryden went out in his coble and saved the crew of five from the brig *John & Ann* in seas so heavy that, after a safe return to Whitby with crews from several wrecks, the lifeboat put out again but capsized only 50 yd from the pier. One by one her crew were drowned, despite gallant attempts at rescue; only one man, H. Freeman, wearing the new cork life-jacket, was saved by men wading in the breakers arm in arm. Ship after ship drove ashore; from one the crew were rescued by rocket line, from the brig *Urania* all hands walked ashore as the tide ebbed, to be followed by another brig *Tribune* after nightfall. Rocket lines having failed to reach her, the east-side boat was launched into the harbour, hauled out on to the west side and launched to the rescue, manned by master mariners, fishermen and others, and saved all but one of the crew. This boat had capsized in 1841, drowning four of her crew of 13, but there was never any lack of volunteers when other seamen were in peril.

Whitby also had a number of pilots who went off in their cobles seeking vessels in need of their services. One winter's day

Page 107 (*above*) *Lily May* of Lowestoft, LN 230; (*below*) mule *Dora Ann* at Scarborough. Note thafts resting on inwire and the short, or mizzen, mast lashed to the mast as a bowsprit

Page 108 Lowestoft shrimper, 395 LT. Note oars worked in double thole pins, small jacky topsail, transom stern, two reef pendants rove and beam trawl to port

two pilots set out and were never heard of again, but their coble was washed ashore near the Skaw. Pilot cobles were painted black with the letter 'W' followed by a number in white. *Helena*, W1, a double-ender, was the last, and subsequently bore the fishing registration letters WY. Fitted with an engine, she was sold to Seaham in 1953.

The herring fishing flourished during the second half of the nineteenth century and the big cobles were joined by Scots luggers, Yarmouth drifters and 'the Penzance men', much of the catch being kippered in odoriferous smoke houses.

Robin Hood's Bay is situated between Whitby and Scarborough with the village towards its northern extremity, the houses clustering on the very edge of the cliff. The ancient name of the Bay was Fyling, but Leland called it Robin Hood's Bay 'a fisher townlet of 20 boats'. Legend says that Robin Hood used to be in league with the fishermen and when things got too hot for him in Sherwood he made tracks for some sea air and fishing! A steep road lined with cottages leads down to the shore and here cobles were drawn up in bad weather. In 1840 fishing was from about 30 cobles and five-man boats. Smuggling was rife but a lieutenant and seven men of the coastguard did their best to put a stop to this nefarious practice.

The principal ground for cobles lay 8 to 16 miles offshore, but in winter the men did not venture so far, shooting their lines 6 to 10 miles out. A crew normally consisted of three men. When the wind was unfavourable two men at the bow each rowed a single large oar, while the one on the thwart nearest the stern pulled a pair of smaller size. In light winds the steersman pushed an oar with one hand, the others pulled, and the sail gave some assistance.

The 1838 Report says:

> The lines are shot across the tide, left on the bottom for several hours, usually during the time of a tide's ebbing or flowing, say six hours. While the lines are shot one man keeps a lookout, the other two wrap themselves in the sail and go to sleep in the bottom of the coble. Each man has three lines, each line 200 to 240

G

fathoms, 240 to 300 hooks to each line are tied or whipped to a length of twisted horse hair called 'snoods', each about 2½ ft long, fastened to the line 5 ft apart.

When the lines are baited they are regularly coiled up on an oval piece of wickerwork like the bottom of a clothes basket, called by Yorkshire fishermen a 'skep', at Hartlepool in Durham a 'rip'. The lines are baited by wives and children before the coble proceeds to sea, all are fastened together and when each is 240 fathoms the length of the whole is nearly 2½ miles. An anchor and buoy are at the first end of the line and the same at the end of each man's set of lines, or four anchors and four buoys to each coble's entire line. The buoys at the extremities are tarred dog-skin, inflated like bladders with pole and flag, intermediate buoys are usually cork. The anchors are large stones, as an iron anchor is liable to get fast among rocks.

The five-man boats were about 46 ft long, clinker-built, sharp at the bows like a coble and partly decked. Each boat carried two cobles on deck.

On arrival at the fishing ground the boat is anchored and the cobles launched, three men to each, one left on board. The lines used for this more distant fishery are called 'haavres', from 'haaf', Swedish for main sea. The lines are about the same length as for inshore but thicker, with hooks at greater intervals. As the six men who fish have each two sets of lines, they can shoot one set immediately after they have hauled the other. The hooks are always baited at sea.

Although these five-man boats still retained the old name, the crew numbered seven owing to the increased size.

Five-man boats are laid up during the winter, fitting out about the beginning of March . . . after a successful season the fishermen indulge in festivity, shared by the humbler class of tradesmen, who receive payment for debts by families during absence. When five-man boats are laid up the men employ themselves in coble fishing.

Robin Hood's Bay, or to give it the local name Baytown or just Bay, has no harbour and the cobles were hauled up a steep slipway into an open space called 'the dock'. The coast is rocky and the boats put out from the 'landing', the name given to a stretch of deep water between two reefs, or scars, running out seawards. Wooden posts were fixed on these scars to mark the entrance, as at high water the rocks are covered. Many a coble was lost trying to get ashore in bad weather.

Scarborough, with Whitby, was the registration port and in 1872 153 2nd-class boats are listed, Whitby having 277. More a seaport than a fishing station, little mention is made of the activities of cobles but in 1840 it is described as 'a pleasure resort and bathing place' and Thos Armstrong, Robt Skelton, James & Thos Smith are given as boat builders. The herring season brought drifters from all parts and the big sharp-sterned 'mules' were a typical sight in the harbour. (Pictures, pp 89 and 107.) During the hot summer months, when the gentry—'toffs' —and other visitors came to enjoy the sea air and bathing, the local boatmen made a living taking out pleasure parties.

Filey, eight miles to the south and somewhat sheltered by Filey Brig, was an important station. In 1840 'upwards of 40 boats and 100 men and boys are employed in the fishery, which is famous for lobsters, cod, ling etc. About 13 six-men boats go from Filey every year to the Yarmouth herring fishery and there are several curing houses.'

Each man provided his own line about 90 yd long, with a hook at every fathom, and he cleared and baited them. The cobles were pulled up on wheels by horses who got so used to the job that they would go unattended into the sea up to the boat, turn for the traces to be hooked on, and at a shout all pulled together, two or three in tandem—'line ahead' to use a naval expression. Donkeys carried the nets and lines.

Flamborough, the next village, is thus described in 1840: 'The landing place for the fishing boats is a small creek half-a-mile to the south of the village and is both dangerous and inconvenient in stormy weather. In 1794, 20 fishermen perished in the sea, yet so powerful is the force of custom that the survivors are as adventurous as ever on the strong element and now amount to about eighty men and boys.'

In later years there were two landings; at the north the cobles were pulled up a steep slope by a steam-engined winch.

Being sheltered by a chalk headland, the north landing was used when winds were from the nor'ard. At the south landing the cobles were hauled up by horses. Photographs sent to me by Mr Mellor show upwards of a score of boats on each, facing seaward, a gay sight with their brightly coloured strakes shining in the sun, all having Hull registration.

I was extremely fortunate to find willing correspondents in Flamborough during my quest for information in 1953. Mr Geo B. Bayes wrote:

> The trade of coble building in Flamborough I am sorry to say came to an end with the death of Mr Hopwood several years ago. He was a most remarkable character. He was a wonderful craftsman and most of his work was done with an adze. He built all the Flamboro' cobles and others for Bridlington, Filey etc, all single-handed with no help other than from his wife, who was probably called in to hold the end of a heavy piece of timber whilst he fixed it into place. Mrs Hopwood is still living . . . today there is only one sailing coble and this is only used as a ferry boat. The last one to go to sea, that I can remember, was sometime around 1936.

I at once wrote to Mrs Hopwood, who replied that as her husband had died in 1939 she was unable to give much information, but she sent a very faded newspaper cutting from which I quote and offer my thanks to R.C.S., the unknown interviewer. In her postcript she said, 'as for time it took to build, I'm afraid I could not say as they had to leave off so often for unseen things happening, repairs etc . . . did not work by the hour, worked from 8 to 5. . . . Mr Hopwood died in 1939 and all the boats are still going to sea, only some have been fitted with engines.'

On looking up some old notes I found the name of Hopwood as a boatbuilder at Flamborough in 1888.

> Like a bunch of herrings on a string, the cobles lie on the steep-pitched slope of Flamborough North Landing. Perhaps 18 of them now, counting the one bobbing to the tide, and the two chugging somewhere out behind the headland. Once 40 craft were based on this tiny harbour, says their builder. Their builder? Yes—every coble in Flamborough was built by Mr Hargrave Potter Hopwood, boat-builder . . . you'll look in vain for a boat-

builder's signboard over his workshop . . . somewhere about the premises you are pretty sure of finding Mr Hopwood. If you are lucky you may find him, as I did, at work on a coble, the *Adeline* was her name. Thirty-five years ago his father built her, said this short, sparse, friendly man, a philosopher as all good craftsmen are. And now the *Adeline* was in for repairs—no bad tribute to her builder.

HOW THEY ARE BUILT

For an hour, while he worked, I chatted to one of the last men of his craft on the coast. His talk, like his workshed, is fascinating —full of odd things and old things, rough-grained, seasoned, like the timber his hands have wrought with these forty years and more.

How is a coble built? Well, now, I should be able to tell you, if any man can. There's only three of us left between Whitby and Flamborough, so there's not many that can contradict me, eh? Absently, he picks up an adze. 'That's what I call the shipwright's right hand, you use it see, like a croquet mallet.' He swings the heavy-headed steel thing illustratively. 'A slip, and that will give you a nasty gash. It shapes the timber of the posts and ribs. A coble may be either clincher-built—the planks overlapping each other—or caulker-built, that is with the planks flush and the seams caulked with a mixture of tar, oil and pitch. Lasts for ever, that does. Now, if she's clincher-built, first I make the shell, shallow as a true coble should be, for ease in hauling her up the beach. Then I fit the ribs in. With a caulker-built boat the ribs are put up first, then the shell is fitted on them, but come and see.'

He leads me through the long, littered workshop, which smells of oil and tar, of sawdust and the good smell of wood. 'There' he says, and slaps the half-section of an oak tree, a two-inch sponge-cake slice from a trunk five feet across. His hands run lovingly over the coarse grain. 'The ribs of a good boat are curved to the natural shape the tree grows. They'll never spring, never bend, never break, even when the wood's all but green. And they're best of English oak. Years ago they used to make the bottoms of oak too. Russian stuff it was, but good stuff. Nowadays the bottoms, like the sides, are of larchwood, locally grown. Mine comes from Hackness.

'For smaller boats, river craft for instance, the ribs are made from one straight piece of timber, which is put in the steambox—

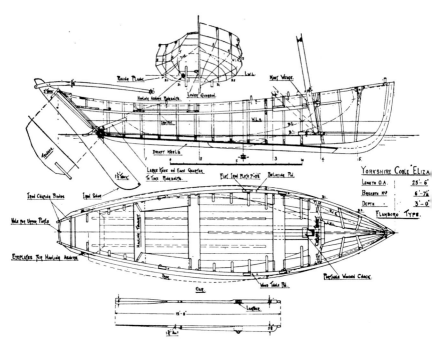

Flamboro'-type Yorkshire coble *Eliza*: plans drawn by W. H. Blake

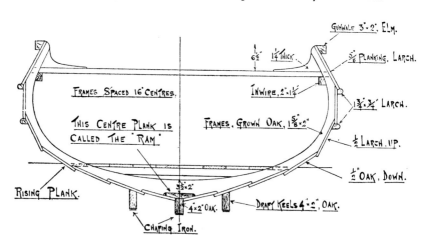

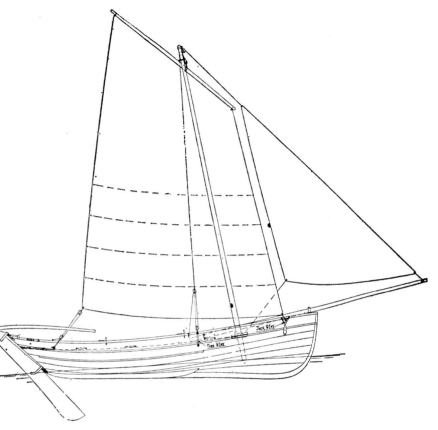

Sail plan of coble *Eliza*

that long, coffin-like thing there—and cramped to shape in a mould. Good enough, but it wouldn't do for a coble.'

I asked him about the plans he worked to.

'Plans?' Mr Hopwood chuckled and slapped his thigh as a wave might smack the bow of one of his boats. 'Just after the Armistice I built a big boat. Nine or ten-tonner. Forty-foot long, she'd be. I built her to the shape of a coble that was in Bridlington harbour at the time. I took one man with me. We had the coble beached and we took moulds off her, from stem to stern, five pairs of 'em, between a tide and a tide.'

He showed me the moulds, thin strips of wood, bent to the shape of a boat's hull and hanging now in his workshop.

'We measured her up and we used the moulds, and built a replica with no more plans to go by than a few chalk sketches on the walls of my old shed here. No, sir, a boatbuilder goes by instinct. Same as I went by when I first had the job of putting an engine into a coble. During the war, that was.' He chuckled again. 'There were three boat-builders in Filey alone at one time, in the days when all cobles went by sail alone. But after that engine went in, they all wanted an engine in their boats. It was a success from the start.

'Yes, rule of thumb does it, IF you know your job, as it did in the days when we sawed all our own timber in the sawpit. From the trunk, do you see? My father used to put his apprentices at work and tell 'em so much was a day's work, and when they'd done that they could knock off. Ah, I've called it a day at two in the afternoon, and' his eyes twinkled, 'at two in the morning in my time'.

'What do you call a day now, Mr Hopwood?' I asked.

'Eh? Oh, well, last coble I built, I started her in November last year and finished her in April. What you might call a longish day.'

'They're never two alike' he said, looking musingly back over the ships he had built. 'You see, a boat's alive and she lets you know it when you're steering her'.

'And when you've finished one, and she's handed over, how do you get her down to the landing?'

'Two pairs of wheels and a lorry to pull them. Once of course it was horses,' and he laughed at some memory. 'And no ceremony about it, either. I hand her over as you might a sack of potatoes. And no bottle of champagne at the launching. Lass in the village paints her name on her, and then the boat's launched, like that. What I call a dry job.'

The late John W. Bayes wrote:

Our cobles measured 15 ft to 19 ft on the keel, the larger would be 27 or 28 ft overall, the others pro rata. They usually carried two masts, a short and a long mast. The short was for bad weather and reefing the sail; they never referred to reefing, it was allways described as 'setting on', yet in sailing they always referred to it as one or two reefs short mast sail. The hull sides usually had five planks—'strokes'—the top plank was well 'tumbled home'.

The rudder came well down under the coble's bottom and

Page 117 Lowestoft pilot gig *Kapiolani*. Note short washboards at bows, strakes in one unbroken length and blobs of white paint on oars

Page 118 Pleasure boat at Great Yarmouth, *c* 1910. Note six
lines of reef points, long boom and lead of peak halyards

Page 119   (above) Hilda, CK 297, built as a cutter at Brightlingsea in 1886 and later converted to ketch rig. Fitted with auxiliary 33 hp motor in 1927. Length 58·5 ft, beam 16·3 ft, depth 8 ft; *(below)* beach yawl, probably *Georgiana*, with 19 men on board. Note size of lugsails, short iron bumpkin and long outrigger

Page 120 (*above*) Robert Aldous and his chief man, Rasbrook, on the daily inspection tour; (*below*) *Polly*, MN 12, on the hard at Maldon, *c* 1950. Note length of bowsprit and boom

really acted as a centreboard. It was detachable and was attached on going out to sea and taken inboard coming ashore. Flamboro' Head is a very tricky place to fish from. There are twelve different sets of tide every six hours, each tide is affected by every different wind which blows. Yet the best of the fishermen had a strange, uncanny knowledge of this peculiar phenomenon. They seemed to sense any change of tide which the lay mind would never notice. I have known them fishing 5 to 7 or 8 miles off the Head on what they always described as 'off to eastward' when they could be caught in a hard westerly gale, which of course placed them dead to leeward.

When finished hauling their lines, they would tack—'ratching' they called it—with all their fish and ballast banked up to windward, with one man with a wooden basin baling water out of the lee side of the boat, and close-hauled drive their small craft on the flood tide to away south of the Head to a place called Hornsea, and then come back with the ebb to the South Landing on the other tack. They could never do this fishing day under 12 hours, it was more often 14 to 16 hours. It produced an extraordinary splendid type of seaman of this class, but the frequent changes (rapid) of winter weather took its tragic toll of their number and it was rarely a winter passed without one of their number being lost. . . . Flamboro' fishing has gone down considerably, sixty years ago we had 45 cobles going winter fishing, today we have only four or five . . . the advent of steam into trawlers destroyed our famous 'off to eastward' ground. I always felt that the sailing coble was really a dangerous craft for the uninitiated to handle, yet it was a glorious sight to see them come in under all sail and even one or two reefs short mast sail, in bad weather it was a thrilling picture especially the way they were handled by experienced seamen.

Mr Eric Mellor of Bridlington sent me further data on coble builders, materials and sails:

Flamborough. 'Arg' Hopwood had no blueprints, used adze, hammer, chisel and maul. Built *Florence* (now 60 years old) and many others. Beam 9 to 10 ft. Beam, sheer and tumble-home varied according to client's requirements. Boats built for Bridlington owners were brought by road and launched here.

Cambridge of Filey used the same equipment as did Chapman of Filey. . . . Filey boats were pulled by horses and launched here. Baker Siddall of Bridlington built many, some with centreboards.

He put extra timbers in the boat compared with Hopwood's and so were stiffer. All Bridlington cobles had one position for the mast.

MATERIALS:

Oak, bottom to waterline, ¾ in thick
Larch, for tops to waterline, ¾ in thick
Bulwarks: pine or hardwood. Capping: hardwood
Rubbing binn: American elm
Listing: American elm or oak
Cuddy, deck beams: softwood or hardwood

The timbers were fastened with galvanised spikes and washers, the spikes were sawn off and clenched to. A thin scantling was used to rest the bottom boards, but there was a 4 by 2 in inwire. The mizzen thwart (thoft here) was of soft wood, the long winter rudder, 9 to 10 ft, was of elm, as was the 7 ft short summer rudder. The long tiller—6 ft—had a hardwood head and the rest was fir, whilst the short tiller was of hardwood in one piece. Both tillers had a bowed rise, 18 in in the long one and 12 in in the short one.

The boats carried 30 cwt. or two tons of granite stone ballast according to the fishing, for trimming four sand ballast bags.

TIME TO BUILD. Six months. Hopwood worked by himself and used assistance only when fitting stomach piece. Siddall took a similar time.

COST. 27 ft keel, 32 ft mast, 28 ft bowsprit or short mast. £90 in 1914, sails roughly £25.

FITTINGS. The builders put in the deadeyes, the gammon and belaying pins for the tacks.

BLACKSMITH. Wiles of Flamboro' or Tom Rowntree of Bridlington did rudder gudgeons, pintles, stem iron, keel irons, draft irons and travellers for bowsprit, mizzen and main mast.

Sails were made in Bridlington by Bill Raddings and then by Bill Broadmeadows who came here from Burnham-on-Crouch and fixed his sails by running a fold down the centre of each canvas, so the sail hung straighter and was stronger.

MATERIAL AND SIZE.

A lug with 110 sq yd of cotton duck, 5½ or 6½ reefs
A big jib with 90 sq yd unbleached calico
A second jib with 40 sq yd of stronger unbleached calico
A third jib with 20 sq yd of 18 canvas
A storm jib or 'spitfire' 15 sq yd heavy canvas
Mast not stayed save by halyards and back stay
In Bridlington harbour the big cobles always downed the jib in

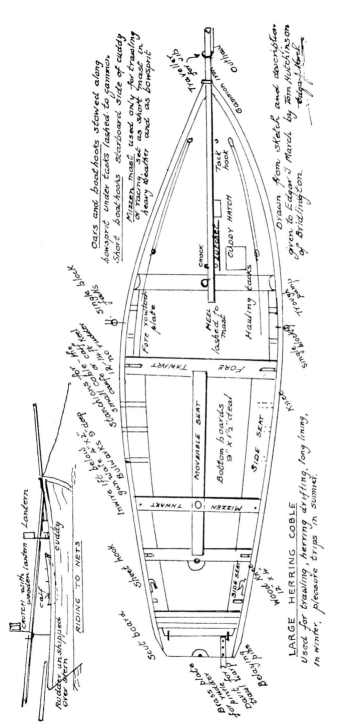

Large herring coble, Bridlington

the harbour mouth in a westerly wind, sail aback and rounded up to the jetty, down tiller, spun round and lowered the lug at the same time as a 30-ft boathook was taken out to come to the jetty.

USE OF THE COBLES. Herring fishing swim nets, 24 to 30 nets, 60 yd each net, lower bottom boards used for this.

Crab pots, 150 worked in fleets of 18, 20 or 25 pots.

Long line fishing with small coble—calf (caulf)—stowed inside for hauling lines.

Pleasure fishing and sailing, average 36 people with seat down the middle of the coble.

Trawling with beam trawl, 22 ft beam.

Recovering anchors lost by ships, up to 30 cwt.

Carry coal and food to ships in the bay, coal 5 to 8 tons according to the weather.

The 1838 Fisheries Report makes no mention of Bridlington as a fishing station—'the old name, Burlington Bay, a secure roadstead in NE gales, often 300 vessels sheltering by the promontory of Flamboro' Head. On SE is partially sheltered by Smithwick Sands, run in line with the coast . . . ships leave the bay as soon as wind changes to E or SE'.

On the north-east coast attendance on shipping in the offing was known as 'foying', a term also used at Broadstairs and Ramsgate; at Deal it was 'hovelling'. The name 'foy' means allegiance, and a boat chosen by a shipmaster supplied provisions, stores and so on whilst the vessel was sheltering, a period which might well run into weeks during prolonged spells of bad weather. Mr Mellor writes:

> In bad weather, sheltering steamers were bunkered with coal supplied by Wm. Gray, and carried out in cobles. Six or seven tons were carried at a time and loaded by means of 5-cwt baskets or bags. The task was risky, for a fisherman was killed in the coble *Hetty* in 1901 or 1902 when a basket fell on him; 12s a ton was paid for ferrying the coal out. Hutchinsons and Champlins had their own baskets which were slung with ropes and hauled up by the ship's derricks.

From my notes, I see that bunkers were 10s a ton in the Humber in the 1880s, at Plymouth, Welsh steam coal was 22s 6d, Durham unscreened 17s a ton in 1912, all FOB. In 1907,

Scottish anthracite was 14s 6d a ton, and many a ton of the best Yorkshire household coal was shot into our cellar at Westgate-on-Sea at 16s to 18s a ton.

To go back to Mr Mellor's recollections of Bridlington:

> When ships were windbound or in distress, Robert Gray commenced baking bread and ship's biscuits and he paid a bonus to the fishermen for taking them out. Mark Wilson supplied meat.
>
> There was a profitable trade in recovering ships' anchors. Tom Hutchinson's father went as far as Hartlepools to grapple or sweep for anchors and chains, which were then heaved up and capsized aboard. The heaving was done in a coble using a hand winch with double gear and tackles. Stays were on the mast trunk and the davit, stepped in the stern, was fastened on skids, all were properly fitted. Unclaimed anchors were stored at the south end of Clinda Road in an anchor yard.

The owner of one of the first engined cobles had an eye to making 'baccy' money by taking tow ropes from cobles going out of the harbour in adverse winds and calms, charging his pals 3d or 6d a time.

Tom Hutchinson left school at 12, worked in a shop for two years, then went to sea with his father until he was 18, when he sailed in coastal schooners, brigantines and billy-boys. The first time he took charge of a coble was the Whitsuntide when King Edward died (1910), taking over his father's *Hesperus*. He made some excellent sketches of cobles, naming various items, and wrote that in 1954 there were no sailing cobles left, all—

> fitted with motors . . . a lot manning them don't know how to set a sail . . . however we all have had to go over to the motor business, but I can assure you that sail dies very hard with us because that was our early upbringing in cobles and under the kind but stern scrutiny of our fathers or seafaring relatives. These cobles were tricky to sail and always griping into the wind on account of their build, but easy to sail when you know how and of course the trim made a lot of difference too. Some were built with centre keels but they were nearly always taken out for different reasons, most jamming with mud and small stones when aground. . . . I always try to tell the rising generation that a bit of sail soothes, humours and helps a boat in its labouring, especially in heavy

weather. We never had to beach our cobles, because we always had a harbour, but we knew what to do if we had. Flamboro' and Filey always had to beach their craft. . . .

Tom served 40 years with the Bridlington lifeboat, being in turn bowman, second cox'n and cox'n, and proud to have taken part in the rescue of 63 lives. He retired in 1950 on reaching the age limit.

FISHERIES

In 1817, according to the Government Report, these were the fisheries on the Yorkshire coast:

> The great fisher towns of our coast at present are Staiths, Runswick and Robin Hood's Bay. . . . There are 28 five-men boats employed, viz: 14 belonging to Staiths, six to Runswick, five to Robin Hood's Bay and three to Scarborough . . . the number was more considerable three years ago, six large boats having been lost during that time and not yet replaced. Each large boat is provided with two cobles besides which there is nearly an equal number of fishing cobles for the winter fishing and several other cobles, not connected with the large boats, employed both in summer and winter, among which are some lobster boats used near the shore for catching crabs and lobsters. The number of cobles belonging to our three great fishing towns, including the cobles attached to the large boats, may be nearly as follows: Staiths 70, Runswick 35, Robin Hood's Bay 35, in all 140, to which if we add the cobles of Scarboro', Whitby, Sandsend, Skinningrave, Saltburn, Marsk, Redcar etc the total number will be found to be from 250 to 300.

Describing the five-man boats, crew seven, the Report gives the cost as £600 and upwards, fishing gear £20 for each man, the proceeds being divided into shares; nets were used only for catching herring and mackerel.

> The larger fishes are taken with strong hemp lines . . . the common lines and the haavres . . . the common line is about 200 fathoms long, furnished with from 14 to 20 score of hooks . . . snoods each a yard long. . . . These hooks are baited with mussels, sand eels etc. The task of procuring the mussels and sand eels and

baiting the hooks before the boats go to sea devolves principally on the women. Each fisherman generally has three lines, which are carefully coiled in a flat, oval piece of wicker work called a skep . . . the haavres are coiled in a round piece of wicker work called a swaitch. The fishing ground is chosen at various distances between the coast and the Dogger Bank . . . the large boat is anchored and its two cobles are employed in shooting the lines, stretching them across the current and sinking them with small anchors or perforated stones. All the lines belonging to each boat are fastened to one another so as to make one range, or at the most two ranges. . . . The cobles not connected with the large boats fish after the same form . . . they seldom venture so far from the shore . . . fatal accidents too frequently occur . . . one of the most melancholy ever known was that of Friday, 14 April 1815, when three Runswick and one Staiths boats containing in all 29 persons perished in a tremendous storm.

After naming the numerous kinds of fish caught, the Report continues.

The holibut, turbot and skate are amongst the largest of these fishes. The holibut sometimes weigh 17 or even 20 stone, the turbot 10 or 12 stone and often more, skate is sometimes about the same size. Cod and ling seldom exceed 3 stone. Great quantities of cod and ling are cut up and dried during the summer, skate and coal fish are also often dried but only for the home market . . . the average quantity may be stated at 6 tons from each large boat . . . 150 to 180 tons in all. The proportion at Robin's Hood Bay and Scarboro' is less, the boats there sell more fresh fish. About 500 to 550 fish are required to make a ton. The London merchants or their agents purchase them on the spot at from £20 to £30 per ton in good years, at present the price is only from £13 to £20 . . . the greater part of the fish caught during the summer is sold fresh . . . great quantities are forwarded to the interior in every direction, Malton, York, Leeds etc being supplied by means of pannier men and other fish carriers. . . . The large boats are laid up for the winter and the winter cobles are used till March following. A coble carries three men, furnished with three lines each, and six men forming the complement for a large boat are therefore sufficient to man two cobles. . . . The surplus winter fish is not dried but salted in barrels, each barrel containing from 22 to 24 stone of cod or ling, and sells at about 40s or 42s . . . average Staiths 280 barrels, Runswick 140, Robin Hood's Bay 120 . . . the quantity sold fresh may be estimated at three times the quantity barreled. . . .

The cargoes of the cobles are sold to fishmongers, pannier men and fishwives at so much per score. The price varies exceedingly, haddocks are sometimes sold at 1s 6d to 2s per score, at other times as high as 8s and upwards. The average wholesale price of cod and ling, 18s per score. The women sell the fish by retail in the fish market and often carry them about to private houses. Turbot and holibut are sold at from 2d to 4d per lb.

The taking of crabs and lobsters, which are caught in bag nets called 'trunks' fixed to iron hoops, 20 in in diameter, is carried on both summer and winter, chiefly by the elder fishermen. There are eight lobster boats at Staiths, five at Runswick, and as many at Robin Hood's Bay. Crabs sell from 1s 6d to 3s or 4s per score. Lobsters at about three times that price. Shrimps and prawns are taken on the sandy shores, but not in great quantities. The net used for that purpose resembles the lobster nets, but its hoop, instead of being circular, is flat on one side: a person wading in the water pushes the net before him by means of a pole fastened to the hoop, the flat side of which grazes along the bottom while the arched part stands erect to keep the net open.

Before the 1914 war I frequently saw men shrimping in this manner at Westgate-on-Sea and Birchington.

Salmon and salmon trout were once plentiful in the river Esk but are now very scarce, the quantity being diminished since the establishment of inland alum works. The price of salmon trout varies from 6d to 1s per pound. The fisheries yield employment and support to about 400 fishermen and their families and to a considerable number of fishmongers, fishwives, pannier men etc. The fishermen are a hardy race and although their gains are precarious, it is no uncommon thing for a careful fisherman to become a respectable shipowner. It is difficult to calculate the annual amount of the whole proceeds of the fisheries in the district, but the annual average value can scarcely be less than £25 or £30,000, supposing the fresh fish to sell at from £10 to £15 per ton, which is probably below the average. The value if stated according to the price paid to the consumer, might be doubled, if not trebled.

A Government Report of 1840 had this to say of Tees fishing:

The Tees abounds in excellent fish such as flounders, eels, smelts, trout etc, but the principal fishery is that of salmon which

Page 129 Lowestoft yawl *Georgina* flying 10 winning flags, including five cups. Note length of outrigger, iron tiller, fine entry and run, bags of shingle ballast on staging, sett below, lifeboat in background

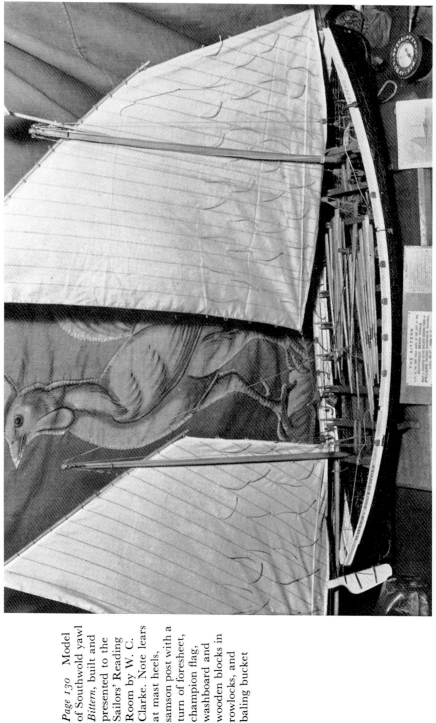

Page 130 Model of Southwold yawl *Bittern*, built and presented to the Sailors' Reading Room by W. C. Clarke. Note lears at mast heels, samson post with a turn of foresheet, champion flag, washboard and wooden blocks in rowlocks, and baling bucket

may be taken by any of the fishermen from Nov. 22 to Aug. 12 on their paying to the Vicar of Stockton a small tithe for each boat pursuant to an Act of Geo. I . . . sea trout ascend the Tees as far as Barnard Castle to spawn. . . . About 60 cobles are sent yearly from the Yorkshire coast to the herring fishery at Yarmouth where they are employed by the merchants of that port. . . . The poor inhabitants of the northern parts of the coast are occasionally employed in gathering and burning kelp for the use of the glass and alum works.

This wholesale capture of salmon in nets is still carried on today and has long been, and still is, a bone of contention between the fishermen and those who own fishing rights farther up the rivers and catch the lordly salmon with rod and fly.

To quote Mr Hay:

Salmon nets are similar to mackerel drift nets, ie, corks on head rope and leads on foot rope, but a larger mesh (5 to 6 in). One man takes the corks, the other the leads and a third at the oars, one end of the net, having a buoy at the surface and a large flat stone at the bottom for an anchor, is dropped just off shore and the net is shot as the boat moves seawards, then the rower doubles back on his tracks and then again heads seawards, thus laying the net in a sort of S, the idea being that the salmon swimming along-side the net will suddenly find a net in front and becoming frightened will either try to rush the net or head away from it at speed to become enmeshed in the part of the nets behind him. Having laid the net, the boat lays-to, keeping watch on the corks for signs of fish striking and occasionally rowing up and down. When hauling, the coble is backed down the net by the oarsman, the others hauling, one at the corks and one at the leads, this brings the net into a sort of bag as it comes over the side and prevents the fish wriggling free.

Another way of salmoning is 'jazzing' and is carried on at the harbour mouth after a heavy rain has brought a 'fresh' down the river, the local name for a sort of small flood or what is known as a 'spate' elsewhere. The salmon spawns in fresh water and these freshes enable it to get up the river to the spawning beds. After spawning the fish are in poor condition and are called 'kelts' and look scabby on the back, many die but the rest return to the sea in the early part of the year where they clean up. The salmon are attracted to the harbour mouth by the fresh water and try to get upstream, the cobles therefore shoot their nets across and then haul

H

them practically straight away, they are not allowed to shoot
within the harbour mouth but must be outside, by the fishery
laws. As there is often some sea running, it is sometimes a risky
job and cobles capsize. Salmon also enter the river with the flood
tide and then, if there is no fresh running, are unable to get far up
the river and return with the ebb. Jazzing is also employed to
catch the fish doing this.

With 'trouting', the nets have a smaller mesh and are shot and
anchored at the mouth of the deep lagoons formed by the scars at
various places or near rocks or stones where trout are known to
lie. The boat is then rowed up inside the net and the crew begin
'blashing', that is hitting the water with the flat of an oar blade to
startle the resting fish which rush seawards into the waiting nets.
Trout are, of course, sea trout or salmon trout, not the angler's
kind. Trouting is only done at night, salmoning day and night . . .
fishing begins in May and ends on the last day of August, no
fishing is allowed from Saturday noon until Sunday midnight.

When working lines under sail, care had to be taken to watch
that the speed of the coble was not too fast; usually the lines
were set while rowing. When hauling, the boat was pulled up
to the line, one man aft hauling in, the rowers keeping speed so
that the line came up with an 'up and down' pull, otherwise
there was a danger of it fouling. In calm weather the coble
would sometimes be 'backed up' the line—rowed stern first,
also when hauling pots.

When working herring nets, the 'plosher' was put before the
wind and the nets shot; if there was not enough breeze to keep
her going sufficiently fast a pair of oars was put out to increase
her speed. Ploshers were big cobles ranging from 30 to 40 ft in
length.

Mr Hay continues:

Another type much in use for herring fishing was the 'mule', a
big clinker-built double-ender, about 40 or more feet in length,
decked in for'ard, but more or less an open boat aft. She carried a
single mast with a dipping lug and a jib on a bowsprit. The mast
was lowered on to a crutch when riding to her nets. A small lug
sail was used in bad weather to save reefing down . . . usual crew
five men. At Whitby, the mules and ploshers were laid up in the
winter time, either up the line side, ie, on the west bank of the

river Esk in the upper harbour, or else in Spital Beck, a small stream flowing into the upper harbour on the east side . . . as the herring season drew near the craft were painted and got ready for sea, and then moved down to the Bell, the local name for an island of mud in the upper harbour which dries about half ebb. Here the plugs were removed and they were allowed to sink, the tide being able to flow in and out until it was decided the topsides were tight. The plug was replaced and fitting out began, getting mast and sails aboard. To get out of Spital Beck it was necessary to pass under Spital Bridge and as this has a small arch mules were worked through by the crew who laid on their backs and pushed on the stonework with their feet. . . . With the coming of motors, as mules were the largest craft in use at the time, naturally they were converted and used all the year round. . . .

You would not think that a coble was much of a craft for rowing races in . . . an old list of events for Whitby Regatta gives races for yachts, large fishing cobles or mules, open sailing boats, fishermen's cobles, a rowing match for 4-oared boats, sculling match, rowing match for dinghys and a rowing match for cobles, one man in each. In 1866 four Blyth miners, who had already rowed and beaten Blyth and Newbiggin fishermen, rowed a race from Staithes to Whitby, about 10 miles, against four Staithes fishermen for a £200 stake, a silver cup value £15 and the Championship of the German Ocean. Staithes rowed the coble *Jane*, Blyth the *Temperance Star*, and *Jane* won, taking 1 hr 25 m 30 s for the whole course and covered the distance from the Rock Buoy to Whitby Bridge, somewhat over a mile, in 12 m 30 s. They had the flood tide under them, but a headwind for part of the way. Blyth was just behind them, 1 m 12 s as they rounded the Rock Buoy.

In 1873 Redcar fishermen, accepting a challenge by Staithes, rowed a race between Coatham Pier and Saltburn Pier for £100 a side, a distance of about six miles. Redcar cobles were used, Staithes rowed the *Rising Sun*, Redcar the *Gentle Annie*, Redcar won in 40½ minutes. Another race over a four mile course was rowed in 1874, all Staithes cobles, and a win for a Staithes crew in *Sarah Jane*, another Staithes crew were second in *Sir Titus Salt* and Redcar last in *Brotherly Love*.

Lots of things have changed . . . the shipyards are now finished, the old kipper houses almost a thing of the past, the roperies and sail lofts are gone, the fish hawkers with their ponies and flat carts are almost finished . . . two from Staithes are the last and can still be seen (1954) in the Cleveland district shouting 'fresh herrings etc' . . . my grandfather often used to tell how these carts used to race from Staithes to Grosmont to catch the Whitby–York trains, the coast line via Staithes was not then built, with their fish for the inland markets, often coming to the station at a gallop with just a second or so to spare.

The women had a very hard life, up long before dawn, walking over slippery rocks to gather limpets into oval-shaped baskets, often staggering home with a weight of five or six stones on their backs. The fleshy part of the limpet had to be extracted from the shell before they could start baiting the hooks. If bait was scarce even snails did not come amiss, beasts' offal; at the worst, mussels had to be obtained from as far afield as Holland.

Tom Hutchinson wrote to me that mussels from Harlingen cost from 1s 6d to 3s per 10-stone bag, carriage paid. They were kept in tubs filled with half fresh, half salt water and fattened with oatmeal. For crabbing, a favourite bait was 'gurnets' obtained from Grimsby, Hull or Fleetwood and costing about 1s 6d per stone, carriage paid. They were cut up and pickled in strong brine, and the men aimed always to have two days' bait in hand.

When Tom was a young boy his father sold his crabs on commission at Hull; an average price for four-score crabs to a kit was about 6d per score after expenses, rail carriage, commission and porterage had been paid. A day's catch was about six kits, each coble setting some 150 pots. Twine then cost 1s 6d a ball and a shilling bought an eight-fathom warp.

Describing the method of fishing the crab and lobster pots, Tom wrote:

> The pots are attached by a strop to the 'legs' which are approximately 1½ fathoms long and these are attached to the 'tow' every eight to ten fathoms. A 'fleet' consists of from 25 to 50 pots according to size of boat working the gear. The tow is made up in lengths of 20 to 16 fathoms to make easy handling ashore and to enable kinks to be removed. 'Enders' are usually made of cork and the corks on the end tow are to prevent the rope getting down on the bottom at low water slack, fouling and holding the ender down when the flood tide starts.
>
> The same pot is used for both crabs and lobsters. In winter

time they are found in deep water, coming in to shallower water in spring and early summer. In middle and later summer they cast their shells and are therefore scarce at this time, indeed many are 'soft shelled' and consequently unsaleable if caught. They become more plentiful in autumn and then move into deep water. They seem to be sensitive to extreme cold and consequently burrow in the sand or hole up at such times.

Generally, when working for lobsters inshore, the pots are shot into holes or underwater pools fairly close to low-water mark. These are bad places to be caught in when the wind comes on shore with any force and pots are then moved into deep water or brought ashore. Pots caught in shallow water on rock soon smash up, if on a sandy or mud bottom they tend to run up into a heap and lifting them is difficult as 10 or 12 pots and even more at times may be brought up at a time and pots are always half full of sand, small stones and the netting scrubbed about. In deep water they ride pretty safe, but there is always danger of losing them, say if the enders smash up and the fleet shifts it may not be easy to get them again by 'grading' (or towing a grapnel).

Crabs will eat their way out of pots left at sea for a day or two. Lobsters can swim pretty well and can get out of pots in shallow water when the sun is up, so pots are best hauled before sunrise. If the water is 'thick', eg after a storm has stirred up the bottom, they do not get out so easy and also are generally pretty active at these times feeding.

Ten to 12 big cobles sailed from Bridlington for the herring fishing from 1 October to the end of November, using 24 nets, each 60 yd long, 9 to 14 score meshes deep, 36 meshes to a yard and costing £1 to £1 10s ready for sea.

The herring were sold by sample on Crane Wharf at prices often as low as 6d per long hundred, sometimes up to half-a-crown. All were counted out two in each hand, 31 warp of 4 to a long hundred—124 herring. Buyers took anything from a hundred up to a last, nominally 10,000 fish, actually 12,400 or about two tons.

Line fishing started in November and each coble carried 24 to 40 pots to catch whelks for bait out in the Bay. Each man had three lines, 120 hooks to a line of six 'half-pieces'. Prices ruled low, from 9d to 3s a stone, livers were dumped overboard and roes given away. Tom ruefully remarks 'now 30s per stone. Phew!' Each fisherman sold his own catch; there were no salesmen. Six men got a meagre living carrying the fish from the cobles to the place of sale, each coble giving them a few fish in payment. These men were called 'cads'. Winter cobles set nine lines of the same length.

Shares were: if three men and a lad, one line was shot for the boy. Crab fishing, two men and a lad, one fleet of crab pots—eighteen—for the boy. Herring fishing, two men and a lad, the boy a half-share.

The men made their own oilskins, tanning and oiling the sheepskins to make them supple and waterproof. When hauling lines or pots a leather apron—a 'barmskin'—was worn. They used a language 'that the stranger does not know'. Mussels were 'skaaned' from their shells, the pot warps were 'tows', a line without hooks was a 'balk', with hooks—'heeaks'—a 'line balk', with the old bait removed, a 'caved' line. 'Sprags' were young cod, 'brats' turbot, 'doggers' green crabs, a 'gog stick' was a piece of wood used for removing the hooks, a 'lanthron' the lantern, the standard length of line—45 fathoms at Bridlington—was 'a hauf piece', 'dag cleeats' were gloves used for handling lines, made of 'fearnought' or dag cloth. A 'lipper' was a slight swell, the sky was 'harden-faced' when a storm threatened, a boathook a 'clep', while a poor sailing coble was a 'bruzwater', only bruising the water, not slipping through it. The heavy pieces of timber running fore and aft from the mast to the rowing thwart were the 'gantrys or gauntrees' and kept the mast in position when lowered into the crutch aft.

CONSTRUCTION

Cobles can be divided into three classes:
1. Salmon cobles, small light craft about 23 to 24 ft long.
2. Cobles used for winter lining and potting from 26 to 28 ft.
3. 'Ploshers' or 'splashers', used for herring fishing, and ranging from 30 to 40 ft in length.

Few cobles were built exactly alike, most fishermen had their own ideas as to size, depth and so on, but all except the 'mules' were constructed on the same principle, and to beach stern foremost in heavy surf. The true coble is built up on a 'ram plank' not a keel as in other types of boat; forward the bow is lofty with a considerable rise and sharp and hollow below. A rounded forefoot is scarphed into the keel which continues aft to the ram plank lying horizontal.

The old boats were measured for length from the heel of the sternpost to the scarph of the stem or forefoot, and this length was called the ram. It varied from 15 to 40 ft, and was always made from the finest baulk of oak obtainable. The stern was practically flat-bottomed, the bow the usual form of a normal boat. The ram plank was cut out of the solid with the after end curved up, broad and thick, tapering forward to suit the scantling of the keel; here it had a slight curve downwards, giving a graceful wave-like form. The hull was now built up on the ram plank and keel, the first planks for'ard rise vertical; aft they lie horizontal until sufficient width of bottom is obtained. Then the strakes are given an upward tilt aft as well, the first strake to do this being called the 'rising stroke' or strake. The number of strakes varied considerably, even in boats of the same size, and much depended on the timber available; but they were always as wide as possible. The planks were of local grown larch, the trees selected having a slight curve towards the base; the trunk was sawn up over a sawpit, the lengths being about 12 ft, width 18 in and 1 in thick for a large coble, and fitted so that the curve gave the bold sheer required. Nails were of copper or galvanised iron, clenched over rooves. The upper plank—the sheer strake—was given a pronounced tumble-home, particularly aft of amidships.

After fitting the frames, stern, thwarts and gunwale, the hull was turned over and the side drafts—old name 'skorvels'—were fitted aft and a false keel fastened to the underside of the ram plank forward, and generally shod with iron. When a coble was aground she was slightly hollow and rested on the deep side drafts. Elm rubbers, or 'binns', were spiked to the timbers with special nails made by the blacksmith and shaped like a lino brad. These rubbing strakes were protected by a half-round iron, and beading was fitted to preserve the edges of the planks from damage.

In a big coble the forefoot was 9 in deep, scarphed to a keel 6 in deep, with a 1-in iron on the forefoot. The gunwale was always outside, bottom boards were of 9 in by 1½-in deal.

SAILING QUALITIES AND RIG

Cobles were either sharp- or square-sterned, the former being favoured by pilots and fishermen who could use a harbour and not have to beach their boats. Square-sterned cobles were faster on a wind; sailing to windward in a breeze, a square-sterned boat would carry more sail than she could run with, a sharp-sterned would run and go to windward under the same quantity of sail, steer better off the wind and run more safely. Pilots preferred a sharp stern as they frequently towed astern of steamers; a square-sterned coble was always towed stern first. When hard pressed, the water was thrown off at the shoulder and amidships owing to the tumble home, with the gunwale at times below the water level without shipping any water.

Generally speaking, the flatter the bottom the faster the coble would sail, being at her best with the short mast set and a 'double reefed' breeze. Running was always the weak point as, if sailing too fast on a sea, steering became difficult and in inexperienced hands a broach-to was certain. As in the Shetland sixerns, there was always a man at the halyards ready to drop the lugsail if the boat 'ran away'. The pins for belaying the halyards projected from the underside of the gunwale, the bight was put round the pin and 'set light', the fall being jammed between the gunwale and the standing part of the rope so that one pull would release it. There were no cleats or belaying pins in the early boats and no place to make the mainsheet fast; cobles were never luffed in a squall. The bottom halyard block had clip hooks, the tack hook and sheet hook were always moused when sailing. The backstay led from an iron ring at the top of the mast to a single block fall.

The rig was simple. In the small cobles only a mast raking aft and a dipping lug provided with several rows of reef points. The halyards were always set up on the weather side to stay the mast, and the tack to the weather bow. When coming about, the falls were slacked off, the tack unhooked and halyards let go, the yard was passed round the mast, the tack hooked on opposite bow, halyards shifted to weather side and the sheet moved over by the helmsman. Bowlines were used to keep the luff taut.

The bigger boats carried two masts, a long one for fine weather and a short on which the double-reefed lug was set; this was used as a bowsprit when a jib was set. A few had a mizzen mast, but it was of little use on a wind except to balance the jib, and it was always the first sail stowed if the wind increased. There were two, sometimes three, steps for the mast which had considerable play fore and aft when the clamp was on, and by means of a wedge before or behind the mast it could be raked to the exact amount required, as much as 10 ft in a heavy sea. When sailing fast the tiller, mast and boat quivered and hummed. In light winds, the mast was upright; if a fair breeze it was in the middle step; in a heavy gale well raked, thus easing the bows. Some boatmen favoured five reefs, some six and a half, tiller ropes were always used when sailing hard, 'a round turn, round tiller and held in the hand'.

The 18-ft yard was slung about a quarter of its length by an iron sling 2 ft long, not nailed but lashed and covered with leather; when set, the bowsprit was well steeved up. When tacking, the backstay was handed, jibsheets changed, tack let go and bowsed down to wind'ard, mainsheet tackle unhooked and carried over to leeward, the boat making much leeway unless kept sailing fast.

The oars were of peculiar shape. The blade of ash was scarphed to a deal handle—'oarwash lashed to clog'—working with an iron ring on a single thole pin, the wide part of the

loom resting on the gunwale. Cobles were light to row. Filey
boats built by Cambridge were noted for their good qualities
under canvas.

Lack of communications and the isolation of these small
fishing villages until the coming of the railway account for the
local differences in the build of cobles and the wide variety of
names given to the same piece of equipment. About 1860, these
picturesque spots began to attract summer visitors and taking
them to sea on pleasure trips broke the age-oid tradition of
keeping the Sabbath. Against the white chalk cliffs the gaily
coloured cobles, lined up facing seaward, blue sky, white horses
coming in on golden sands, all made an unforgettable picture.

CHAPTER FIVE

THE EAST COAST: LINCOLNSHIRE, NORFOLK AND SUFFOLK

IN the Humber area, boats known as 'gold-dusters' attended on shipping, 'seeking' incoming vessels and boarding them to take their ropes to buoys. As the first boat on the scene secured the work, they needed to be fast under oars or sail. Some of the watermen had their regular customers, the masters of sailing ships frequenting the Humber. At times a steamer asked for their services, then a boatman used an iron hook on a 12-ft pole to catch any projection before hanging on to the rope attached; the steamer never slackened her speed and it was a hazardous job to pay out the rope and keep clear of the wash, and more so the death-dealing propeller.

In the 1880s these boats were about 18 ft long, 6 ft 6 in beam, clench-built with oak or larch planking $\frac{1}{2}$ in thick. Frames, of American elm, steamed not sawn, were spaced about 6 in apart, floors flat, four to five thwarts, little ballast, a transom stern, wooden thole pins, and heavy rope fenders.

With the decline in the number of sailing ships entering the Humber, the tendency was for the boats to be built smaller, but few survived into the twentieth century.

The rig of the Hull boats was two masts of equal length, about 2 ft shorter than the dimensions of the boat so that they stowed snugly inside when the craft was being pulled. Then masts, yards and sails were rolled up in a bundle and secured by a chain to the middle thwart. The foremast was stepped about one-fifth of the length from the bow, the mainmast amidships. Two equal spritsails were set, high-peaked with the spars on the

A Humber 'gold-duster'

starboard side of the masts, two lines of reef points, and one brail leading to a block at the top of the mast.

The Grimsby 'dusters' ran up to 22 ft in length with a beam of 7 ft, 8 to 12 cwt of inside ballast, rockered keel with up to 3 cwt of lead, and were rigged with two standing lugsails. As trade declined, the foremast was removed and a lofty, dipping lug set on the mast amidships. It was made of unbleached calico with 9-in cloths and four reefs, the tack being taken to a similar number of points in the bow to give the correct set when the sail was reefed.

At Grimsby and Hornsea there were a number of Norfolk fishermen who had come north with their crab boats; nearly a score could often have been seen lying at moorings outside a small lockpit at the Fish Dock, and others at Spurn and Withersea.

Along the Lincolnshire coast the fisheries were of little importance, except in the Wash for mussels and shrimps, stownets being used for sprats, trawls for shrimps and soles. Up to the 1870s, the mussel 'scaups' gave much employment, but the demand for young mussels for manure led to a serious shortage of large ones for bait. So acute did the problem become that at times Staithes fishermen were paying up to 5s a bag, sufficient to bait only two lines, plus labour of 1s a line for baiting. It paid them to get mussels from Hamburg at 4s 4d a bag, sufficient for four lines.

Mussels were 'the poor man's oyster'; average length 2 in when two years old, about 39 to the lb, 87,360 to the ton—16 bags or 32 bushels—value £1. The close season was June, July and August, and minimum size had to be over 2 in. Whelks were the great enemies, clearing a large acreage in a few hours; strong easterly gales also played havoc with the beds. In 1871 about £5,000 worth were sold at Boston, but in 1874 some 195 acres were killed by fierce gales. Fortunately, whelks were eagerly sought by cod smacksmen working on the Dogger Bank and elsewhere, the measure being a 'wash', 21 quarts and 1 pint, about three-quarters of a bushel, average price 4s. Huge quantities were landed at Sheringham and sold for bait.

At Lynn, 17 'mussel scalps' were under the control of the Corporation, the largest being Lower Daisby, ½ mile long, 300 yd wide, bottom mud. During the winter of 1873-4 the quantity marketed was 2,480 tons, the following season, 4,452 tons. The large cockle beds also provided a living.

For shrimping, all the fishing craft were cutter-rigged, and easy to handle as they had to work in intricate channels between vast sandbanks drying out at low water. From Boston on the river Witham and Wisbech on the Nene, the smacks often had to beat against foul winds in narrow, winding channels. These conditions naturally influenced the design, the Boston boats having raking sternposts and long, overhanging counters, rockered keels, high bows and low sterns for ease in working the beam trawls. A raking sternpost enabled the underwater lines to be carried out more finely without resorting to long counters, thus adding to speed and turning powers.

At Wisbech they were somewhat smaller; all had big, powerful windlasses for'ard. The cutters were about 30 ft long with a beam of 9 to 10 ft and draught around 4 ft 6 in. The keel was straight, forefoot square, good sheer and rise of floor.

At Lynn, on the Ouse, the largest cutters went up to 50 ft overall, good beam, clench or carvel build and completely decked. The 'shrimpers' were smaller, some 36 ft overall, no windlass, and a long, open hatch amidships as they were used chiefly for cockling. The third class consisted of the double-ended, clinker-built cutters known locally as 'yolls'. These were of shallow draft and built to lie easily on the mud while being laden with cockles. *Baden Powell* and *Edward VII* were the last working yolls. (Picture, p 107.)

A pole mast, a little over one-third from the stem, had a gaff and boom, the loose-footed mainsail having three lines of reef points. A long, reeving bowsprit, set to starboard of the stem-head, carried a jib of varying sizes, and a foresail was set on the stay. In light weather a big 'jacky' topsail was hoisted.

In 1872, Boston had 5 first-class and 89 second-class boats

registered; Lynn had 11 and 100, one of my photographs showing a registration number as high as LN 235.

The beam trawls were up to 20 ft in length, and a buoy was
sometimes attached at the cod-end so that, should the net become full of mud, the cod could be picked up and emptied
without hauling the whole trawl inboard. Generally the net
was hauled for comparatively short periods to prevent un-
wanted fish being killed; these had to be returned alive to the
sea.

Inshore the brown, or common, shrimp was sought in
summer, and during the winter in deeper water a few miles seaward. The catch was sorted—'culled'—in a riddle which was
swished about over the side on the surface of the water, thus
allowing small fry to escape through the narrow oblong slits.
The measure was a curious one, from 1½d to 4½d, or the number
of pennies or halfpennies, new or old, held face together which
could pass between the wires. The mesh varied in different
localities, at Yarmouth it was three halfpennies, old, or three
new pennies, in the Thames three pennies for large, a penny-
farthing for small. The shrimps were thrown into a copper and
boiled immediately on board.

Little is known of the smacks working from Wells and
Blakeney in the nineteenth century. In 1821 an extensive bed of
oysters was discovered off Happisburgh and hundreds of tubs
were brought in by these vessels. In 1870, 18 decked oyster
smacks were owned in Blakeney and 14 herring luggers owned
in Sheringham and Cromer used the harbour there. The
number of fishing boats registered in Blakeney was 300. The
last of the local oyster smacks was *Pelican*, which dredged up to
1935. She was a double-ended cutter with an overall length of
about 35 ft, a small cuddy for'ard and a large cockpit aft.

At Cley and Blakeney the boats used mainly to convey very
heavy loads of mussels from the 'scaups' to the Carnser were
known locally as 'canoes', probably derived from the 'canots'
carried on the decks of the French cod-fishing schooners.
Several drove ashore at Cley over the years and their boats were

much sought after and copied by local builders. Length overall varied between 13 ft 6 in and 16 ft, with a beam of between 4 ft 10 in and 5 ft 9 in. The bottom was not absolutely flat,

> a good canoe having about 2 in rocker and about ¼ in kammel, and usually three longitudinal rubbing strakes on the bottom with a toe and heel piece to save the main planks from abrasion. The sides consist of four, or sometimes three, sometimes five planks a side laid clinker-fashion and meeting the bottom at a chine. The great peculiarity of these boats is the broad heel given to their transom sterns . . . about 8 or 9 in wide. This is necessary to provide a lot of buoyancy aft to cope with heavy loads of mussels: without the buoyancy given by the broad heel even gentle poling or rowing would put the stern of a heavily laden canoe—which will have a freeboard of no more than 6 in—under water.
>
> The wood preferred was elm for the bottom and deal for the topsides, with oak knees. Fastenings were often galvanised nails, although early ones were usually copper-fastened. For rowing, they have thole pins, though later ones have rowlocks, some carry a lugsail but they do not sail well. 'They are cows under sail, steer with an oar over the stern', Mr Peter Catling tells me, 'When light they row badly, loaded they are poppets. They can stand an incredible amount of rough water—if the crew don't get rolled out.'

So wrote Mr R. W. Malster.

North Norfolk fishermen and boatbuilders spoke of crab boats as so many feet 'on the keel'; a boat with an overall length of 16 ft would be 12 ft on the keel.

Bigger boats with a keel length of 15 ft—'hovellers'—worked from Sheringham and Cromer beaches. The name suggests that originally they attended on ships and engaged in salvage work, but in later years they were used for herring and mackerel fishing and for cod-lining. Cod were laid out on the beach beside each boat and the fisherman acted as auctioneer. 'He would pick up two stones off the beach and when he couldn't get another bid he would bang them together to signal that the sale was concluded.'

For'ard was a removable cuddy, shipped for the herring fishing, to give some shelter for the crew who went far seaward

Page 147 (above) Rowhedge Regatta, 1904. *Elise*, CK 299, built by P. Harris and owned by J. Green; *Maria*, CK 21, built by P. Harris and owned by J. Gunn; *Sunbeam*, CK 328, built by Howard and owned by W. Cranfield. Note three different types of topsail and trawls on board; (below) *Sunbeam* leading *Neva*, 86 CK. *Neva* is setting her big staysail and her new mainsail has stretched badly

Page 148 (above) Armorel, CS 5, a Colne cutter sold away; (below) William & Emily, CK 212, hauled up on slipway, c 1950. Note sharp floors, rounded bilge, straight stem and rounded forefoot

to fish with long lines or nets. The for'ard oar ports were blocked with a chunk of wood known as the 'cork'. Similar boats were used for whelking at Wells, the grounds lying some 10 miles from the port.

Many of the crabbers and whelkers were built at Sheringham by Lown, whose business was taken over by John Johnson, or by Robert Emery. Other builders were Howard Brett of Cley, William Starling of Blakeney, Tom Dack of Wells and Gaze of Mundesley.

At Sheringham and Cromer were fleets of luggers similar to those at Yarmouth where many were built, and in the 1870s the majority were converted to 'dandies'. These 'great boats' followed the herring shoals from Scarborough to Yarmouth and also went lining for cod. From the last week of March until June or July, they would be crabbing off the Yorkshire coast, taking a couple of crab boats on deck to work the pots. These were also used when working the cod lines, the hooks being baited with 'lampor eels' brought alive in tubs from Holland.

When the men returned to Cromer for the spring crabbing they brought back from the Yorkshire coast live crabs which they shot overboard off Cromer to replenish the local stock. A crab of a light brown colour was called a 'Yorkshireman'. These boats were owned by families and carried a crew of ten for the herring voyage, four being local men paid by the share, the rest capstan hands paid per last.

Cromer and Sheringham were noted for crabs and lobsters, the sea bottom being rocky, but until the coming of the railway and the rise of the villages as watering places thronged by visitors in the summer months, sales were mostly local, two or three buyers from Norwich having it all their own way.

In the 1870s, the crab season lasted from 1 April to 20 June, most of the catches being sent inland. The lobster season was from mid-July to Michaelmas. Catches were sold locally, their value ranging from £5,000 to £6,000.

The men agreed among themselves that no crab measuring less than 4½ in across the shell should be brought ashore, under a

I

penalty of £1, a big sum in those days of golden sovereigns. Heavy fines were also imposed on any man bringing in a 'berry' lobster. The fishermen kept a close watch on one another, being convinced that such regulations were essential for the preservation of the fisheries.

Crab pots were replacing the old-fashioned hoop net by the middle of the nineteenth century and 30 years later about 50 boats worked out of Cromer, setting from 30 to 25 pots each.

The boats were, and still are, double-ended, short, deep and beamy, with no thole pins or rowlocks in the upper strake; instead the oars were worked in oar ports—'orrucks'—cut in the top plank. After landing on the shore, the men pushed the looms of the oars through the opposite hole, lifted the boat and carried it up the shelving beach. When launching, the boat was run down over the pebbles and pushed out into the water, the men scrambling in over the stern quarters. The crew usually numbered two, sometimes three.

Hulls were clench-built of oak, later larch, the length varying from 15 ft to 19 ft, beam 5 ft to 7 ft, stem and stern posts were rounded with the rudder projecting about 2 ft below the straight oak keel. Planking was about $\frac{1}{2}$ in thick, no gunwale, but the sheer strake was protected with cope iron to take the chafe when lifting pots. There were no floorboards except small triangular ones in the sternsheets on which the crew stood to haul the pots or lines; three thwarts and a parting board amidships. Ballast was beach shingle carried in four or five canvas bags, shifted to windward every time the boat went about and emptied before each beaching.

The mast, short enough to stow inside the boat, was fitted well for'ard in a wooden step notched down on two deep floors. The large dipping lug, dressed an almost black colour, was short in the luff, long in the head, leech and foot, with an area of 100 to 120 sq ft. The only rigging was the halyard, always set up to windward. When sailing close-hauled, the tack was made fast to the stemhead, but with the wind aft it was taken to a hook on the weather side inside the sheer strake just for'ard of the mast. The sheet was led through a hole in the top of the stern-post, along the boat's side and in through the after oar port; it was never made fast but held in the hand.

The yard was slung at one-third of its length and when fishing was in progress the sail was rolled round it and placed for'ard out of the way of the crew. Under sail, the boats were reputed to 'fetch where they point' and could get off the beach in any weather.

Bait for the crab pots was brought from Lowestoft, a middle-man supplying fish offal which was retailed in small hampers to the Cromer fishermen at an average price of 5s each, including carriage. One hamper baited 40 pots, which had to be fresh-baited every day.

The Sheringham crabber *Star of Peace*, measured up by W. H. Blake early in the 1930s, had larch planking, oak keel and stems, bent floors, 1 in thick, between every frame extending to

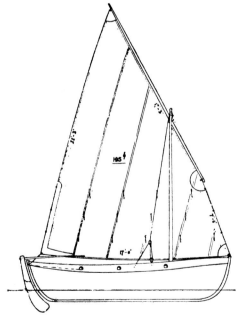

Sail plan of the Sheringham crabber *Star of Peace*

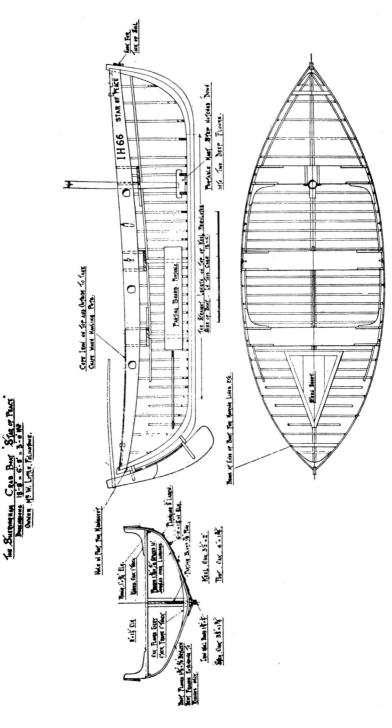

The Sheringham Crab Boat "Star of Peace"
Dimensions 18'8" × 6'8" × 3'0" MB
Owner Mr W. Little, Falmouth.

Home Port
Zack of Peace

IH 66   STAR OF PEACE

Portable Mast, Step, No Chees Down
Into Two Deep Floors.

Cert Iron on Top and Bottom To Take
Chafe When Hauling Pots.

Parting Board—Bottoms.

The Straight Length of Top of Keel Regulates
The Size of Boat. In This Case 13'-0".
Size of Boat.

Beam of Eden of Boat, For Working Lines, etc.

Keel Shoe.

Hole in Port For Mudhook?

Beams 1¼", No Steam to
Angled over Lambing.

Parting Board 6 or 6½" Thick.

Risers ¾" Elm

Risers ¾" Elm
Keens, Oar, Vanes.

Keel, Oak, 3½ × 2.
Stem, Oak, 4 × 1¾.

Boat Timbers 1½ × ¾ Bent in
Boat Timbers Excluding 2
Risers only.

Lead Keel, Bottom Plate,
Stem, Oak, 3½ × 1¾.

Plans of the Sheringham crabber *Star of Peace*, drawn by W. H. Blake the rising, which was 1 in × ¾ in elm. The lugsail had six cloths and three lines of reef points. The boat could carry 3,600 mackerel, 38 wash of whelks, three wash weighing about 1 cwt. Ballast was stones from the beach, and the parting board prevented the bags from shifting. *Star of Peace* was built by Robert Emery at Sheringham in 1912, price complete £19 2s 6d.

South of Happisburgh a different type of boat worked from the beaches, double-ended and clinker-built, resembling the famous yawls of the beach companies. These 'punts', which varied in length from 18 to 20 ft, had one mast and a dipping lug, but the largest, about 25 ft long, had two masts and set a dipping lug on the foremast and a standing lug on the mizzen.

A typical punt had an overall length of 19 ft 7 in and a beam of 6 ft 9 in, and cost, complete with sails, about £27. The timbers, spaced at 6-in centres, were 1¼ in by 1 in, joggled to fit the strakes.

These boats were used principally for drift-net fishing, but some had gaff mainsails for seasonal trawling. For drift-net fishing close inshore, beach skiffs were used, clinker-built pulling boats with a length of about 12 to 14 ft, beam about 3 ft, and worked by two men.

Fleets of transom-sterned shrimpers sailed from the harbours of Yarmouth and Lowestoft, mostly cutter-rigged and clinker-built. The mainsail of the Yarmouth boats was rigged in an unusual manner, being set loose-footed on a boom whose heel had neither gooseneck nor crutch, but was fixed with a heel-rope. To stow the sail, the heel of the boom was cast off, the peak of the gaff lowered and the sail furled in to the mast. In light weather a big topsail—a 'jubilee'—with a long yard laced to the luff and a short one at the clew was set above the pole mast. A big jib with its head close up to the masthead and leech parallel to the mast was often set instead of the usual smaller jib and foresail.

The Yarmouth shrimpers averaged around two tons and used beam nets 9 to 10 ft long with no ground rope. In 1878 fifty were registered. The red shrimp was first discovered in Yarmouth

Roads by beachmen sweeping for anchors early in the nineteenth century and the season was from February to August.
With the development of seaside resorts following the introduction of railways, the demand for shrimps increased by leaps and
bounds, costers selling them at twopence a pint.

Lowestoft men worked two trawls, one for'ard with the warp
leading from the end of the bowsprit, the other aft, the boat
lying broadside to the tide and driving with it.

Also fishing from Yarmouth were the 'wolders', boats of $3\frac{1}{2}$ to
10 tons and up to 40 ft in length, which worked the inshore
trawling grounds—they got their name from the Would, a clear
channel 8 miles in width, separating Haisborough Sand from
the shore. The boats were either cutter- or ketch-rigged.

At Yarmouth, the big open boats were known as 'punts' although they ran up to 37 ft overall, beam 12 ft 3 in, depth 4 ft
9 in. The clench-built, copper-fastened hull weighed 5·8 tons,
ballast 5 tons, and cost £75; fitted with two lugsails, a fore and
mizzen, with stores ready for sea the boat cost £125, 'and will
last, with care, from 15 to 20 years' wrote the builder, W.
Teasdale, in November 1848. 'Some of her size are decked and
it is talked of laying decks to many more, but they do not sail
so fast when decked.'

Yarmouth and Lowestoft having harbours, the boats were
naturally larger than those working off open beaches; at the
Suffolk port, the average size was 35 ft overall. 'The fishermen
prefer the open boats because they can fish with two men less
than in those with decks. The number is four men and a boy,
which, supposing each to have an equal amount of fish, makes
considerable difference in sharing the proceeds.' The cost was
about £165 with deck, £150 without, including masts, sails and
rigging, according to the builder, Samuel Sparham.

In place of the two dipping lugs favoured by northern fishermen, the rig here was to have a standing lug on the mizzen, and
a wide, almost upright, transom stern.

The Lowestoft shrimpers were around 20 ft in length, beam
8 ft, depth 4 ft. In later years many had a small cuddy for'ard,

iron ballast stowed inboard, a crew of two—sometimes one—
and worked a 15-ft trawl. The rig was a dipping lug on the
foremast, with two lines of reef points, and a curious standing
lug on the mizzen mast which raked sharply for'ard; the sail
had a short yard, a long loose foot, tack at the foot of the mast
and, some 18 in up the mast, a boom going to the clew and
sheeting almost centrally to a short outrigger. Others had a
longer yard and an outrigger at the foot of the mast. The
decked boats were cutter-rigged. (Picture, p 108.)

At Aldeburgh, the small 'sprat boats' were about 4 ft shorter,
with a beam of 6 ft 3 in or thereabouts, clench-built, a wide
transom stern with the mizzen mast stepped against it and an
outrigger to starboard. At the stemhead was a short iron boom-
kin with a hook to take the tack of the fore dipping lug. The
oars were worked in double thole pins, four a side, three
thwarts; amidships were parting boards to divide soles, plaice
and roker, aft was a space for the nets.

Oak was largely used in the construction as the boats were
subject to heavy wear when hauled up and down the beach.
Around the turn of the century Critten of Southwold was
building 15-ft spratters for about £30. Although some of the
boats ran up to 18 ft in length, the fishermen preferred the
smaller type to save the extra hand. The usual crew of three
went fishing for herring and sprats in winter, shooting about 18
nets, each 30 yd long and 18 ft deep. An average catch of sprats
was 40 to 45 bushels. In summer, the men trawled for soles,
plaice, dabs and roker, using a 16-ft beam trawl.

A 20-ft oak, clench-built, lug-rigged beach fishing boat
built by Reynolds of Lowestoft for H. C. Barham of Aldeburgh
cost: wages £16 15 5d, fastenings £2 6s 1½d, centre plate £2
9s 6d, wood for hull £9, ironwork £1 6s 4d, nett cost £31 17s
4½d. These figures were in a notebook given to me by the late
William Parker, date about 1903. A usual price was about £1
a foot, including hull and spars.

The prices charged for a 23-ft cutter-rigged shrimp boat,
clench-built of oak by Reynolds in July 1905 were:

	£	s	d
Wages to hull	16	2	2
Fastenings	1	8	8
Wood to hull	17	13	11
Spars & blocks	5	17	4
Smithwork to hull & spars	3	19	6
	45	1	7

An 18-ft oak-built, half-decked sailing boat:

	£	s	d
Wages	16	17	11
Wood hull	10	10	
Fastenings	2	7	6½
	29	15	5½

No lead or sails supplied. Contract price £38.

Two 15-ft rowing boats of spruce:

	£	s	d
Wages	10	10	5
12-ft sailing dinghy: wages	6	14	8

Reynolds also built boats for the Royal Navy. The net cost of a 32-ft steam cutter was £275 13s 8d, and this price included £5 7s 8d railway carriage to Chatham. A 30-ft sailing cutter cost £121 14s, including a rail charge of £3 10s, one 32 ft long cost £134 14s 7d, including £4 15s for 'gun cone'.

These prices include masts, spars and sails, and the hulls were probably clench-built as the next entry for a 36-ft sailing pinnace is carvel, with two diagonal skins of teak, and the price was £324 9s 7d.

A 27-ft special surveying whaler, built of silver spruce, was priced at £97 3s 11d, and a 30-ft whaler cost approximately the same. All costs are net, no mention being made of contract price.

It is interesting to compare the prices for a heavy sailing cutter and a light-built gig with the charge for an admiral's 32-ft galley:

1906:	30-ft cutter			30-ft gig			32-ft admiral's galley		
	£	s	d	£	s	d	£	s	d
Wages	33	3	2½	34	8		28	16	6½
Stores	8	17							
Timber, hull	28	5	11½	19	1		19	13	7½
Fastenings				1	17	7	3	19	4
Sparmakers	5	13	11	3	10	5	3	10	5
Ironwork	7	—	6	1	19	3	1	19	3
Sails, covers, & awnings	10	19	4	6	3	4	7	15	6
Metalwork	6	13	6	6	16	10	6	16	10
Leathering		6			6			6	
Blocks	1	1	8		12	4		12	4
Wire rope		13	2		2			2	
Hemp rope	2	14	9	2			2		
Galvanising	1	5			10			10	
Rail carriage	1	7	6		17	6		17	6
Paint, lab. & mat'ls	6	17	6	3			3	10	
Riggers	2	10		1	10		1	10	
Launching, labour		15			7	6		7	6
Carriage to Chatham	3	10		2	4		2	4	
Net cost	121	14		85	5	9	84	10	10

The price in 1900 for a small boat for a smack or drifter was £9 11s 11d net. For a sailing drifter with boat, £454 15s 3d. Contract price, £575.

In January 1904, an 18-ft, clench-built boat for the coast-guards cost:

	£	s	d
Wages	6	18	1½
Wood	4	15	
Fastenings		15	9½
Ironwork	1		
Net cost	13	8	11

Contract price, £22

Yarmouth has always been associated with herring and as far back as 1614 it is known that cobles from Yorkshire came south for the autumn fishery. Writing in that year Tobias Gentleman says: 'also the fishermen of the north countries beyond Scarborough and Robin Hood's Bay, and some as far as the Bishoprick of Durham, do hither resort yearly, in poor little boats called five-men cobles, and all the herrings that they take, they sell fresh unto the Yarmouth men to make red herrings'.

In the parish registers at Wells are references to three men who perished in a cobble boat in 1584; four men 'being perished in a cobble sunk off ye haven' in 1590, and frequent later records tell of accidents to cobles. In the 1875 Report Frank Buckland refers to these boats as fishing from Wells.

In 1822 three men were lost when a coble put off from Corton beach to obtain passage in a passing vessel for four shipwrecked seamen from Sunderland. The coble was drawn under when a rope was flung from the brig and eight occupants were thrown into the water; only five were rescued. Again, a Yorkshire coble in the employment of Mr Shuckford rescued the crew of the Yarmouth lugger *Walter & Ann* in 1838. In 1857 ten men put off in a coble to rescue three people from the Lynn sloop *Alpha*, wrecked off Winterton. 'The coble was hardly ever used and the wonder was how the gallant men collected oars and trusted themselves in such a boat on so perilous an adventure,' to quote from the RNLI citation making an award to the men who again went out some months later and saved the crew of a Whitby brig.

I am indebted to an article by R. W. Malster in *The Norfolk Sailor* for the information on cobles.

E. W. Cooke drew a Yarmouth coble in 1828, and the engraving is before me as I write. There are differences in build; the forefoot is not so deep and the planks are narrower. Such boats may well have been built by local builders. Half-models and crude plans have been found in local boatyards and at Ipswich, but that is not evidence that any were in fact built. Undoubtedly cobles were used on the Norfolk coast, but I hesitate to say that the local boatmen preferred them to their own punts or 'wolders'.

In the days of sail, collier brigs, billyboys, snows, brigantines, topsail schooners, ketches and spritsail barges passed up and down the coast in an endless procession. In bad weather hundreds would bring up in Yarmouth Roads to await a slant or ride out a gale. This anchorage, some 6 miles in extent and about 1 mile wide, with depths ranging from 5 to 12 fathoms, has a bottom of sand, mud and stones, affording good holding ground except close inshore, and protected from the east by the Scroby Sands, some 2 to $2\frac{1}{2}$ miles seaward. The northern end, known as Caister Road, has the Caister Shoal running nearly parallel to the coast for about 2 miles within the 2-fathom boundary, the centre drying out at low water. The Cockle and Winterton shoals were further hazards. To the south lay the Corton Sand, a shoal with only 12 to 18 ft of water over it, steep-to on the east, but deepening gradually northward. The approach to the Roads was through the narrow Hewett Channel between the Corton Sand on the south-west and the Scroby Sands on the north-east, a fairway with a least width of barely $4\frac{1}{2}$ cables and subject to constant changes, as are all the sands in this locality. To navigate them safely demanded local knowledge or familiarity from constant usage.

These were similar conditions to those in the Downs off the SE Kent coast and the East Anglian beachmen were akin to the Deal boatmen, both famed for their skill in handling open boats in the most appalling conditions, renowned as pilots, always ready to go to the assistance of vessels in distress and rescuing thousands of lives, long before lifeboats were thought of and stationed at danger points. And both suffered the calumny of poets who, sitting comfortably ashore, wrote scathing remarks about those brave men who, risking their all, expected some reward.

The golden years must surely have been during the long French and Napoleonic wars. Men working in 1792 might well have thought those days would last for ever—five, ten, fifteen, twenty years passed and still the fighting dragged on. Ships of the Royal Navy frequently lay for weeks in the Roads and few captains or masters of merchantmen dared to use their own boats to come ashore, lest the crews deserted. Attendance on ships, carrying out stores, and other calls, was undoubtedly a lucrative trade.

The beach yawls—local name 'yols—and pilot gigs were owned by 'companies', groups of from 10 to 30 or more beachmen who handed over all profits to a common fund which was shared out at regular intervals. Certain rules had to be obeyed. Each member on joining paid his share and was then entitled to take his place as one of the crew whenever the yawl was launched, but was allowed to take his share of money earned in piloting or salvage work if he was present at the time the yawl floated. It was not uncommon for a man to run into the surf in order to touch the boat, or climb into her, but then he had to be on the beach on its return.

Beach companies are known to have been in existence at the beginning of the eighteenth century. The Old Company of Lowestoft Beachmen was established early in the 1800s. Eight were operating from Yarmouth in 1858: the Young, Diamond, Star, Denny's, Holkham, Standard, V.C., and Layton's, later Robert's. At Lowestoft the Old or South End Co, the Young and the North Roads Co. Others were at Caister, Winterton, Palling and Southwold.

The yawls and gigs were always ready for instant launching. In bad weather the men sheltered in a long, wooden shed adorned with figureheads, and the trail and name boards of ships that had gone to pieces on the treacherous coast. Outside was a half boat upended to serve as a shelter, while adjoining was a lookout tower, sometimes an elaborate structure with a staging surrounded with wooden screens; here a day and night watch was kept. Others had a mast with rough steps nailed to the sides and a crow's nest at the top. Keen eyes searched the offing for any glimpse of a signal for a pilot, a distress rocket or a vessel standing into danger. Then came a wild rush to the shore from every quarter to get afloat. Some placed skids under the bows, others gathered along the sides awaiting the cry

'Hold her up', then the stools were removed and the boat started down the beach. Meanwhile, others were carrying bags of ballast, and the sails were shipped. The crew tumbled in, each doing his appointed job, placing ballast, setting the lugs.

Once the boat had started over the greased skids there was no stopping her. As she entered the water an extra spurt was given by using a long spar, called a 'sett', which connected to the stern roller at the head of the sternpost. The mizzen was already hoisted, for a moment the yawl would hang as the foresail went up; then she was away at racing speed. Rival boats were also afloat, all vieing to get ahead, and for mile after mile perhaps only a length or two separated them. Superbly handled, these craft were able to live in any sea, and when going to a ship ashore outside the sands never a thought was given to going round. The helmsman fearlessly drove right through the leaping, angry breakers, the bow lifting on a big sea, then diving into the seething hollow. Here in a maelstrom of broken water the greatest caution had to be taken, the foresheet slackened and the bows eased to the seas which drenched the crew with flying spray. Seven or more men would be baling furiously, flinging water overboard as fast as it came in. At times the stout oak keel touched bottom with a judder, shaking the boat from end to end, but still she flew on until she reached deep water and turned to seek the vessel in distress, the leading yawl dropping her sails and men leaping on deck, grabbing any shroud or handy rope. Men indeed!

John Annis went to sea as an apprentice to J. D. Palmer of Yarmouth, but was taken by a press gang at Lisbon and served for nearly six years in the sloop-of-war *Sabrina*. After peace was proclaimed he went for a time in merchantmen, sailing from his home town before becoming a beachman. On one occasion in company with the yawls *Sovereign* and *Beeswing* he put off to the assistance of the brig *Aid* of Sunderland. Being unable to get near the vessel owing to the surf, he offered to veer the yawl *Seaman's Assistance* down to the brig, and there being no other volunteers he did so single-handed, boarded and saved the lives of eight men and a boy.

Another gallant service was when he put off to a brig near the Scroby Sand, jumped on board with two others, put a spring on the cable, cast the brig clear and thus saved the vessel and ten hands. On two occasions of a similar nature he received no reward. In his old age he petitioned the Lords Commissioners of the Admiralty to 'spend his few remaining days as a pensioner in that noble asylum, The Royal Hospital at Greenwich, to which all true-hearted sailors look as one of the proudest rewards he can obtain. And your memorialist will ever pray (Signed) James Annis X his mark.' The mayor, aldermen and common council, as well as many influential inhabitants, testified to his character.

Early in December 1859 the smack *Gratitude* of Grimsby struck a wreck off Haisboro' and sank on the edge of the sand. The crew took to the rigging at 10 pm on a bitter night and remained there all the following day, when the lad fell to his death. A brig sighted the wreck and put out her boat but it could not fetch owing to the strong tide. After trying vainly for over an hour, the master picked up his boat and hauled in for Winterton, hoisted a 'waif' and told the beachmen who came off the whereabouts of the wreck. The Bacton yawl was immediately launched and rescued the skipper and three hands after they had been exposed in the rigging for 60 hours, clinging to 8 ft of bare mast. The men were practically naked, having used most of their clothes as 'waives' to try and attract attention.

For the saving of life there was no reward, yet the beachmen sent £1 to the Sailors' Home to which the destitute smacksmen were taken.

In October 1854 a ship was seen to be ashore on the Holm Sand. It was blowing a strong ssw gale when the yawl *Happy New Year* put off with a crew of 12. A tremendous sea was running with heavy breakers on the sands making it exceedingly dangerous to come alongside. Suggestions were made that it would be better to wait for the lifeboat, but the beachmen feared that the ship would soon go to pieces. Without hesitation they entered the broken water and, passing alongside two men jumped into the yawl, but the captain fell into the sea and had to be hauled into safety. The yawl had barely turned away from the wreck when the mainmast went by the board and soon afterwards the vessel disappeared. On landing the captain asked if the beachmen would receive any money, and was told 'no'. He took their names and later sent a cheque for £13. Countless similar instances could be told.

There were three types of beach boat, all double-ended:

1. The pilot yawls, with either two or three masts, both sailing and rowing, carrying large crews, at times as many as 40 men if much salvage work was likely, so that four or five could be put on board to assist in bringing a distressed vessel in to safety. Long, narrow, fine-lined boats, they were undoubtedly the fastest of their kind in existence. Mr J. Combes wrote me:

> During the 1850s and '60s they were mostly used in taking pilots, naval officers and government officials to and from the British Fleet which at that time often anchored in Yarmouth Roads. Pilot yawls were only stationed on a four-mile strip of the Norfolk coast from the mouth of Yarmouth harbour to Winterton beach, so that they were directly opposite where the Fleet anchored. . . . Several of the old-time Yarmouth shipbuilders specialised in building these yawls . . . Beeching's, Mack's and Hastings Bros. . . . James Beeching had much to do with the design of the famous pilot yawls and they had a great reputation for speed and seaworthiness . . . it is said he designed them on the fine lines of the 'Long Ships' used by the old Norsemen in bye-gone days when raiding the Norfolk coast. . . . J. & H. Beeching built a large number of beach yawls of all types . . . they finally went out of business in 1920.

2. Ferry or bullock boats, shorter in length and with more beam, were used for landing cargoes from brigs and schooners lying out in the Roads, taking out stores and provisions, anchors and gear. Their chief use, however, was to land catches of herring from the luggers which anchored in the Roads, but after the fish wharf was built in 1869 by the Yar-

mouth Corporation the catches were landed there and this type went out of existence.

3. Pleasure boats. With the rise of Yarmouth as a holiday resort large, clinker-built boats were built for pleasure trips during the summer season, taking visitors off the beach for a sail around the Roads and back. In winter the boats were laid up. Their rig was a huge mainsail with six lines of reef points and an enormous boom, projecting many feet outboard. In fair weather a big jib was set on a reeving bowsprit with its head to the top of the mast. Packed with 'gents' wearing straw boaters and women in long skirts held a few inches off the sand when boarding the gangway, these boats were manned by four or five beachmen. They were hauled off the beach by means of a hauling-off rope and when they returned were dragged up on skids or rollers by rope tackles. (Picture, p 118.)

One of the largest of the beach pleasure boats was the *Britannia*, built by Beeching Bros, with a length of 42 ft 6 in and a beam of 12 ft, depth 4 ft 9 in. Cutter-rigged, her spars measured: mast, hoist 30 ft; boom 35 ft; gaff 27 ft; bowsprit outside stem 14 ft. She was manned by a crew of four, or three in fine weather.

Owners reaped a rich harvest when the Fleet visited Yarmouth, by taking crowds of trippers round the warships. On one never-to-be-forgotten occasion they took so much money that the crew emptied their ballast bags of shingle and filled them with coins, carting the money home in the late evening on net barrows.

The confidence of visitors was shaken for a time following the disaster to the *Skylark* on 1 September 1903. While sailing near the Scroby Sands north-west bell buoy on a fine, clear sunny day, the London collier *F. E. Webb* crashed into the stern of the pleasure boat which instantly capsized, drowning three of the crew and three passengers. The survivors were picked up by boats sent from HMS *Hearty*, the fishery protection cruiser anchored in the Roads. An inquiry was held in Yarmouth town hall but little light was thrown on this inexplicable disaster—the steamer should have kept clear.

Page 165 The Great Frost of 1895 with Gravesend clench-built bawley and steamers frozen in the ice. Cory collier and Watkins tug to left. Note bawley's topmast is housed, gaff hoisted at throat to give clear space amidships, dandy wink amidships

Page 166   (above) *Iris*, LO 246, August 1931. Two reefs are down, tack of main-sail has been hauled up with the truss and the small jib set half-way out on the bowsprit; (below) Gravesend bawleys frozen in the ice, 1895

Unquestionably the finest yawl was *Reindeer*, 75 ft long, beam 12 ft, built in 1838 by Jermyn of Yarmouth. Eighty-five people were on board at her launch and this magnificent open boat could make 16 knots with a stiff breeze on the quarter—always a yawl's best point of sailing—as their shallow draught made them poor when going to wind'ard. So proud of her prowess were the beachmen owning her that when the yacht *America* won the Queen's Cup at Cowes in 1851 they issued a challenge to sail a match for a stake of £200. Mr Stevens sent one of his friends to Yarmouth but when he saw *Reindeer*'s speed on a reach he was so surprised that he advised declining the challenge, the ostensible objection being that the yawl was an open boat, not a yacht. The stake money was therefore proposed at £1,000, an impossible sum for the beachmen to raise, so the match was called off, but the men felt rather proud of the rebuff, considering it a compliment to the sailing powers of their magnificent yawl.

Other yawls credited with a good turn of speed were the 50-ft *Thought* which once sailed the 8 miles from Lowestoft to Yarmouth in 34 minutes, while the old *Happy New Year* covered $1\frac{3}{4}$ miles in $7\frac{1}{2}$ minutes.

The Yarmouth yawls were larger than those on other parts of the coast, many exceeding 60 ft in length.

The late S. G. Aldrich wrote to me:

> Regarding the beach yawls, a very attractive item around the coasts, and the gigs that used to work with them in calm weather . . . at the annual regattas they were the chief event of the day. I have seen five or six of them in the race, which was nearly always a triangular course which tested their quality in sailing, running, reaching, close-hauled. The main rig was fore and mizzen, they also carried an extra mast and sail which they used when the winds were very light, rigged amidships, but of the latter years this extra item was very seldom seen. These yawls were 49 to 50 ft in length and had a washboard above the gunwale with detachable sockets, which filled in the apertures to receive the oars when not in use. They were built with a very deep hog, or inner keel, to take the strain of the long length. In a flash breeze when they were carrying on with gunwales under now and again, the crew

K

were fully occupied in bailing the sea out. Most towns and villages possessed one of these boats; some had two. There used to be some excitement when these boats were launched as the ways or skids were well greased and when they commenced to move there was no stopping them until they were afloat.

The statement that at times the yawls sailed gunwales under intrigued me, and when I met Mr Aldrich we had a long talk about construction. Then he took me along to meet some venerable stalwarts who, from their own experiences, confirmed that at times, when hard pressed, the lee gunwale would sink from six inches to a foot *under water*, but so fast was the boat going that only a trickle came aboard. Their eyes lit up as they spoke lovingly of their beautiful yawls; often twenty-five men were needed, as each time she came about the big dipping fore-lug had to be handed round the mast, others shifted over from bilge to bilge the bags of shingle, nearly always painted white canvas, and perhaps eight to ten would be bailing as the yawl thrashed her way to wind'ard. When sailing free all sat on the floor boards to improve stability.

DESIGN AND CONSTRUCTION

Yawls were built for speed and easy launching, and their design varied to suit the beaches where they lay. Some had an easy rise of floor, others were rather flat; beam and depth also differed. Double-ended, the bows were sharp and graceful, a good sheer fore and aft, long, fine entry and run.

A few had a little iron ballast, the majority used bags filled with sand or shingle, well roped; when beaching in heavy surf it was easy to open the top and shoot the contents overboard, thus lightening the boat. Some of the waterlines tended to be slightly hollow, and hulls, being lightly built, were apt to wring considerably in a seaway.

The early yawls had three masts, the later ones two, the mainmast with its dipping lug being removed. Two suits of sails were provided, one of light material for summer, the storm suit of heavy canvas, with three or four lines of reef points.

The big forelug had a very long yard, slung at one-third of its length, the tack went to a hook on a short iron bumpkin outside the stem, the clew sheeted well aft. The storm lug hooked inside the stem. The standing lug on the mizzen was sheeted to the end of a long outrigger, and in summer the tack went to a hook on the thwart for'ard of the mast; in winter to the foot of mast which was raked forward. In light weather a jib was sometimes set on a long reeving bowsprit. (Picture, p 119.)

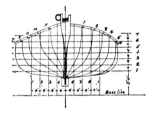

Body plan and section
of the Southwold yawl
Bittern

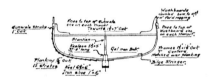

A 50-ft yawl of 10 ft beam had a 28-ft foremast, a 25-ft mizzen, and an outrigger 18 ft outboard. The storm foremast was 22 ft long. Masts were grown spars, young fir. The foreyard measured 27 ft, mizzen 23 ft—about 3 ft shorter in winter.

The masts were stepped on the hog—keelson—and supported at the thwart by timbers called 'lears' running fore and aft to the next thwart, also known as 'mast guides' and 'tracks'.

Gear consisted of an anchor and cable, buckets, bailers, compass in box, lantern, flag, hatchets, boathook, fenders, hand spikes and oars. Spare gear was kept in the tarred boat shed where some men were always on watch.

The rigging was simple. On the foremast the halyard and a burton were always set up to wind'ard, the mizzen was stayed

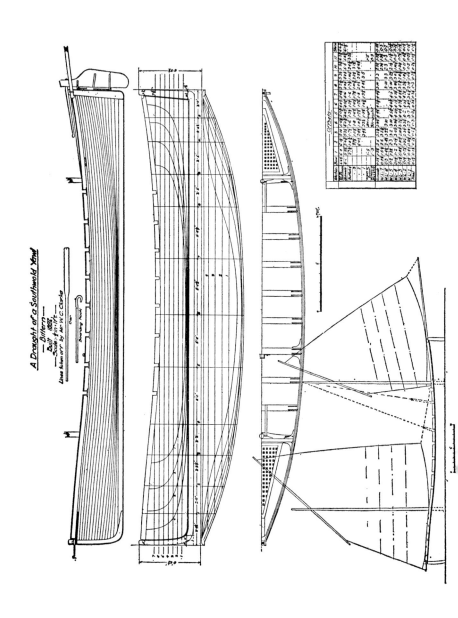

A Draught of a Southwold Yawl
— Bittern —
Built 1832.
— Scale ½ in. = 1 ft. —
Lines taken off by Mr. W. C. Clarke

with a burton a side and another set up to wind'ard, sometimes taken well for'ard. An iron tiller, with a handgrip, was shipped in an iron rudder head. Gear was always the best manilla.

Mr Aldrich said that, when going about, the halyards were eased, tack unhooked, yard and sail passed aft of the mast, sheet unhooked, halyards and burton shifted over; then the lug was rehoisted on the opposite side of the mast, sheeted home and the fall given a turn or two round the sampson post.

Nil Desperandum, built in 1856 by Critten of Southwold for the Kilcook Cliff Co, was 50 ft long, 8 ft beam, 'of good American board and timbers, with knees, inside village pieces, stern and headsheets, kelsen board, steps and tabernacles, rudder, light cheeks aft, main lears etc, for the sum of £1 6s 6d per foot, copper-fastened'. Shares in her were £3 each, sons of old members £1 13s. In 1892 the same company had *Bittern* built by Beeching Bros at Yarmouth, waterline length 48 ft 7 in, beam 9 ft 7 in, depth 3 ft 6 in. (Picture, p 130.)

It is interesting to compare her scantlings with those of *Baden Powell*, built by Spence Bros of Yarmouth: length 40 ft, 6 in, beam 11 ft 6 in, depth 4 ft 3 in.

	Bittern	Baden-Powell
Keel, oak	6½ in × 6 in	7 in × 4½ in
Hog or keelson	37 ft 6 in × 5½ in × 5 in	6 in × 5 in
Upper keelson		17 ft 0 in × 9½ in × 4 in
Planking	15 strakes ⅝ in	18 strakes ½ in
Sheer strake	1 in	¾ in
Frames	7-in centred 1½ in × 1¼ in	6½-in centred 1¾ in × 1¼ in
Bilge stringers		for half length 3¼ in × 2 in
Thwarts	1 in × 7 in	2 in × 8 in
Knees		2-in thick
Lears		4 in × 4 in

All timbers were oak, and copper-fastened. Considerable skill was required to keep an auger, making a hole 22½ in deep, dead central through the upper keelson hog and keel.

In *Baden Powell* the mizzen mast was stayed for'ard by a tackle known locally as a 'Tommy Hunter'.

Mr E. Cooper wrote that:

Prior to 1846 the Trinity pilots and 'Pullicans' owned the yawls and gigs, but afterwards they were owned by the men of the crews themselves . . . three at Southwold—Long Island Cliff, New York Cliff, Kilcook Cliff. Each company had its yawl, locally built, five of them between 1846 and 1870 by James Critten who came of a long line of boatbuilders. His first yawl *Reliance* in 1846, was followed two years later by the *John Bull* and the *Swiftsure*. The *Young Reliance* was launched in 1870 . . . the lovely 49-ft yawl, *Bittern*, the last of her kind, lay decaying on the beach near the pier in 1929. Alderman A. J. Critten, for the love of boat building handed down from his ancestors, rescued her rudder, which stands outside the Sailor's Reading Room. Her bow was converted into a shed and stood in Benstead's garden under the cliff. . . . To sail these yawls properly a crew of 20 to 25 was required, to shift round the big fore lug and pitch all the ballast from bilge to bilge each time she was in stays. The foresheet was never made fast, but was held in hand with two or three turns round a sampson post in the main tabernacle, the lives of all depended on the foresheet man.

It was essential to take seas stem-on, never amidships. When tacking you had to wait for a smooth; if rowing, all the oars on one side pulled, the others backed water and the boat was quickly round. Very few were lost at sea.

One of these was the *Increase*, belonging to the Layton Company of Yarmouth. At 1 pm on 6 October 1835 she was launched to a vessel flying a signal for a pilot, distant about 12 miles due east from the jetty. At 4 o'clock they spoke the Spanish brig *Paquette de Bilboa*, laden with general cargo, leaking and working both pumps. After a good deal of haggling over salvage, the pilot and a couple of beachmen were put on board to take her into Yarmouth harbour. The yawl then made for home, but passing the Newarp lightship the crew were asked to take a sick man ashore. This they did, and hoisting all three lugs in a fresh wsw breeze they were soon smoking along and reckoned to be on the beach by 10 o'clock. Suddenly, without the slightest warning, a terrific squall from the nor'ard put the sails flat aback, the ballast trimmed to wind'ard was now to leeward, and the yawl capsized in an instant.

One man, Samuel Brock, struck out, the time about 6.30 pm, the nearest land some 6 miles distant. It was dead low water, soon the flood was making off the shore to the south'ard, and he reckoned it would take him about 15 miles before the ebb could assist him. Luckily a rush horse collar, used as a fender, floated by and he got his left arm through it, cut away his petticoat trousers, then his frock, waistcoat and neckcloth went, but he dared not try and free himself of his oiled trousers, drawers and shirt, lest his legs became entangled. He now started swimming, after abandoning the horse collar. Gradually the tide carried him out of sight of Winterton light, so he watched two bright stars until they went behind heavy cloud from which rolled peals of thunder and forked lightning. Then the moon, almost full, came out. Brock now decided to cut away his heavy boots as he could see Lowestoft high light. He drove over the Cross Sand ridge and, sighting a buoy, got his exact position, the chequered St Nicholas Gat buoy, by irony, directly opposite his house but 4 miles out to sea. He had now been in the water about 5 hours as near as he could judge and he debated whether he would clamber up and hope to attract the attention of a passing vessel. He decided against this, fearing his limbs would be numbed—and would he be able to swim again if necessary? The tide was now easing and the wind was from the eastward when he struck out again for the shore. To his horror, large grey gulls dived to attack him, but by splashing he drove them off into the darkness. Then he sighted a ship at anchor a great way off. To get within hail meant going across Corton Sands, over which angry crests were breaking; the wind flew round and he met the full force of the swell. 'I prayed that the wind might change, or that God would take away my senses before I felt what it was like to drown. But in less time that it takes to tell, I had driven over the sands into smooth water and my strength returned to me as fresh as in the beginning.'

The ebb was now running towards the shore, but also carrying him to the nor'ard. Brock began to wonder if he could get out of the surf breaking on the beach, be able to walk, or climb the cliffs and find a house. He therefore turned back towards the brig *against the tide*, and succeeded in getting within 200 yd, but no farther, so he called out at the top of his voice, and was lucky in that a good anchor watch was being kept. A boat was lowered and at 1.30 am he was picked out of the water, having swum for 7½ hours and nearly 15 miles from the spot where the yawl capsized. Landed at Lowestoft, he was cared for in the house of a relative for five days; then he walked back to Yarmouth.

The regattas engendered intense rivalry and in hard-sailed races in heavy weather masts and gear frequently carried away. In 1892 the Young Co of Lowestoft decided to replace their *Young Prince*, now getting past work. A local man, Capps, designed *Georgiana*, which was built by Allerton for £150, length 48 ft 6 in, beam 9 ft, depth 5 ft. (Picture, p 129.) The day after her launch she easily defeated *Bittern* at the Lowestoft Regatta and only twice was she beaten by the Southwold yawl, winning in all 15 first prizes, value about £12 each.

Determined to have a faster yawl, the Old Company asked G. L. Watson, designer of Lord Dunraven's *America's* Cup challenger *Valkyrie* and the famous royal cutter *Britannia*, to draft the lines of *Happy New Year*—the fifth to bear that name, and Henry Reynolds built her in 1894. Somewhat bigger than her rival, her length was 50 ft 2 in, beam 10 ft 5 in, and depth 3 ft 6 in, but the yawl never came up to expectations, finishing well behind the two cracks in her first race. Photographs in my collection show her with a raking stern. *Georgiana* had the normal straight sternpost, the stem was shorter and a long rounded forefoot merged into the keel quite a distance aft, while her rival had a deep, straight stem with only a slight round where it joined the keel. Were these innovations the reason for the poor sailing qualities? Or had the skill of Jack Swan, skipper and helmsman of *Georgiana*, something to do with it, as he was acknowledged to be the finest handler of a yawl on the East Coast?

The last race at Lowestoft was in 1907, but at Yarmouth the

following year there was an unhappy dispute about *Bittern* slipping her anchor instead of recovering it and the result was declared a draw. *Georgina* was now laid up until after the war, when she was sold for conversion into a houseboat on the Norfolk Broads. About the same time *Happy New Year* foundered while being towed down the coast.

Conditions on the beach changed rapidly following the increase in the number of powerful tugs and the stationing of lifeboats along the coast whose design was based on that of the yawls. Towards the end of the nineteenth century many yawls had been sold away to seaside resorts for conversion to pleasure boats and, re-rigged as ketches with gaff mainsail and mizzen, their popularity was soon established among holidaymakers. Some were hauled up alongside the tarred sheds and left to rot away, others were broken up for firewood.

For boarding and taking off pilots, gigs were frequently used; long, narrow boats, very fine lined, rowing six or eight oars, each marked with a circle of white paint so that every man had the correct length of oar for his place in the boat. The boat, steered by a yoke and long lines, fairly flew through the water under the powerful strokes of the crew, and in light weather could easily beat a yawl making for the same ship in answer to a signal to land a pilot. These gigs were the equivalent of the Deal galleys, and occasionally set a big lugsail on a mast stepped amidships. (Picture, p 117.)

Suffolk punts differed markedly from those in the Yarmouth area, although of about the same size and lug-rigged. The hull was clinker-built with a wide transom stern. The Southwold punt *Maria*, built in 1886, had an overall length of 17 ft 2¼ in, keel 16 ft, extreme breadth 7 ft, depth amidships 2 ft 6 in, but many ran up to 21 ft overall. *Rapid*, built by James Critten at Southwold in 1850, had 13 strakes a side, frames joggled to fit the planking, and three doublings on each bilge to take the wear when beaching. The bags of shingle ballast were placed under and aft of the third thwart; for'ard was a pound for the nets and catch.

The foremast carried a dipping lug with the tack hooked to a short iron bumpkin on the stemhead. There were five lines of reef points and when fully reefed the tack went to a hook inside the stem. The short yard had two positions for hooking to the traveller. The standing lug mizzen, with three lines of reef points, was sheeted to a single block on a long outrigger fitted to starboard and belayed to a cleat on the port side of the transom. Each punt had two pairs of thole pins a side for rowing.

There were two ropewalks at Southwold, a short one on which short lines and twines for shrimp and trawl nets were spun, and a long walk for making long ropes. The yarns were first drawn through a copper of boiling Stockholm tar, then bound on bobbins and placed in a large frame where they revolved freely. They were then drawn through a board with a number of circularly-placed small holes; then through a heated iron tube and fixed to the revolving pinion of the jack which had at one end a cogged iron wheel to which cogged pinions could be engaged. At the other end was a tapered grooved capstan cogged at the top and connected with the cogwheel. A strong rope, fastened at the other end of the walk, was then placed round the capstan in a groove, a horse hitched on and as it was led down the walk, the jack, on wheels, would be drawn along causing the cogwheel to turn, thereby giving the right number of turns to the strand. When the three or four strands were made they were laced together and formed a rope.

For spinning twines, a man with a large bundle of hempen fibres round his waist walked backwards spinning a rope yarn. Henry Oldrings' rope ground closed down in the 1880s, Goodwin's about 20 years later. Then his foreman, Button, set up on his own account, using his garden path, some 40 to 50 yd in length, as a walk for spinning twines. He devised a machine so that as he walked backwards spinning, it gave him sufficient turn without the aid of the boy who had previously been employed to turn the wheels. The wheel was about 4 ft in diameter with a broad rim around which ran a tape band which ran over small reels or 'whirls', thereby giving the requisite number of revolutions for the spinning of a thread. Snoods and norsels were produced by the thousands and used by the fishermen for their cod lines and herring nets.

Southwold's fishing industry is recorded in the Domesday Book. The annual due of 20,000 herrings paid in the time of Edward the Confessor was increased to 25,000 in 1087. In the old Walberswick church account books, mention is made that in 1493 there were 18 fishing vessels paying fishing 'doles' and a list of 23 'maysters' is given.

Before the 1914 war great efforts had been made to improve the harbour and in 1908 fishing and curing began. Some 300 boats, mostly Scottish, came and 300 trunks of trawl fish, 4,500 crans of herring and 125,000 mackerel were landed, while two local ships sailed for Germany with 2,100 and 3,212 barrels of cured herrings. The following year the season was poor owing to constant gales, but over 7,000 crans of herring, 1,200 trunks of trawl fish and 350,000 mackerel were landed. In all, 761 fishing craft used the harbour, while longshore boats landed hundreds of bushels of sprats. Although over £60,000 had been spent on the harbour by the London contractors, plus a grant of £21,500 from the Board of Trade, the harbour was not a commercial success and fell into disrepair; it was a sorry sight when I visited it after the second world war.

In earlier years, after the fish market was established at Lowestoft, a small class of boat, 20 to 25 tons, with a crew of eight, was started, called 'half and halfers', the owner taking half the earnings and keeping up the boat and nets, the crew the other half which was doled out in shares after provisions had been paid for. They made the spring North Sea and Home herring voyages, with good mackerel fishing in the summer. *Native* was the first of this class, launched in 1850 at Blackshore; others were built on the beach near California Cottage and on the river bank by Henry Ladd and others. When they were out-classed by the bigger Lowestoft boats, most were sold away and not replaced, the local men shipping in the Lowestoft vessels.

The hard life bred a fine race of men. William Herrington,

born in 1848, was the son of Benjamin, coxswain of the South-wold lifeboat for 38 years. William started work at the age of eight, coiling ropes in a small trawling boat and going to school in the winter. Apprenticed to a collier brig at 14, he sailed all over the world before settling down to longshore fishing with occasional voyages as chief mate in coasting ships. For 30 years a Trinity House pilot for 60 miles of the East Coast, including the dangerous sandbanks adjoining the Yarmouth Roads, he assisted on 20 occasions in the saving of 140 lives and aided many a ship in distress.

Samuel Charles May went fishing in the 'half and halfers', but after marriage only went longshore fishing. In 1891 he was appointed second coxswain of the lifeboat *Coal Exchange*, built in 1855, and with John Craigie was chiefly responsible for planning her successor, the *Alfred Corry*, last of the sailing lifeboats. Elected coxswain in 1898 he never failed to get her launched nor missed sailing in her until she went out of commission in 1913.

Many surnames show their Norse origin and a few words peculiar to East Anglia were: 'bermskin'—an oily to cover the berm or bosom and reaching down to the petticoats; 'brabble' —a tumble of water, as over a shoal when currents cross; 'bristock'—a small knee to strengthen a boat's bow; 'cade'— a measure of 1,000 sprats; 'mand'—a large open wicker basket used to carry fish; 'punt'—a lugsail longshore boat, sometimes called a 'trim-tram' at Yarmouth, a name also frequently given to shrimping boats; 'redcaps'—the master boat among the luggers by earning the most money and whose crew were distinguished by red woollen caps; 'rippier'—a fish hawker selling fish inland; 'shale'—a netting pin used to gauge the mesh of a net; and 'waif'—plural 'waives'—a waft, or piece of bunting, hung in the rigging as a signal that the vessel required the services of a boat, pilot etc.

Some idea of the number of lives saved by beachmen, who also manned the lifeboats, can be gauged from the number of wrecked seamen received in the Sailors' Home at Yarmouth.

1861: 209, 1862: 240, 1863: 336, 1864: 393.

Eloquent figures which tell their own story of the gallantry of a race of seamen who, afloat from a very early age until too old to take a place in a boat, knew the waters, shoals and dangers of that treacherous coast in sunshine and storm, by day or night.

CHAPTER SIX

THE ESSEX COAST

ALTHOUGH every coastal village had a certain amount of inshore fishing, the fisheries along the Essex shores were of little importance except at Harwich, the Colne area, and at Leigh, where shrimping and spratting were extensive. The Colne fishery for oysters dates back to the Roman occupation of Britain.

The constant demand for whelks as bait for the cod smacks gave considerable employment in the Harwich area. The method of capture was known as 'trotting'; long lines were used but, instead of baiting hooks, common crabs were threaded on the snoods, up to 20 on each. The whelks seized this bait ravenously and took a firm hold while devouring the tasty flesh; after a short time the lines were hauled with scores of whelks clinging to the snoods.

Another method was by means of baskets baited inside with fish offal; a net was stretched over one end with a small opening to allow the entry of whelks. Also hoop nets, similarly baited, were lowered to the bottom and picked up after a time full of whelks. This trade died out by 1885–90.

In Essex, hoop nets were used for crab and lobster fishing, and in Kent, cage-pots. George Bates said the reason was because cage-pots were often lost through bargemen and others sending the attached buoy adrift, or dragging them up. The iron ring was flat, 1 in deep, 18 in in diameter with a three-roped bridle attached, spliced on a thin line 13 to 16 fathoms long. The net was 15 in deep, not conical as in a dab-net, but basin-shaped in order not to injure the lobsters. The mesh was 1 in from knot to knot, numbering 40 to 42 round the hoop. The

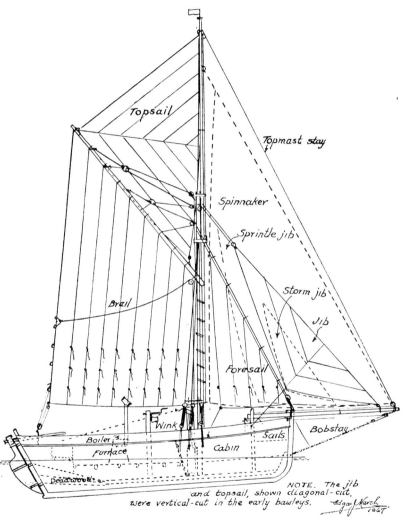

Topsail

Topmast stay

Spinnaker

Sprintle jib

Storm jib

Jib

Brail

Foresail

Wink

Sails

Boiler

Bobstay

Furnace

Cabin

Deadwood

NOTE. The jib
and topsail, shown diagonal-cut,
were vertical-cut in the early bawleys.   Edgar March
1967.

Sail plan of a bawley

line was corked from one end to the other, each a long diamond shape, about 1 ft apart, terminating in a larger oval-shaped one which was the float or buoy. Three lines hitched together stretched about three-quarters of a mile. Colne and Blackwater men never fished commercially for crabs and lobsters.

The Harwich lobster craft were similar to the bawleys at Leigh and carried heavy dinghies, 12 to 15 ft long. The men went out on the ebb and returned with the flood. The West Rocks were the favourite area; bait was small slips—young soles. The bawley anchored and two men got into the dinghy, one rowing, the other dropping the hoop-nets overboard. It was essential to drop so as to sink the net downwards; to this end the bag of the net was given a turn over the rim of the hoop. The nets and corked lines were piled towards the stern, each clear for running, 15 hoop-nets being the usual quantity. The boat was rowed as straight as possible: 'put down five rounds in a tide, otherwise work four on ebb, one on flood'.

In hauling in the lines, the corks were grabbed hand over hand and the nets covered with sacks to keep the lobsters from fighting; their great ripper claws were tied later. When all nets were in, the dinghy returned to the bawley. The catch was usually sold to agents at about 10d a lb in the 1890s.

The majority of the Harwich bawleys were built by J. and H. Cann, a typical one having a length overall of 39 ft, moulded beam 13 ft, and depth 5 ft 6 in. Draught for'ard was 3 ft 6 in, aft 5ft.

The keel was elm, sided 5 in, moulded 12 in, floors and frames oak, sided 3 in, oak deadwood, keelson oak, sided 6 in, moulded 8 in, throughbolted with ¾-in iron bolts. Stem and sternpost were of oak, sided 5 in, beams oak 4½ in sq, the oak coamings 2 in sided, 8 in moulded, were bolted to the deck and beams on hair felt and tar.

English elm, 1½ in thick, was used for the garboards and the two adjacent planks, then 1½-in pitch pine with 2-in oak at bilge and sheer strake, fastened with 4-in galvanised spikes.

The deck planking was 4 in by 2 in fir, with an oak covering

Page 183 (above) H.J.T., LO 284, off Leigh, July 1928. Her biggest jib—the spinnaker—is set, jib and foresail dropped and foot of mainsail is tied up to give clear view ahead. Note brail and net hoisted to mast-head to dry. Smoke from funnel shows that shrimps are being boiled in the copper; *(below)* bawleys trawling for shrimps. In foreground 21 MN has dropped her foresail and boomed out a jib as a spinnaker from the fore shroud. Bawley in background has her jib set as a spinnaker with boom to bitts. Note warp over stern and amidships, wink on post, big jib. May 1889

Page 184 (*above*) *Gordon*, 382 LO, off Leigh, August 1931. Built at Brightlingsea in 1883, 11¾ tons. Note length of bowsprit and topmast, and net hung athwartships over gaff to dry; (*below*) *Gordon* dried out at Leigh, note rubbers on cod end of net over gaff, and the long open hatch

board 7 in by 2 in, shelf pitch pine 3 in sided, 6 in moulded, oak knees and transom, 3 in sided, oak stanchions and cap.

The deck was kept as clear as possible; the bowsprit, to starboard of the stem, was secured by an iron pin through two oak bitts stepped on the keelson and secured to the deck with oak knees. A handspike barrel windlass extended to either rail. The foresail worked on an iron horse for'ard of the mast which had wooden cleats at the base. Two stove funnels, the 'wink', and a sliding hatch to the companion completed the normal deck arrangements. Across the quarters was the iron horse for the mainsheet.

Ballast was about 7 tons of pig iron, all inside, ground gear was a 130-lb anchor with 30 fathoms of ⅝-in chain. The shrimp trawl beam was 21 ft long with iron heads weighing 65 lb each, the warp was 56 fathoms of 3-in rope.

Below deck, sails, paint and gear were stowed in the forepeak, next came the cabin with bunks, locker seats, coal stove and lockers for food and lamps. Immediately aft was the space where nets and ropes were stowed. On the centre line of the after bulkhead was a 7-in sq oak post stepped in the keelson, at its head was the 'wink' with a handle geared into a small barrel for working gear.

The copper in which the shrimps were boiled had a wooden lid and rested in a cast-iron furnace standing in a brick surround with a coal bin aft, to port was the bilge pump. Light hatches covered the opening 10 ft long, 5 ft wide for'ard tapering to 3 ft. Aft was the steering flat with a tiller rack into which a pin was dropped in the appropriate hole to hold the tiller, then the bawley could sail herself when the crew were otherwise engaged.

Pink shrimps were abundant in the Harwich district and conditions differed from those at Leigh. The depth of water and the state of the tides had little or no influence on the time of starting; the men went out and came in as suited their convenience. Usually a start was made at early dawn and trawling went on till sundown. Unless good hauls or blustery weather set in, they aimed to be back in time to catch the 8 pm goods train

L

for Billingsgate. Crews lived on board, spending only Saturday and Sunday nights ashore. The Leigh fishermen often brought their families to Harwich. They began to go to the port early in the 1860s when shrimps were scarce in the Thames; the first three boats were *Rosa*, *Helen* and *Frederick*, unique in having a boom mainsail. On arrival, they found three boats from Milton in Kent, and began work the following day. On the third day *Rosa's* trawl was caught up and badly torn, the men lost heart and all returned to Leigh. The Milton men stayed on, returning in force the following spring and continuing to do so thereafter. The Leigh men soon followed the same practice.

Spratting has been carried on off the Essex coast for many centuries. In 1547 the owners of 'stall' boats fishing out of the Colne were running their catches to London. The word 'stall' meant fixed or anchored, and referred to the method of fishing; the word gradually became corrupted to 'stow' and the net used was known as a 'stowboat' net. The favourite grounds for the Colne and Tollesbury smacks were the Wallet, the Swin, Barrow Deeps and the Kentish shore between the Reculvers and the Swale. Sometimes they worked the Sunk and approaches to Harwich and occasionally large hauls were made in the estuaries of the Colne, Blackwater, Crouch or Orwell.

Stowboating was often carried out at night, and at dusk the skippers watched for the tell-tale cloud of gulls feeding on a shoal of sprats. The smack was brought up some distance down tide of the shoal and the stowboating anchor, weight about 4 cwt, was let go and the cable paid out. This was of hemp until the 1890s then usually chain, sometimes chain and hemp. In autumn the length of Rowhedge High Street was often filled by fishermen 'woulding' hemp round chain cables to ease the strain on the bitts when riding to the net in a seaway. Some fathoms along the cable a large iron ring was let in, and to this were shackled the four 'handfleets' which led to the ends of the baulks at the net mouth. When the lower handfleets came tight the cable was checked and the net shot.

First the two baulks were got over the bow and held separ-

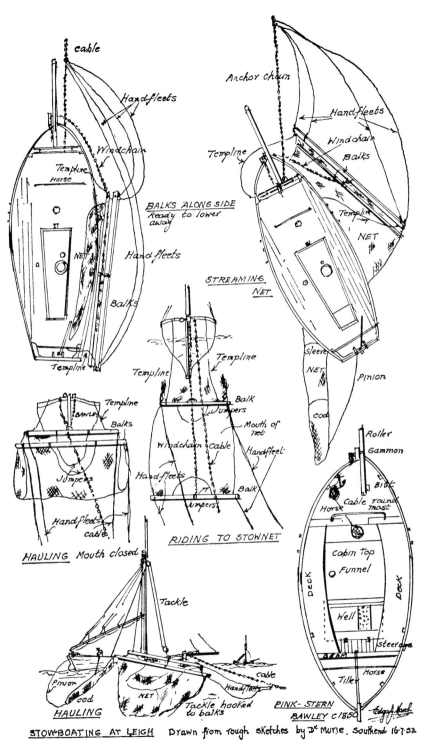

cable

Handfleets

Windchain

Templine

Horse

BALKS ALONG SIDE
Ready to lower
away

Handfleets

NET

Balks

Templine

Anchor chain

Handfleets

Windchain

Balks

Templine

Templine

NET

STREAMING
NET

Sleeve

NET

Pinion

cod

Roller
Gammon

Bitt

Templine

Templine

Balk
Jumpers

Mouth of
net

Windchain Cable

Handfleets

Handfleet

BAWLEY

Balks

Jumpers

Handfleets
cable

HAULING Mouth closed

Balk

Jumpers

RIDING TO STOWNET

Cable round
mast

Horse

Cabin Top
Funnel

DECK

DECK

Well

Steerage

BEAM

Horse

Tiller

PINK-STERN
BAWLEY C 1850

Tackle

cable

Pinion
cod

NET

Handfleets

HAULING

Tackle hooked
to balks

STOW-BOATING AT LEIGH   Drawn from rough sketches by Dᵉ Mune. Southend 16.7.52

Streaming and hauling a stow net

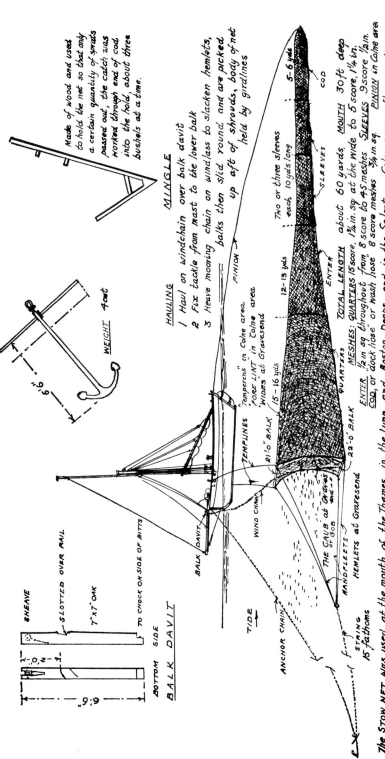

ately by stoppers to the bitts. The net was wetted and streamed overside, then the stoppers were cast off the weighted lower baulk, allowing it to sink as the 'winchain' was paid out over the 'baulk davit' until the mouth of the net was fully open. Casting off the stopper on the upper baulk and lowering away on the 'winchain', the crew secured the net at its most efficient depth for fishing by the marks on the two 'temperens' secured to the forward rails to prevent the net from 'windmilling'.

The net was now held square to the tide by the handfleets and the crew went below to snatch some sleep whilst the skipper frequently felt for a light weight on the 'pinion line' made fast to the quarter. If there was a slight 'pull and lift' the net was fishing well and after two to three hours it would be time to haul, earlier if the smack were lucky and the shoals thick, for to take a catch of live sprats is far easier and more profitable than heaving a dead weight of crushed fish which may split the net or be fit only for manure.

The crew shortened in the cable, then manned the windlass, raising the winchain and closing the mouth of the net. This was secured and a hand abaft the shrouds fished for the net with a boathook. The net was then made fast to the shrouds by a strop somewhere near the middle of the 'enter'.

Some skippers of small smacks had to heave the closed net forward to the bowsprit end with the jib outhaul in order to bring the 'sleeves' and catch within reach. If the sleeves were full it would be necessary to empty them in several parts to avoid bursting the net. This was done with a 'mingle' which was passed under the sleeve and pinion, parting its contents into measures known as 'cods', three bushels making one cod.

With the catch aboard and stowed in the hold, the net was shot again and this was repeated until the smack 'filled'. This was hard and tiring work with a bitter easterly wind freezing the crew handling the icy contents of the net. A good catch might be 300 or more bushels. If other boats were getting under way, sail was cracked on in the race to be first in and so obtain the best price. On her maiden voyage the Rowhedge smack

Ellen returned with a full hold, her decks awash and the net, crammed with sprats, lashed to the rail aft. Catches of 400 to 500 bushels were not uncommon. Prices varied from 2s 6d to 3s per bushel, depending on quality, but not always, as prime sprats were frequently dumped in tons to be carted away in farm 'tumbrils' for manure at 4d to 6d a bushel, inclusive of unloading by the crew who, arriving dog-tired after a hard trip, had to unload in baskets. Colne smacks were never owned by firms.

Over 100 sail of spratters from Brightlingsea, Wivenhoe and the neighbourhood, with scores from Leigh, Queenborough and Gillingham, were a common sight. In later years extensive use was made of the large cutter smacks and many of the fleets belonging to big firms caught sprats and carried them for others to the London market. Cooke's engraving of smacks landing catches at Billingsgate shows them to be fine, able vessels. It was not until about the 1840s that bawleys went after sprats, occasionally buying mackerel from Kentish boats. Before going re-buying, the men first cleaned out all fishing gear and sometimes lightened the boat by removing part of the ballast. Only a few of the small pink-stern bawleys risked going so far afield. It was a race to learn if any spratters had fish for sale, the bawleys tacking hither and thither until fortunate. When a willing seller was found the proceedings varied according to the state of the weather, day or night. The buyer moored astern, or in calm made fast alongside and began the 'chaffering'; sometimes a rival would drive up, heave-to and bid against the first-comer. A bargain struck, no time was lost in transferring the cargo, two men shovelling together and measuring the sprats into baskets while another lifted them out of the hold with a hook rope and passed them over to the purchaser's boat to be shot into the hold. At times 50 to 60 bushels would be boarded, and payment was made in cash. When the sea was too rough seller and buyer ran for the nearest shelter.

If a boat was unable to get up to Billingsgate through fog or calm, the catch would be sold for manure at Erith. At the market there was a special dock for sprat boats, but many had to lay out in the stream, selling to petty dealers, costers and fish women, all well able to drive hard bargains and taking anything from 1 to 50 bushels. The mate or second hand, called the 'holdsman', measured and sent up the fish in baskets or tubs. The skipper on deck acted as salesman and he had a mitten into which he slipped the money.

This practice continued until the early 1870s when consignments sent from the north by rail caused a big drop in prices and buying became a precarious speculation.

The sprat season usually began about the middle of November, the boats spreading out and keeping a keen watch. If in 'company' signals were made, flares being used at night; if not, it was every man for himself.

All the Colne smacks worked on the share system. The usual crew was three, but at Tollesbury four, the shares being: one for the net, one for the boat, one for the owner, and one for each of the crew. The smacks from Brightlingsea, Rowhedge, Wivenhoe and Tollesbury went spratting, but those from Mersea and Maldon did not to any extent. By February, sprats gradually became scarce and many of the smacks were laid up whilst their crews joined the big yachts. Others went shrimping in the Goldmer gut, a 4-fathom channel between the West Rocks and the NE Gunfleet, or else worked around the Cork, Cutler and Sunk sands. At times they went farther north and landed catches at Harwich. These prime pink shrimps were sold for 4d to 8d a gallon.

Working constantly amongst the shoals and lee shores of the Thames Estuary, the Essex men evolved a fore-and-aft-rigged craft able to beat to windward well. Their handling of smacks was well nigh perfection; little wonder that they found employment as yacht skippers and hands in the big cutters and schooners of Victorian and Edwardian days.

As far back as 1377 and earlier it is known that Brightlingsea fishermen were using a trawl net, as in that year a royal commission held an enquiry into its legality. Well-smacks were introduced in 1701, three being engaged in the fish carrying

trade to London. Many of the large smacks went coasting when
not fishing; their size ranged from 14 to 40 tons, all clinker
built. They were constructed locally for £10 a ton for the hull,
and a 20-tonner needed a further £180 to equip her for fishing
and was reckoned to last from 30 to 40 years, with care. Crew
numbered from three to five, including at least one apprentice.
Oystering was only one side of their work; trawling and spratting were carried on in the appropriate season.

One of these old vessels has survived in her original hull and
rig to the present day, the West Mersea *Boadicea* built at Maldon
in 1815. In the 1880s her clench planking was replaced by
carvel, but the old frames, notched for the 'lands', are retained.
With a length of 28 ft, the hull form is a very full 'cod's head
and mackerel tail', ending in a small, narrow transom, no topmast. Mr John Leather writes, 'I can vouch for her handiness,
having sailed aboard her in races for smacks at the West
Mersea Regattas when she won several prizes against vessels of
her own size.'

Another working until well into the 1920s was the Wivenhoe
Eliza, which retained her clinker planking to the end, although
the lands were doubled flush in the 1890s. She differed by
having a topsail and lute stern, and was 38 ft in length. She was
built for trawling and spratting, with the old wooden barrel
capstan worked by handspikes, and treadstrips on the deck to
save the crew from slipping.

Fine, able craft, a fleet of 40 were dredging for oysters in the
1820s off Falmouth, Guernsey and other Channel Islands.
These were deep-sea oysters taken in the spring, a practice
leading to many disputes with the French who alleged that the
smacks were poaching when they worked in Caen Bay. As an
average catch yielded up to 50,000 oysters, it is not surprising
that at times feelings ran high. In 1886 *Heiress* in five trips
caught some 155,000 oysters. Another ground lay off the Terschilling Light on the Dutch coast which gave its name to the
vessels working there—'Skillingers'. Lying about 180 miles to
the eastward with depths up to 22½ fathoms, this ground called

for powerful cutters, able to face any weather as they were often away for weeks, storing the catch in wells. The ground lay exposed to the full force of westerly gales and, with innumerable sandbanks and low shores to leeward, ability to claw to windward was vital.

Disaster struck in March 1883, when some 15 smacks were dredging in calm weather. Without warning the light nor'-wester increased to a furious gale with blinding snowstorms. As it swept over the Dogger Bank it claimed 43 big smacks with all hands, seriously damaged 38 and left 51 disabled. Finally the tempest reached Terschilling and the Colne men were fighting for their lives. Days later the *Express* and *Glance* bore up for Brightlingsea in a battered condition, having lost one man washed overboard from *Express*; others followed at varying intervals including *Vanduara* but *Conquest* and *Recruit* never made port; likewise *Mascotte*, a Yarmouth vessel with a Colne crew, mainly from Brightlingsea. In all 19 fishermen were drowned and 32 children left fatherless.

According to the 1865 Report, prolific beds of deep-sea oysters were discovered in the Channel shortly after the enforcement of a close season, *c* 1852. They lay in deep water, 15 to 24 fathoms, in all parts between Cherbourg and Dunkirk. The oysters were large and coarse but they improved on being laid down on inshore beds; they would not stand the winter on the Kentish Flats. Immediately the news spread there was a wild rush to cash in and soon 'upwards of 300 vessels engaged, each about 25 tons, crew six. Colchester, Rochester and Jersey men take the oysters to Shoreham, Newhaven and beds at the mouth of the Thames, stocking the beds during the open season sufficient to last, if possible, through the close season. During the summer these large oysters are in great demand at fairs and races. Fine weather in mid-Channel during work is precious, so dredge day and night . . . carry four dredges to a boat, 2¼ in diameter ring, so few small oysters. . . . Large supply exported from Newhaven to France, French work same grounds, no disagreement.'

This 'Jersey Oyster Fishery', as it was known, paid well for a time, but within a decade the product of centuries was practically exhausted as the following returns show only too well.

1st Sept. 1855 to 30 April 1856: 99 English, 86 Jersey, 22 open boats. Carrying smacks: English 35, Jersey 14. Total 256 boats, 1,301 men.

	£	s	d
Tubs of oysters 179,194 @ 3s 10d a tub	34,345	10	4
Freightage Jersey to England @ 10d ,,	7,003	18	4
	41,349	8	8

The following season saw 261 boats on the grounds; oyster catches were about the same but were now fetching 4s 1¾d a tub. Then came a steady decrease year after year, with prices increasing, until 1863–4 saw only 8 Jersey cutters and 15 open boats bringing in 6,196 tubs at 6s 3¾d a tub. 'About 3,280 tubs were dredged in British Channel and brought to Jersey by cutters working in the Channel.'

Scallops were sought on the Beachy Head grounds, with Shoreham and Newhaven as bases. Often the harvest was so prolific that prices tumbled from 4d to 1½d a dozen. At times the smacks worked from Boulogne, sending catches by cross-Channel steamers.

A profitable trade was dredging for 'cement stone', known to the Romans as 'septeria' and used for making builders' mortar. About 30 Colne vessels worked with hundreds of others off Walton and Harwich for this chalky stone, valued at 5s a ton. Copperas, a petrified 'twig' used in the manufacture of sulphuric acid, was found off Whitstable.

Smuggling and salvaging were remunerative side lines. No Preventive men or coastguards could be expected to watch all the maze of creeks, or search every boat, and many a consignment of contraband was landed on the marshes and hidden until it was deemed safe to take it along paths known to a few and placed in the cart or waggon of a 'wellwisher'.

By the 1820s, the growth of trade following the end of the

Napoleonic Wars brought a new activity to smacksmen—
rendering assistance to, and salvaging from, the scores of wrecks
on the treacherous sandbanks. With no lighted fairways and
few shore marks, innumerable collier brigs, Baltic timber ships,
coasters, emigrant packets and even Indiamen were driven
ashore every winter, and the summer toll was high. Warehouses
were crammed with goods brought ashore and some naturally
found their way into other storehouses but, as elsewhere around
our coasts, many a life was saved at considerable cost to the
salver.

A typical example was that of the Brightlingsea smack *Fair
Traveller* which lost her boat containing the skipper and boy as
they were going off to a Dutch vessel wrecked on the Gunfleet.
Only the mate was left on board. Helpless to rescue his friends
in a boiling sea, he could only watch the other crew drop one by
one from the rigging into the surf and death. The smack had to
be sailed back single-handed through a gale.

That was in 1838 and by then over 50 smacks were working
from the Colne, but a more able type of craft was needed to
combine fishing with salvaging. The old clencher-built 15–20
tonners were superseded by a larger and more powerful type,
capable of knocking about the North Sea in weather which sent
other vessels running for shelter. Special emphasis was placed
on speed and windward ability, for what was the use of arriving
after another man had got there first? They dredged oysters
from the Firth of Forth to the Bristol Channel and Solway
Firth, or went trawling and spratting, for which a hold capacity
of 1,000 bushels was stipulated, not easy conditions to fulfil.

The local builders, Aldous and Root and Diaper of Brightlingsea, Harris of Rowhedge, Harvey, Barr & Husk at Wivenhoe
produced a type of powerful cutter, 20 to 40 tons and 50 to 70
ft overall length. Carvel planking was introduced and within a
few years the old clench-built hull was out of favour. The quality
of work was high at that period—1840 to 1880. The men were
accustomed to designing, building and maintaining half the
yachts of the day, and this yacht influence was apparent in the

high, lean bow, the graceful sheer sweeping down to a low counter stern, a fine entrance and finer run, and the cutter rig with a big topsail and loose-footed mainsail.

Aldous built 36 big smacks between 1857 and 1866, in addition to yachts and a large number of smaller craft. Nothing but the best was good enough and so high was his reputation that orders flowed in from Liverpool, Hull, Bosham, Anglesey and even Mumbles, despite the intensive fishing by Essex smacks which dredged millions of oysters from the local beds. Speed meant profit for the fisherman, and careful building a minimum of repairs. Everything was done by hand, heavy and shaped timber being pit sawn. From his draughted lines a section and ribband model was often made to enable owners to approve the design, then the lines were laid off in the mould loft.

A typical smack was *Aquiline*, built by Harris at Rowhedge in 1867 for Harry Mills Cooke, length 65 ft, beam 15 ft, deep draught 8 ft 6 in, hold capacity 21 tons. The main boom was 45 ft long, bowsprit 30 ft outboard, and she spread about 2,000 sq ft of working canvas. When sea dredging, the mainsail was lowered, the boom stowed in a crutch and a large trysail set, sheeted by tackles to the quarters to avoid danger to the crew if an accidental gybe occurred. Then the heavy boom could easily maim if not kill a man. The topmast was often struck.

For'ard was the usual hand-spike windlass for handling the anchor and, in season, the stowboat gear. Just for'ard of the mast was a large geared hand-winch with four barrels for working halyards, running out the bowsprit, working fishing gear or whipping out cargo, as potatoes were at times brought back from Jersey, or coal from northern ports. Another winch or geared hand-capstan stood amidships and was worked by two or more hands when dredging or working trawl warps. A 15-ft clench-built boat was carried on deck or lashed, capsized, over the main hatch in foul weather.

Below deck, the forepeak was the cable locker, abaft was the 'mast room' where a large scuttle butt for drinking water and racks for bread, vegetables etc were housed. The hold, about one-third of the ship's length, had a capacity of 21 tons on the ballast, clean shingle with a proportion of iron pigs covered by a wooden ceiling.

All hands berthed in the cabin aft, entered by a sliding hatch in the deck. In a space perhaps 14 ft by 9 ft, six men lived for months on end. Locker seats ran down each side, four bunks, each with a sliding panel, and a big double berth across the counter—the 'Yarmouth Roads'—held a couple of apprentices. On the coal stove stood a kettle and a huge teapot, only emptied when it would no longer hold six mugfuls of water. Knives and forks were stuck in cracks of the deck beams, while saucepan lids made excellent plates in a seaway. Then, rested on the knees, they could be gripped between them by the handles and the rims held the gravy from spilling. Five, sometimes six, hands were carried. Often as many as three apprentices, who lived in the master's house when in port, went to sea at the age of 10 or 12, bound for five, seven or nine years and paid £10 to £12 a year. They were found in food but not clothing, which consisted of a cheesecutter cap, white canvas jumper or smock over a thick Guernsey, duffle trousers tucked into leather seaboots with cobbled soles. When out of his time, a trustworthy lad could have a smack of his own, paying instalments to the builder.

Dredging in deep water was a hard, back-breaking life— hauling in huge dredges with 6-ft hoeing edges from 25 fathoms by hand. Frequently six were worked at a time on 65 fathom, 3-in bass warps leading in through multiple rollers on the rail or through a port in the bulwark. Hour after hour would be worked with little respite, until perhaps the early hours of the morning when the gear would be laid in and the crew snatched a brief sleep, keeping half-hour watches.

The fisheries flourished after the coming of the railway which gave direct access to Billingsgate, and by 1874 there were 132 first-class smacks of 15 to 50 tons registered at Colchester, 250 second class under 15 tons and 40 third-class vessels. Of these big smacks 89 were owned at Brightlingsea, 20 at Rowhedge, four at Wivenhoe and six at Tollesbury, average size 21 tons. West Mersea fishermen were chiefly interested in the Blackwater oyster dredging, using smaller smacks.

Many of the big smacks were employed on contract for £12 a week as fish carriers for the great fleets of Grimsby, Hull, Yarmouth and Lowestoft ketches trawling on the Dogger Bank. Others carried fresh salmon from the western Irish ports of Sligo and Westport round the northern coast of Ireland to the Liverpool market. Exposure to the full force of North Atlantic gales necessitated chain reef pendants to stand the hard driving. The round trip was frequently made in four days, 100 boxes being the normal freight. A few smacks even brought cattle from Jersey to Weymouth, and in the early nineties the owner of *Aquiline* contracted to supply all the shingle required for the new drydock at Wivenhoe, 22 tons per trip, dug out by hand from Colne beach.

Equipment varied with the nature of the work, but a good store of cables, warps and tackles was carried; some men shipped a brig's anchor for use in kedging off stranded vessels. Stored in the hold, it was swayed overside with tackles when required. These craft were always smartly kept and fitted out in the autumn, replacing worn gear and sails with new; 'the hards must have been a brave sight, for in 1848 there were 160 owned locally'.

First Fruits was built by Barr at Wivenhoe behind the Greyhound public house and launched down the High Street on ways. In these craft speed was paramount, so when Peter Harris of Rowhedge built *Bluebell* for Jack Spitty it was stipulated that she should beat *Aquiline*, his previous best. She succeeded, but Harris improved on her in *New Unity*, a real flyer, owned by Thomas Barnard, which finally outsailed the lot.

What was life like aboard these daring craft, racing each other out into the flying spray of a roaring gale and what sort of men were these salvagers? (writes John Leather).

Probably the best known of all was Thomas Barnard of Rowhedge, my great-grandfather, whose stocky figure with sou'wester jammed down over his ears, winter and summer alike, was well known on both East and South coasts . . . born of a good Essex family he ran away to become boy in a Colne smack. The wild nature of the work in those days evidently suited his adventurous spirit for whilst still in his twenties we find him owner and master of the *Prince of Orange* . . . that was in the 1830s.

Marriage and a new smack followed, the *Thomas and Mary* engaged in fishing and salvaging, and for a time he carried on a large oyster business at Chichester. His great name for life-saving and daring salvages was made in the next 40 years . . . there were many terrible wrecks on the Long Sand and Kentish Knock shoals and Tom was always in evidence on these occasions. In company with other smacks he went to the assistance of a ship ashore on the Long Sand (17½ miles long, up to half a mile wide and drying out in places at low water). At dusk all attempts at rescue had failed owing to the tremendous seas running and the other smacks left. The *Thomas and Mary* remained hove-to nearby; at 11 o'clock the ship lifted and quickly smashed herself to pieces on the hard sand, finally sliding off and sinking, allowing the smack just enough time to sweep alongside for her crew to jump aboard.

Racing out to a wreck on the Kentish Knock one wild and bitter night he found the victim to be a huge German barque, crowded with emigrants bound for New York. She was pounding her bottom in and no time was to be lost if all were to be saved, so Tom ran alongside in the terrifying surf and the human cargo was transferred to the wildly pitching smack. It was not until he had made three 'runs' through the maze of sands to Walton-on-Naze, and another to a passing steamer, that the whole complement of over 300 was saved from the great ship which was matchwood in 48 hours.

His fame grew as he rescued more and more crews from what seemed almost certain death, medals were awarded by life-saving societies and foreign governments and he and his sons were several times 'chaired' round the streets of Harwich after spectacular rescues. During the sixties Trinity House, recognising his ability, chartered him and his smack for pilotage work off the Suffolk coast, where he found time to rescue the crews of six vessels.

Into the *New Unity*, the last and finest of his smacks, he put all his 40 years' experience, and Harris produced a splendid sea boat

of 39 tons register. She proved a powerful craft and many a shipwrecked crew, lashed to the rigging, was glad to see her rakish
spars plunging alongside.

One of the toughest jobs he ever tackled with her was at the
wreck of a barque, when not only his own boat but the boats of
all the other smacks at the wreck were lost in boarding her. What
a hopeless situation! A dozen salvagers trapped aboard a wreck
whose crew were half crazy with fear, a vessel fast breaking up in
the gale which screamed above the thunder of seas breaking clean
over her. Away to windward hovered the six smacks, powerless to
get near in the shoal water. Tom set to work and drove the others
to make a boat out of the wreck's topsails and spars. Launched
over the lee rail, this held 27, floated and drove about until picked
up by the *New Unity*.

This fine smack met her fate during the great gale of 1881
which overwhelmed so many craft. Her 11 years of salvage ended
going to the wreck of a vessel in the Whittaker when, after letting
out both anchors to wait for water, she was parted from the
cables in the rising gale which forced her to run for the Medway
to leeward. They could do nothing else in that hurricane, to
attempt beating to windward was impossible and soon a blizzard
raged. With Tom at the helm and the crew, which included
several of his sons, peering through the howling snow squalls, the
gallant smack ran before the gale with her new sails bursting in
rags from the ropings. Through the network of swatchways she
raced to the mouth of the Medway when, with safety so near, she
struck the Grain Spit in a snow squall and drove on to be
smashed against the Spit Fort. Tom and his crew leaped to the
fort from the bowsprit end and, as he said afterwards, he could
not help shedding a tear at the sight of his swift smack pounded
to splinters.

A few years later he retired from the sea, though his sons
carried on the tradition of smack owning and, together with his
grandsons, made their name as yacht skippers. At his death in the
'nineties, he had saved over 900 lives from shipwreck and drowning. All vessels in the Colne struck their flags in memory of a fine
seaman.

What a magnificent story, and how it gives the lie to those
many traducers who try to suggest that smacksmen had an eye
only to the main chance, leaving men to drown while they
helped themselves to the cargo.

The salvagers had their lighter moments (continues John Leather), such as when Henry Cook of the *Aquiline* was spratting in the Wallet with the rest of the fleet on a very thick night. Being the first boat to 'fill', he quietly got his net and, placing an empty coal sack over the Knoll lighted buoy, sailed off into the Colne, leaving the rest of them at anchor until daylight before getting their bearings.

Jack Spitty of the *Bluebell* was another noted salvager, fisherman and occasionally smuggler. Several times when working off the Dutch coast he poached in adjacent German waters, being often chased by the patrol boats and finally caught and imprisoned. He was also a great smuggler and had a topsail made from two thicknesses of canvas. This was thrown down the fo'c'sle with the other sails when returning from the Continent and however hard the Customs might search they never found the contraband stuffed in the sail! He often laid 'tails' of smuggled spirits in the Colne, these were retrieved later after the Customs men had gone.

Mr Jack Owen, the veteran West Mersea seaman, recalls dredging five-fingers in Jack Spitty's *David and Eliza*, landing at £1 a ton. Spitty chanced on a thick patch of them off Frinton, just below the telegraph cable to the old Gunfleet lighthouse. Word went round and a few days later a score of Rowhedge, Wivenhoe and Tollesbury smacks appeared to reap the harvest. However, the cunning Spitty anchored a skin buoy right over the cable and dredged around with dredges hanging just below the surface. Down came the others, some with 16 dredges apiece and with warps straining, fouled the cable and each other, losing many dredges and their tempers. With a satisfied grin Jack Spitty retrieved his buoy and sailed off to Harwich, returning early next morning when he filled his hold without another smack in sight. He died from exposure about 60 years ago when digging up sand under the lee bilge of his smack *Annie* after she had got ashore on the Ridge when he was trawling alone in his old age.

Mention must also be made of Fred Salmon of the Brightlingsea *Emily* who saved many lives in the 'sixties, for which he received many tokens. Such were the brave and skilful salvagers, they feared neither men nor weather and were magnificent seamen, but by the 1880s the improved coastwise lighting, buoying and the provision of coastal lifeboats was reducing the number of wrecks and though the big cutters were outmoded the curtain was about to rise on the last and most active use of fishing under sail.

M

The deep-sea fisheries declined during the last decades of the nineteenth century and in 1890 the Brightlingsea fleet had fallen to 52. Several poisoning scares killed the demand for sea oysters and the end came during the 1914–18 war. By then, most of the cutters had converted to ketch rig.

The new factor influencing the design of smacks was the increasing number of local seamen skippering and manning yachts, especially racers, with which they were acquiring an international reputation. This led to the division of the year into two seasons, summer yachting and winter fishing.

The new boats were smaller, handier and handled by a smaller crew than the big old cutters they replaced. Suitable for winter spratting, in summer they could be more inexpensively laid up or worked by a crew of two for fish trawling or shrimping. These smart and rakish craft of from 12 to 20 tons register were turned out in large numbers by Aldous of Brightlingsea and Harris of Rowhedge, though several of the smaller ones were by John James and Root & Diaper of Brightlingsea. Husk of Wivenhoe and Howard of Maldon were building the 8- to 10-tonners favoured by Maldon and Mersea fishermen for their work in the Blackwater. (Pictures, p 148.)

A typical smack of the Brightlingsea, Rowhedge, Wivenhoe and Tollesbury fleets would be of about 18 tons register. These became almost a standard type and formed the backbone of the Essex smack fleet, which numbered several hundreds before the first world war. As early as 1872 the fleet under Colchester registration comprised: 132 first-class, 250 second-class and 40 third-class vessels. This compared with London's 149, 56 and 0, or Harwich with 17, 60 and 49.

The improvements then being made in yacht design were reflected in these new, fast cutters. Forefoots were rounder making them quicker in stays, beam was reduced, area of sail plan grew larger and jackyard topsails, big jibs and balloon staysails and spinnakers made their appearance on light days. Most of the orders resulted from the large sums of prize money won by local racing skippers and many craft bore evidence of their origin by such names as: *Valkyrie, Neva, Volante, Sunbeam, Shamrock, Xanthe, Deerhound* or *Foxhound*.

Take the typical example of a skipper ordering a new 18-tonner. After discussion of the dimensions, hold capacity and rig an agreement was drawn up and signed by owner and builder. The lines plan was drawn and approved by the owner and, after a few elementary calculations for displacement and trim, these were lofted and building commenced. Occasionally a model of the hull would be made and lined out to assist in planking up, but the vessel was never built from it as is so often stated . . . a fair hull or a set of 'shams' would never be achieved without laying the vessel off. The scantlings for an 18-ton smack were:

Item	Material	Scantling
Keel	E. elm	sided 5 in, moulded 7 in, 1½-in iron keel under as shoe
Stem	E. oak	sided 5 in, moulded 7 in, apron to suit
Sternpost	E. oak	sided 5 in, moulded 8 in at head
Breasthook	E. oak	
Frames	E. oak	sided 3½ in, moulded 3 in at sheer to 3½ in at floor heads
Floors	E. elm	sided 3 in, moulded 6 in on centre line
Hog	E. oak	sided 6 in, moulded 4½ in
Shelfing	larch	sided 4 in, moulded 7 in
Sheerstrake	E. oak	2¼-in thick
Topside planking	fir	1¾-in thick, generally 8-in wide
Bottom planking	E. elm	1¾-in thick, shift of butts at least 8 ft
Deck beams	E. oak	sided 3½ in, moulded 3 in in way of foc's'le and cabin, 3½ in at coamings to 3 in at ends
Deck planking	red pine	1¾-in thick
Timber heads	E. oak	3½ in at deck to 2⅞ in at top
Covering board	E. oak	1¾-in thick, generally 8-in wide
Rail	E. oak	2-in deep × 4 in wide, with top of rail 14 in above deck
Quarter timbers	E. oak	9 in at transom, 6½ in over top
Bowsprit bitt	E. oak	5½ in × 3¼ in
Pawl	E. oak	5½ in × 4¾ in
Arch piece	E. oak	5 in wide × 3 in thick
Windlass	E. oak	cheeks 7 in chocks 10 in × 6 in

Rudder post and blade of English elm
Spars, Oregon pine. All fastenings galvanised iron bolts and spikes.

Normal methods of building were employed. The frames, sawn

from local timber in the yard's sawpit, were erected and held fair by harpins and ribbands. Skin planking and decking followed and the vessel was usually completed in about four months. Ballast was stowed below the floors in the form of pig iron; the fo'c'sle was used as a sail and gear store, next was the fish hold, bulkheaded off and fitted with a heavy ceiling, abaft was the cabin with bunks for three, two fore and aft and one athwartships for'ard of the rudder trunk. The smaller oyster dredgers had a tiny cuddy for'ard in lieu of a cabin. One of the bowsprit bitts formed the pawl bitt of the windlass, which was worked by handspikes. Between the fish hatch and the after cabin hatch stood either a double-handed geared capstan or a 'wink', a 9-in diameter barrel geared to a handle and supported by a 6-in square post. The tiller rose abruptly in a sharp curve to a height of about 3 ft; at the end of the counter was the mainsheet block and a 'mitch board' to support the mainsail when stowed.

When new, smacks were invariably painted on topsides and bulwarks, favourite colours being grey and blue respectively, they were only tarred after age and use had roughened the planking.

An average sail plan had a working area of 825 sq ft for mainsail, 162 sq ft staysail, 210 sq ft jib, 210 sq ft topsail. The big jib, balloon staysail and jackyarder were for use in light weather, the small jib or 'spitfire' for a three-reef breeze.

The runners and fish bag tackles set up to chainplates on the bulwarks; the Colne and Tollesbury fleets rarely had channels to spread their main shrouds, but the smaller dredgers and Blackwater smacks had them to compensate for their reduced beam. You could always tell a Wivenhoe-built smack from one launched across the river by the round rubbing strake her builders fitted, the Rowhedge smacks having flat ones.

Occasionally an owner would feel the need for a larger craft and, lacking the means to build a new one, resorted to lengthening the old. The Rowhedge *Wonder*, CK 40, owned by Capt James Carter, was a 15-tonner built by Harris in 1876. She was slipped, cut in two and had 6 ft put into her amidships in 1893. After the hull had been sawn down, the forward end was drawn ahead on ways and securely shored up; the keel was cut back in long scarphs and a new centrepiece and hog fitted, backed by a keelson, always as near the parallel middle body as possible. The new frames were spiled from a harpin and ribbands. With these in place the skin planking and deck were cut back to give a shift of butts of at least 4 ft. After the planks had been caulked the vessel

was relaunched, the mast stepped in its original hole, but a new
mainsail and longer boom were required. The increased after sail
area was offset by a longer bowsprit.

Fitted with a motor, *Wonder* was still fishing 88 years after her
first launch.

When I visited Essex in May 1952 I was fortunate enough to
meet many old men who told me of their experiences. One was
Mr Albert Wm Mann, apprenticed at the age of 14 to Robert
Aldous on the 7 April 1885 for seven years, receiving 3s a week
for his first year and then a rise of a shilling every year, making
9s for the last year. When out of his time, a joiner was paid 4d
or 4½d an hour, but there were various rates in the yard, some
men having 5½d, and one 5¾d. No wages were paid if a man
was away ill.

The chief man was Rasbrook, a wheelwright, who lined out
the keel, 6-in sided and the stem, using moulds from an old
smack; a rabbet was cut two-thirds along, the stem was
tenoned in as the keel lay on its side, then the sternpost. Next
all were erected and shored up, the rabbet at forefoot put in
line by batten, and the apron inside the stem was fastened with
iron bolts and deadwood set up aft. The frames were made up
on the floor after ribbanding span frames, Nos 1 and 2 futtocks,
then the floor, all bolted together. Made thus, the frames were
up in a week, spaced 1 ft apart. On every other frame was a 'set
hole for ⅝ in bolt to set planks down'.

With a twinkle in his eye Mr Mann said, 'I bought a brace
but had to use an auger as the men said it was too fast and
would do them out of a job.'

Then followed the shelf, clamp and beams let in or half-
dovetailed to the shelf, next knees and breasthook 'homeletted'.
For'ard of amidships the fore face, aft the face looking aft, of the
frames were given the required bevel, one man putting on the
batten. Stern timbers were bevelled on the transom, quarter
timbers set in by eye, stanchions erected and covering board
marked by mould.

Planking began at the garboard, a wider plank, then on

round the bilge, 1½-in elm, the planks ripped, one man and a boy doing a strake a day each side 'the sheer by eye with a sheering batten'. After the planking had been adzed it was planed up, then caulked, 'two men doing 100 ft a day, two threads of oakum, brown, prison plucked'.

Robert Aldous had the yard for 40 years, leaving a fortune of some £40,000; in his will he directed that Mann was to be given £25. (Picture, p 120.)

Stone Bros built a 31-ft counter-sterned smack in 1892 for £70 in about three months from the signing of the agreement. Bob Stone often built on speculation and it was his custom to leave a smack in frame for a year to season.

My wife and I went for a trip with a delightful crew of old men, all well over 70 but hale and hearty, cracking jokes as they told me of incidents in their varied lives.

Harry Death went to sea at the age of 12 in his father's smack, sailing subsequently in *Vanduara*, 'the biggest smack, could carry 1,200 bushels of sprats, *Volunteer* 1,000; a lucky night's catch was 500 bushels of sprats in one haul of a quarter of an hour'. He had *Masonic*, an 18-ton smack, 'sail set at work: mainsail, jib and staysail when working dredges, topsail on passage to Whitstable flats etc, to catch 10 ton of five-fingers, sold for 14s a ton for manure to farmers . . . mussels 6s a ton, sometimes farmers paid 12s for 100 bushels.'

Masonic was built *c* 1890 by Root & Diaper. 'Aldous let you have a smack without money if a worker.' Reminiscing, he went on: 'rowed from Herne Bay with 400 odd bushel of mussels, 14s a share, after two tides . . . sometimes 5s for a week's work catching small brood, bad . . . easterly gale laid for 10 days and earned nothing . . . a good week £2, dredging for small oysters . . . skipper had 1s in £1 of boat's earnings if not owner, boys got whelk money . . . always help each other willingly . . . in Colne River about 30 smacks 10 to 18 tons, four bob a day for crew, then 4s 6d, work five days, Saturday clean boat and tidy up'.

Masonic was out in the fearful gale of 29 December 1914,

when over £1,000 damage was done to houses in Brightlingsea. 'Sixty fathom of chain out, jumping so much broke bowsprit and chain, three anchors with chain lost . . . west wind gale force, ran down Swin on one sea, halyards unrove so ran to sea with staysail . . . finally got into Whitstable.'

We were chugging along in the cut-down *Native*, built by Aldous as a bawley; all the time they were talking the men continued to haul up the dredges and sorted over the oysters. I asked which he liked, sail or motor, 'I prefer sail as boat then drifted down sideways, all dredges worked clear of each other. In motor, follow in same path, so bow dredge gets most, aft least.' In bad weather in sail he used to lay-to under storm jib, reefed staysail and two reefs in mainsail, which then cost £10 and lasted from six to seven years.

'We used to lay four million oysters in Pyefleet Creek, now about 200,000 . . . 1947 frost was disastrous to oysters . . . from end April till June dredge up, sort, relay the good till September.'

Walter Field was still hard at it at the age of 85 and he spoke of his days 'skilling' for deep-sea oysters. 'For a three-week trip we took 1 cwt pork, 1 cwt beef, a side of ham, for six men working off the German coast.' An aside from another old chap 'nowadays lucky if we gets a sausage . . . rationing, pah' (1s 2d worth of meat a week in 1952), '3 or 4 soles, 1 lb each and over for one man's breakfast . . . get 40 to 50,000 oysters, then home.' At twenty, he went in the Iceland cod fishing from Grimsby for a spell, then back to smacks working for scallops from Newhaven, Boulogne and Dunkirk. '*Hilda* was a beautiful boat, built by Aldous, now a jetty . . . *Fiona* a good boat, built in Jersey, was a coaster in the powder trade before scalloping . . . deep-sea oysters 4s to 5s a hundred, sold at Whitstable and Brightlingsea.'

The oysters were put in nets and kept in the well until required. In the North Sea they worked in 20 to 23 fathoms, eight dredges day and night.

Mr French was skipper of *Volunteer* at the age of 22 when 50

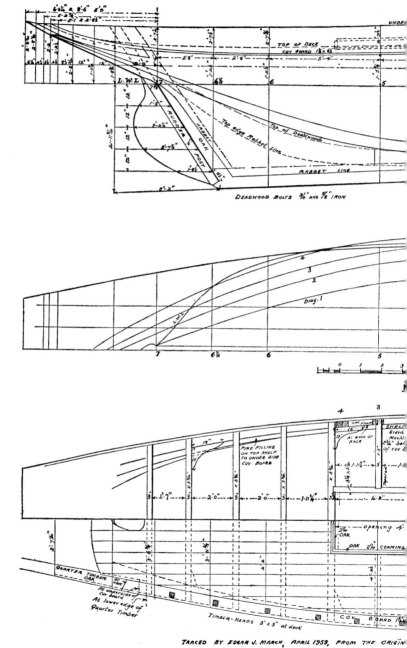

Colne fishing sma

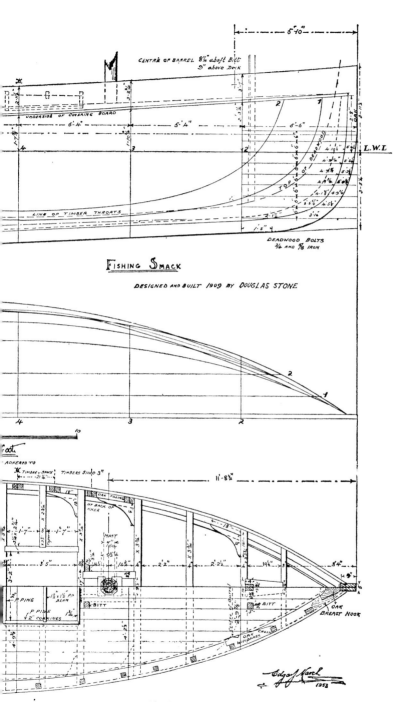

FISHING SMACK

DESIGNED AND BUILT 1909 BY DOUGLAS STONE

CENTRE OF BARREL 8¼" abaft Bitt
9" above Deck

L.W.L

DEADWOOD BOLTS
¾ AND ⅝ IRON

THE POSSESSION OF J. JAMES & C°. L™, BRIGHTLINGSEA

uglas Stone in 1909

or 60 sail went dredging in the North Sea, '70 fathom warp, eight in all . . . at times a hundred would go down Channel . . . I used to read verses of the Bible to the old men when I was a boy . . . go to sea on a Monday . . . if earn 5s a week I was happy.'

Capt Polley told me, 'As a boy I was often heaving the lead eight hours at a time in thick weather.' I also visited Mr Robert Gilbert, a wonderful old gentleman. 'If I live till next year I shall be 100.' He went to sea at 14 in his father's smack *Spray* a 30-tonner, later he bought *Delight* of Jersey, but she was dismasted and sunk. Three smacks were lost in the great gale of 1881 when his brother was drowned, but he was luckily ashore. He went deep-sea dredging, getting 4d a dozen for choice oysters from the fish bars at Hastings, Brighton and other south coast resorts.

At 25 Mr Gilbert gave up fishing and for 50 years was captain of nine or ten big yachts, as well as racing in smaller ones; when he 'left the sea' at 78 he had command of a 200-ton steam yacht.

When I was in West Mersea I called to see Mr E. R. Haward who had sent me Aldous's account for a boat built for his two uncles; then his father bought her and Mr Haward served his apprenticeship in her, finally taking her over. In 1946, after 60 years' fishing, she was sold for conversion to a yacht, thoroughly justifying her name *Evergreen*.

On the walls of the room in which we chatted were hung many photographs of famous yachts. Mr Haward had followed the Essex tradition and he was one of the crew in *Shamrock* when the challenge was made for the *America's* Cup in 1930. Presently he asked if I would care to see an old account book belonging to an ancestor and to my delight he allowed me to take it away for closer examination.

It was a small, dark leather wallet, similar to the old-fashioned bank passbook, the leather still supple. On the flap inside was the inscription:

WILL^m HAWARD Senr

MERSEA ISLAND   April 30th 1791

and on the fly-leaf in writing only slightly faded:

Description of the anchor we had at Harwich No. 3025.
Marked F.S. Wt. 2c 1q 0 lb.

'Teach me to feel another's Woe
to hide the faults I see
That I to others Mercy show
that Mercy show to me'

The first entry reads:

	£	s	d
Dues from			
Chriss Bill	66	1	–
Spring Bill	42	3	–
Freight	9	10	4
	117	14	4
Rec'd at Chriss and Spring	80	–	–
	37	14	4
Lost oysters	2	9	–
	£35	5	4

Then follows similar entries, many in a beautiful script. Some of his debtors never seem to have paid up in full, a small amount on account being a frequent entry. Under 'Freight 1793' comes a list of 43 names with various small amounts, ranging from 1s 4d, 'Mr Wardell £15 2s 4d', totalling £177 1s 0d, but two items were not paid. The following year 12 names, £538 1s 0d. Other entries refunding sums 'for lost oysters' suggests that credit had to be given for oysters spoilt in transit.

A cryptic entry in very faint pencil reads: 'Bonaparte Transmog[d] into a Jack ass and rode to Hell by a Dutch[ss]'

Christmass 1795: 'I pack[d] 9 wash . . . 56 wash', and the account comes to £479 2s 8d.

Now the writing changes, a bolder hand; perhaps his son Adam is making the entries. Mr Ryder continues to be a very slow payer, 'Due more from Mr Ryder £19 19s 8d.'

Towards the end of this fascinating record is a very faint pencil verse, which suggests the passing of a beloved wife:

'She's softly Landed on that
Distant shore

Where Billows never break nor
Tempest Roar
Where peaceful Harbours for the
Ind.............. (indecipherable)
and Crowns repay the long
.... do.

Across what a gulf of time I looked when reading these entries written by a fisherman long dead. When he first penned them, Napoleon was about to rise in the firmament of power, crushing the Austrians and dreaming of the conquest of India. The last entry was made in the year that saw France mistress of the Continent.

I am indeed indebted to Mr Haward for entrusting this precious heirloom to a stranger, as well as the Account, also to all who so willingly told me of a way of life, gone for ever.

Account written on a plain sheet of blue paper, faint ruled. Signed over a Victoria penny stamp, lilac colour.

BRIGHTLINGSEA
1886   Messrs W. Bullock & Co
To R. Aldous & Co

	£	s.	d.
August 21st			
To New 11 tons Boat as Agreed	100	0	0
4–5-in single rope S^t block		5	0
1–5-in double do.		2	6
1–4-in double do.		2	0
3–5-in single iron S^t do.		10	0
2¼ tons iron ballast 55/-	6	3	9
24 lb sheet lead & 2 lb copper N		5	6
Cement, gravel & putting in	1	17	6
	£109	6	3
Rec'd on Acc^t July '86 £25, August	50	0	0
21st £25	£59	6	3
Interest on £59. 6. 3	2	19	3

1887
June 4 To 2-5-in patent rope S^t block   2   6
       2-4-in   do.   do.   2   0
       2 patent sheaves   4   0

                       £62 14 0
Received August 1887 £25   25   0   0

                       £37 14 0
     Settled Nov 19—1887
     (signed) R. Aldous

A visit to the old shipyards showed the great changes which have taken place, and thanks to the interest shown by D. Stone & Son I was able to make tracings from plans of the 8-ton smack *Sarah* built in 1892 for T. Went, another for a similarly named craft in 1902, and *Peace*, designed and built by Douglas Stone for Stanley A. French of West Mersea. (See plans, pp 208, 215 and 224.)

A damp-stained specification was marked in pencil, 'A clean neat copy. D.S.':

DIMENSIONS etc OF A FISHING BOAT TO BE BUILT FOR
MARINER of BRIGHTLINGSEA by
STONE BROTHERS, SHIP BUILDERS, BRIGHTLINGSEA

Length overall   29 ft 6 in
Beam greatest   8 ft 6 in
Draught   3 ft 6 in
Freeboard, least   1 ft 2 in
Depth of Rail & Bulwark   1 ft 0 in
Straight Stem
Transom Stern
Carvel built with Rudder and Tiller and Spars
Keel & Deadwoods of elm   sided 4 in
Stem & Sternpost of oak   sided 4 in
Frame of oak, some floors may be of elm, sided 2½ in & moulded 3 at heads & 3¾ throat
Sheer strake and rubbing band of oak, 1½-in planking of lined 1½-in fir, except 2 strakes up from the keel, these to be of elm
Stanchions, oak. Rail, A. elm. Bulwarks, fir
Covering board of oak
Decks of fir 1½ in in convenient widths, caulked & payed
Deck fittings one hatch & cabin top of fir, fitted with slide

Gear bitts of oak
Shelf, fir 2-in sided
Beams, oak, well rounded; carlines, oak
Rudder post, oak; tail piece, elm and fir
Spars to be one Mast
   one Topmast
   one Gaff
   one Boom
   one Bowsprit and the necessary plain ironwork
    thereto,
All fastenings in plank & deck to be galvd sq. nails, all bolt
 fastening to be plain iron
Channells of oak & chainplates for each side
Spike windlass & pawl

Time required for building, about 3 months from date hereof
Price to be 65£ 10/– sterling
 We the undersigned agree to build & deliver bawley boat as
above as witness here of receipt of five pounds paid by the said
       one
 balance to be paid on taking the boat.
NOTE: The 'five' was struck through and 'one' written below.

Every smack, being fisherman-owned, naturally varied
slightly in dimensions, sail plan and so on; some had short gaffs,
others long, certain men preferred a full body, others a rising
floor; in fact, each skipper had his own ideas and owed allegiance to no company, board of directors, nor anyone else.

 Owing to soakage, many of the later boats built of softwood
lost their speed after a year or two. Fashions changed and some
bawleys built with a square transom stern had a counter stern
fitted in later life to increase the deck area, especially for
dredging.

 Mainsails were loose-footed so that the tack could be triced
up to shorten sail quickly. Staysails worked on an iron horse,
bowsprits were seldom reefed, the storm jib being set with the
iron traveller half way in.

 Halyards were usually of manilla and Mr Death told me that
the main went to port, peak to starboard, jib to starboard side
of the mast and staysail down the centre of the mast. There were

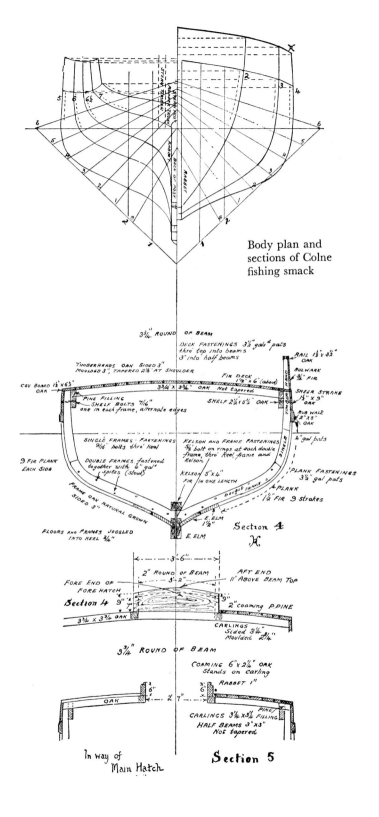

Body plan and
sections of Colne
fishing smack

3¾" ROUND OF BEAM

DECK FASTENINGS 3½" galv⁴ pats
thro' top into beams
3" into half beams

RAIL 1½" x 3½"
OAK

TIMBERHEADS OAK SIDED 3"
MOULDED 3", TAPERED 2½ AT SHOULDER

BULWARK
1¾" FIR

FIR DECK
1½" x 6" (above)

COV BOARD 1½" x 6½"
OAK

3¾" x 3¾" OAK Not tapered

SHEER STRAKE
1½" x 9"
OAK

PINE FILLING
SHELF BOLTS ⁷/₁₆"
one in each frame, alternate edges

SHELF 2½" x 5½" OAK

RUB WALE
2" x 3"
OAK

½" gal pats

9 FIR PLANK
EACH SIDE

SINGLE FRAMES · FASTENINGS
⁹/₁₆" bolts thro' keel

KELSON AND FRAME FASTENINGS
⅝" bolt on rings at each double
frame, thro' keel, frame and
kelson

PLANK FASTENINGS
3½" gal pats

DOUBLE FRAMES, fastened
together with 6" gal
spikes (stout)

KELSON 5" x 4"
FIR IN ONE LENGTH

DOUBLE FRAME

PLANK
1½" FIR 9 strakes

FRAME OAK NATURAL GROWN
SIDED 3"

E. ELM
1½"

Section 4

FLOORS AND FRAMES JOGGLED
INTO KEEL ¾"

E. ELM

H.

3'-6"

2" ROUND OF BEAM

AFT END
11" ABOVE BEAM TOP

5'-2"

FORE END OF
FORE HATCH

Section 4

9"

5"

2" coaming P.PINE

3¾" x 3¾" OAK

CARLINGS
Sided 3¾"
Moulded 2¼"

3¾" ROUND OF BEAM

COAMING 6" x 2¼" OAK
Stands on carling

RABBET 1"

OAK

6"

2' 7"

PINE
CARLINGS 3¾" x 3½" FILLING
HALF BEAMS 3" x 3"
Not tapered

In way of
Main Hatch

Section 5

no runners, backstays or bowsprit shrouds, and the bobstay was usually of chain.

Topsails were jib-headed or jackyarders. A sail plan in my possession shows a pole-masted cutter, mast 27 ft and topsail yard 15 ft 3 in, set almost vertically. The hull is 37 ft overall.

In the palmy days, main booms often projected 5 ft and more over the taffrail, and topsails had yards 10 to 12 ft in length. Many of the big cutters were converted to ketch rig, among them *Hilda* (picture, p 119), built in 1886 and *Vanduara*, built in 1880. Fitted with a motor, *Hilda* was still fishing in 1934 and maybe later, also *Sunbeam*, CK 328, once owned by Wm Cranfield. *Ellen*, built at Wivenhoe in 1886 for Richard J. Cranfield and owned in 1932 by Mrs Emmaretta Cranfield, was still at work in 1966, fitted with a motor.

Mr Redvers Creek talked of the 20-ft oyster skiffs once built for 10s a foot, an 18-footer costing £8 10s. 'In 1939 a skiff cost £70, now £230 to £300 . . . a 60-year old boat was doubled in 1936.'

Apprenticed to Aldous for seven years in 1914, he received 2s 6d a week, rising to 18s in his last year, and worked from 6 am to 5.30 pm, Saturdays until 1 pm. 'Now they start at 37s 10d and get £4 10s last year at age of 20.' A boat builder's wage was 6½d an hour in 1914, 1d an hour overtime for an apprentice, 3d after his first year.

The skiffs were sturdy boats 20 to 21 ft in length, with a beam of 7 ft 6 in to 8 ft 3 in, and a depth from top of keel to rail of 2 ft 4 in to 2½ ft. They were built by eye, without moulds.

A wide keel was fitted in order to press the oysters down in the bed when taking the ground over the beds. Of English elm, sided 3 in, it was in two halves, moulded 8 in for'ard of amidships and tapering down to 1½ in fore and aft, making a total width of 16 in down to 3 in. 'With rabbet there was risk of a leaky garboard, but not when square.'

The oak stem, 3-in sided and moulded, was scarphed to a 4-in moulded forefoot which was scarphed to the keel. The apron of oak or elm, and deadwood of oak, were sided 3 in. The oak sternpost, sided 3 in, was moulded 3 in at the top, 7 in at the bottom, halved to the keel, with a heavy oak knee, 3-in sided. The transom, of 1½-in elm with a 2-in camber on top, was moulded with a graceful curve to a tuck 1 ft 2 in above the keel.

Planking was ¾-in elm taken to the turn of the bilge; then the elm floors, moulded 9 in and sided 3 in, were fitted before the planking was completed; next the grown oak frames, moulded 3 in, sided 2 in, were fitted, and then the oak rail 4½-in moulded, 2-in sided, 8 to 10 strakes of planking being usual.

Flooring was 1½-in fir, fixed thwart 18 in × 2 in fir; barrels were lifted on to this thwart before lifting them on to the rail. Floors were fastened to the keel with ½-in dump bolts, plank lands to floors and frames with 'flat points', with three french copper nails between frames and through garboards and keel, clenched. Rail spiked to top of frames, rubbing strake outside and a 'land listing', to protect the edges of the sheer strake.

Two men could build a boat in three weeks, and its expected life would be 40 to 50 years; after 25 years or so ⅝-in doubling was added, with feather edge filling at lands.

Skiffs were used when unloading sprats from the smacks, 23-bushel barrels at a time, also when dredging oysters over layings.

Probably the last smack trawling under sail was *Polly* of Maldon, MN 12, built as a bawley in 1889 by J. Howard from surplus barge timber at a cost of £70. In 1922 a counter stern was added and nearly 30 years later she was still fishing under a big mainsail, jib and staysail, with E. Pitt, just on 80, at the tiller and his brother, a few years younger working the beam trawl. (Picture, p 120.)

Mr John Leather wrote me:

The years 1870–1914 saw the Golden Age of local sailing craft and seamen. In winter, the Colneside ports were crammed with laid-up yachts, sail and steam, racers and cruisers, their crews manning the several hundred smacks of the fleet and new vessels were coming off the ways every year.

N

In summer, the smacks lay forlorn whilst their crews, many of them great names in yachting history, displayed their perfection of fore-and-aft seamanship when driving the great racers round the coast, in the Mediterranean or off Sandy Hook in quest of the elusive 'Cup', in all the glory of towering spars, sweeping hulls and 40-men crews.

It is not to be wondered that the smacks developed to such speedy and seaworthy craft, for who would wish to sail a hack after handling a thoroughbred all summer? During those settled years yachting and fishing became a way of life having its own customs and traditions. One such was the annual Seamen's Thanksgiving or Harvest Festival of the Sea, when the walls of the church were hung with trawl nets whose dark hues emphasised the gleaming white and gold of yacht lifebelts, flanked by varnished boat oars, whilst from the altar winked the port and starboard lights. The church was crowded with the villages' seamen, families and all, from the racing skippers in the front pews to the smack boys at the back . . . 'Eternal Father, strong to save' always closed the service.

The smack year commenced with the annual fit-out in September and the local smack races and regattas were arranged to coincide with the refitting and no trouble was spared to get the crack smacks into racing trim. Bottoms were blackleaded and the best stretched canvas bent, including big reaching staysails and huge jackyard topsails and spinnakers, whilst only the smartest racing hands shipped for crew.

There was a long tradition of Essex smack racing reaching back to the year 1783 when the first was held in the river Blackwater . . . the heyday was during the period 1880–1914 when tremendous annual tussles took place at Brightlingsea, Rowhedge, Wivenhoe, Tollesbury and sometimes at West Mersea.

Racing was keen, as was to be expected from men accustomed to split-second judgment when handling 300-ton racing cutters, and good sport was assured when they were matched together in their home waters and native craft. Conditions were that competing vessels must be bona-fide fishing smacks, to be sailed in fishing trim, with number painted on mainsail and no lead ballast allowed. The first prize was often a new Ratsey mainsail and always a cup, with second and third prizes in proportion.

The course was from the line off East Mersea stone, out round the Bar buoy, across to the Wallet Spitway, up to the Swire hole and back to the Knoll buoy, then home. . . . The finer points of racing were observed, tactics playing a great part and overlaps or luffing matches were the order of the day.

Every port had its champions, Brightlingsea's *Foxhound*, Tollesbury's *Bertha*, Wivenhoe's *Elise* and *Maria* and Rowhedge's famous trio, Capt William Cranfield's *Sunbeam*, Capt Alf Cranfield's *Xanthe* and, that Champion of Champions, the lovely and incomparable *Neva* which, in the hands of her owner Capt Lemon Cranfield, the 'yacht racing genius', was acknowledged champion of the Essex smack races for over 30 years. So great did her fame become that it was said in the '90s in the Press 'it seems she cannot be beaten'. However, she was often hard pressed by the powerful *Sunbeam*, sailed by his brother William of *America's* Cup fame.

The finish of nearly every race saw *Neva* and *Sunbeam* (picture, p 147) tearing home for the line, heeled to the rails under clouds of canvas and hotly pursued by the other cracks, all fighting it out to the last.... A word on these Cranfield brothers ... all five were crack yacht-racing skippers and were of magnificent physique, the smartest racing men of the day as well-known in American and Mediterranean waters as in this country. Amongst the many craft he brought to the top, Lemon's greatest triumph was the racing schooner *Miranda* with which he was so successful that no one would sail against her after three seasons. William made his name in *Yarana* and earned undying fame with the Cup challengers *Valkyries* II and III. While John was bringing other big class cutters to the head of the list, Richard and Stephen were prominent in the smaller classes. They often let men take their smacks for the winter if 'standing by' a new racer on the Clyde.

In 1892, Colne men skippered six out of the seven 40-raters, big yachts about 60 ft LWL. Sycamore had *Corsair*, E. Gould *Varuna*, Maskell *Irene*, Skeats *Creole*, Jay *Reverie*, and Carter *Thalia*.

Sycamore later made his name sailing the *Shamrocks* belonging to Sir Thomas Lipton in the races for the *America's* Cup.

King Edward VII's *Britannia* was skippered by Capt John Carter of Rowhedge and, in King George V's early ownership, by his son Jack, with her crew from Rowhedge. *Satanita* was sailed by Capt Tom Jay, another Rowhedger, who took his village crew with him into the great racers *Ailsa* and *Rainbow*, one of the fastest schooners afloat.

The speeds attained by working smacks at the regattas were

astounding. Up to the 1880s, the first-class Colne smacks held an annual race amongst themselves with a hogshead of beer as the prize.

This event was quite distinct from the yearly regatta struggles among their smaller sisters. The deep-sea smacksmen scorned an inshore course, though the start and finish were in the Colne: racing out round the Galloper and back with only one rule to observe—port gave way to starboard and, as most of them were pretty evenly matched, it meant exciting moments when two or three of these fine cutters crossed tacks. Then the skippers' bearded faces would set in unwinking stares, calculating, knowing to the inch who would weather who but each brazening it out until, with the bowsprits of some almost at the lee shrouds of others, the whole lot would fling round in a flurry of thrashing jibs and topsails, and the bowlines, jerked free by the boys forward, sent the big staysails slamming across to disappear with a whang into the foam surging the lee decks as they stood off on another tack. Perhaps they got a fair wind home when the great half squaresails, carried before spinnakers were devised, lifted and ranted them back into Colne, the winner proudly fixing his metal masthead cock as the finishing gun boomed from the committee smack anchored off East Mersea stone, announcing him cock of the fleet for that year.

One instance must suffice of the regattas. At Wivenhoe in 1884, *Neva*, *Wonder*, *Eudioa*, *Lily*, *Violet*, *Ada* and *Nancy* started under all plain sail and jib-headed topsails. During the beat out to the Bar buoy *Neva* took the lead, which she never lost. They reached to the Priory Spit before making a board to the Wallet Spitway buoy and running back up Colne to Wivenhoe, a course from mark to mark of 20⅞ nautical miles which *Neva* covered in 2 hr 23 min 4 sec, an average speed of 8¾ knots. *Wonder* finished second, 2 min 56 sec later, and *Eudioa* third, 30 seconds after her.

In 1885 the race was sailed in a gale of wind with single-reefed mainsails and topmasts housed, but all set spinnakers for the run. One ever-to-be-remembered day saw only 6 ft between *Elise* of Wivenhoe and *Ellen* of Rowhedge after a 22 miles race.

After the smack races the long topmasts were sent down and

replaced by the shorter 'chocker poles' for no seaman would dream of sailing a craft 'bald-headed', but topsails were still set.

Two men could handle a 15-ton smack for fish trawling, though some of the more powerful carried a boy. Earnings were divided into shares, one for the boat, one for each of the crew, half for the boy. The usual trawling grounds were the Wallet, the Raysand Channel and the East and West Swin, depending upon the direction of the wind. The little Mersea and Maldon boats worked the Bench Head shoal at the mouth of the Blackwater and the upriver grounds off Osea Island and the 'Stumble'.

The catch varied, but in spring and summer soles were fairly plentiful these, together with plaice and roker, formed the staple haul. Prices were very variable, but 9d to 1s per lb was a good price before the first war.

The beam trawl was similar to that used on other parts of the coast, the length of the beam being determined by the distance between the aftermost shroud and the quarter rail, usually about 25 ft. Iron trawl heads were used and the groud rope of the net was 'woulded'—bound round with old rope to prevent its biting the soft ground. Beams were generally carried on the starboard side and secured to shrouds and quarter by stoppers.

Smacks always trawled down wind. To shoot the net, speed was reduced by either backing the jib, staysail, or rucking the peak down and tricing up the main tack, dependent on conditions. Two hauls a tide were a fair average; a good day's work might be 15 lb of prime soles and larger quantities of plaice and skate. For shrimp trawling, a finer mesh was used. If a big haul was made the net had to be 'parted' and the crew baled the shrimps out with a small net—the 'didall'—until the net could be got aboard. A small dredge with shrimp mesh net known as a 'tell tale' was always towed astern; and it was frequently scanned by the skipper to observe the quality of the catch.

The oyster trade was the background to other occupations. For the first year of its life the oyster is known as 'spat' and up to three years as 'brood'. From three to four years as 'half-ware', 1,600 to 1,800 filling a tub measure. 'Ware' or 'oysters' is the term given to those which require a further year on the fattening beds before they are ready for market. This may be at any age between five to seven years, depending on demand.

When gathering oysters one or two dredges were worked by each man, the usual number being six a smack. The method is to hoe the oysters into the bag or net. In Essex, the bottom of the net is formed with steel rings, but at Whitstable a perforated 'hide' bottom is substituted. The dredge is towed on a bass warp attached to a thole on the rail with a dredgerman's hitch, a round turn with the end backed over. This slips off if the dredge comes fast; 'If you can't free it, the warp is thrown over with its buoy bent on in readiness and you scull after it in the boat to worry it free.' The dredge also serves to clean the beds of rubbish and mud.

The principal pests are the American slipper limpet, imported with some 'bluepoints' at the turn of the century and now the greatest threat to all oyster layings; the 'tingle' whelk which bores holes into the shell and sucks out the oyster, the starfish or 'five-fingers', which inject a poison before eating the oyster; and the crabs which destroy the young brood.

Trade tools are a 'cultar' or large blunt knife used for detaching brood from culch and generally cleaning up oysters, a 'tindal' or flat basket for carrying brood, nets which hold a 'wash' of oysters on a smack's deck, and 'sheards' or two boards used for gathering and disposing of culch from the deck when working. Oyster pits are used for storing fattened oysters, which in winter must be protected from frost.

The fully grown oyster is selected by 'culling'. This is done in the companies' packing sheds by experienced men who sort the oysters into No 1s and No 2s. The Colchester fishery has a silver oyster for standard.

Measures vary with the district; the largest is the 'tub', equivalent to the ancient Winchester bushel which holds 21 gallons, 1 quart and ½ pint. The following are the locally used standards: 2 gallons = 1 peck, 2 pecks = 1 wash, 4 wash = 1 tub. 1 prickle basket = 10 gallons or ½ tub, 1 bucket = ⅓ of a wash, 1 nipperkin = 1/16 of a tub.

The Corporation of Colchester was granted the first charter by Richard I in 1183; others followed subsequently but the fishing limits have remained unchanged from the first. In 1638, when oysters were very scarce, the price rose from 4d to 2s 8d a bushel. In 1758 came the rule 'no dredgerman to take more than five bushels in a day for each dredge used'. The penalty for fishing from 1 March to 15 August was 40s. Brood was being dredged off Falmouth to lay in private beds in the Colne, and between 1718 and 1735 foreign oysters to the number of 213,897 bushels were laid in Essex and Kent beds. By 1806, dredged oysters were fetching 4s to 6s a tub of 2 bushels.

The old company got into low water and were forced to ask the Corporation for a loan and so lost complete control.

The Colne Oyster Fishing Company was founded in 1870 and is managed by a board of 12, six elected by the Corporation and six by the dredgermen or 'freemen'. There are no shares or capital in the ordinary sense, though a dividend is generally paid to members at the end of each year. Only members were allowed to work the fishery and to protect their interests, 13 policemen were employed; sailing in a steam launch and three swift cutters they kept watch day and night.

The smacks used were generally around 10 tons register and comprised about a quarter of the total fleet; many of the Blackwater boats carried no topsail. Up to 1914, about 40 smacks and the steam dredger *Pyefleet* were working. Six hands were carried, each working a dredge, and when dredging brood an average of three wash per man per tide was usual.

The day's work began at 7 am and lasted till dinner time when the fleet brought up for an hour on a signal from the *Pyefleet*. At the close of the day she hoisted a signal for all smacks to transfer their catch aboard her; 'whilst this was in progress the vigilant police boats were darting about among the smacks to see none were slipping a few under the cuddy hatch'. On the return to Brightlingsea, the day's catch was re-laid on the stock grounds in Pyefleet by six dredgermen who received an extra 2s 6d for this work.

When dredging 'ware' in Pyefleet a smack would 'fill' after

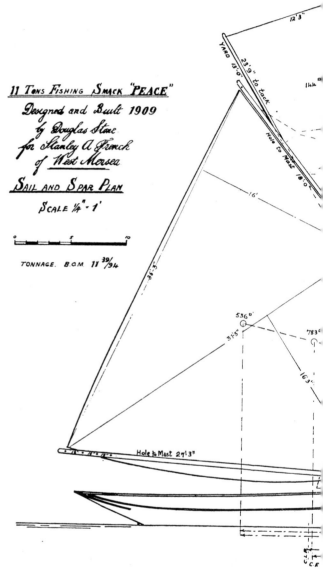

11 Tons Fishing Smack "PEACE"

Designed and Built 1909
by Douglas Stone
for Stanley A. French
of West Mersea

SAIL AND SPAR PLAN

SCALE ¼" = 1'

TONNAGE. B.O.M. 11 39/94

TRACED BY EDGAR J MARCH April 1953 FROM ORIGINAL

Sail and spar plan of smack *Pea*

Lower Sails   Areas & Centres

Mainsail   536°   × 0 =   0
Foresail   108   × 15.75 =   1701.00
Jib   139   × 23.75 =   3301.25
    ———   ———
    783   5002.25

$$\frac{783}{5002.25} = 783)5002.25 \ (6.37 \ ft \ from \ CE.$$
              4698
              3042   of Mainsail
              2349
              6935   (= 6'4½' about)
              5481
              444

Foresail   108°   × 0 =   0
Jib   139   × 7.83 =   1088.37
    ———   ———
    247

$$247)1088.37 (4.40 \ = (4'5' about)$$
     988   fwd of CE of foresail
    1003
     988
     157

To Deck

22'-6"

21'-9"

6'-4½"

139°

108°

8'-9"

9'-6"

10'-9"

14'.1"

To sheave pin   12'.1"

16'-0"

17'-1½"
16'-9"

d built by Douglas Stone in 1909

two hours' work and the catch was landed at the packing sheds on Peewit Island for 'culling' before being packed in wooden tubs and boxes for market. In 1895, 2½ million oysters were sold for over £20,000. 'The present decreased size of the fishery, which employs only four motor craft, is due largely to wartime neglect; there are no river police or sailing smacks left.'

In the river Blackwater were two main companies and many smaller ones, also numbers of private layings. 'The old Blackwater Company is now owned by the Whitstable Company and lies in a state of near disuse, a far different scene from that of 40 years ago when 500 shareholding fishermen were working it and sending over 2 million oysters to market annually. Various private companies and some individual layings remain active in the Blackwater and are worked by fishermen from West Mersea, Tollesbury and Maldon.'

The clink of a hundred and more pawls and the cheep of blocks have given place today to the 'chuff-chuff' of the diesel.

CHAPTER SEVEN

THE THAMES ESTUARY

TIME was when Erith and Gravesend were fishing centres from which the men trawled for whitebait and the brown shrimp abundant in the Thames, but as the water became more and more polluted the fish deserted these reaches of the river and were only found in any quantity lower down the estuary.

At Erith was the well-known barge-building firm of Douglas Stone whose sons started a yard at Brightlingsea. Stone could always be relied upon to build a fast spritsail barge; he also built bawleys, and his *Mayflower* LO 190, which cost about £140 in the 1880s, was reckoned to be the swiftest for her length of 32 ft. The earlier clinker-built boats ran about 22 ft overall, with a beam of 8 ft, oak-built and fitted with wells, but carvel build was now the fashion. All were of light draught for trawling in shoal water, their principal difference from the Harwich bawleys which drew more water. (Pictures, pp. 165 and 166.)

By the turn of the century, over 30 bawleys fished from Gravesend and it was a fine sight to see them beating up Sea Reach. Mr Don Paterson tells me that it was the custom to pickle the early bawleys with Stockholm tar before launching, which may well account for the incredible age many reached. In 1961 the 28 ft 6 in *Ellen*, reputed to have been built in 1760, was still working, her owner Bill Warner, aged 78, coming from a long line of shrimpers which went back to his great-grandfather. Stripped of her sails and spars and fitted with a 15-hp Kelvin motor, *Ellen* was fishing in the estuary during the second world war and twice was nearly blown up. A mere 95 years old is *Lilian*, LO 158.

227

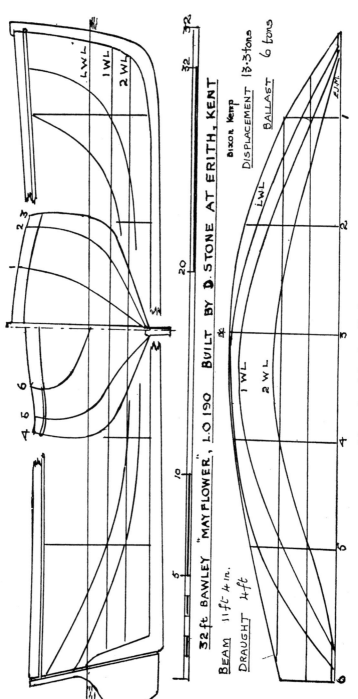

32 ft BAWLEY "MAYFLOWER", L.O 190 BUILT BY D. STONE AT ERITH, KENT

Dixon Kemp

DISPLACEMENT 13·3 tons

BALLAST 6 tons

BEAM 11 ft 4 in.

DRAUGHT 4 ft

Lines of 32-ft bawley *Mayflower*

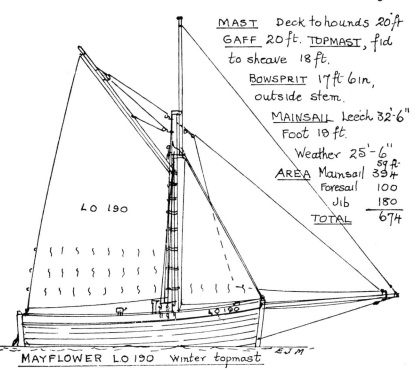

MAST Deck to hounds 20 ft
GAFF 20 ft. TOPMAST, fld
to sheave 18 ft.
BOWSPRIT 17 ft 6 in,
outside stem.
MAINSAIL Leech 32'-6"
Foot 19 ft.
Weather 25'-6"
AREA Mainsail 394 sq ft.
Foresail 100
Jib 180
TOTAL 674

LO 190

LO 190

MAYFLOWER LO 190 Winter topmast   EJM

Sail plan of *Mayflower*

In common with the Yarmouth shrimpers, these bawleys at Gravesend used the trim-tram gear, an adaption of the Leigh shrimping net but having a flat triangular frame fixed in front of the beam with an iron shoe—the 'sluke'—resting on the ground, thus preventing the mouth of the net from falling forward. This net was peculiar to the Thames and neighbourhood, being practically the ordinary beam trawl with a second beam below instead of the usual ground rope. The oak lower beam, about 24 ft long, was some 4 in wide, flat above and below, and weighted with a heavy iron band on the lower surface. A stanchion about 3 ft long was fixed upright in a chock on the centre of the beam and supported the 'bail stick', about 4 ft 6 in long, parallel to the lower beam. The net was fastened to both,

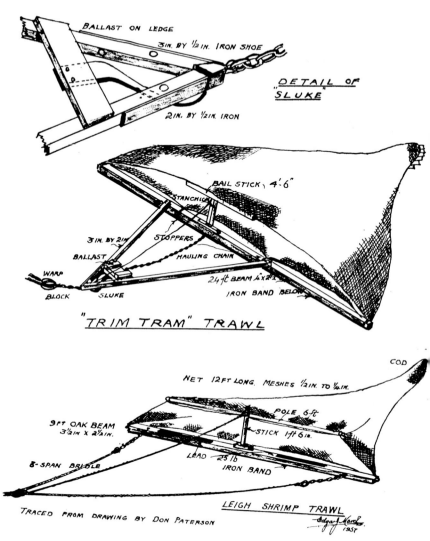

BALLAST ON LEDGE

3IN. BY 1/2IN. IRON SHOE

2IN. BY 1/2IN. IRON

DETAIL OF "SLUKE"

BAIL STICK, 4'-6"

STANCHION

STOPPERS

3IN. BY 2IN.

BALLAST

HAULING CHAIN

WARP

BLOCK   SLUKE

24 ft BEAM 4×2½

IRON BAND BELOW

"TRIM TRAM" TRAWL

COD

NET 12FT LONG. MESHES 1/2IN. TO 1/4IN.

9FT OAK BEAM
3½IN × 2½IN.

POLE 6 ft

STICK 1ft 6IN.

8-SPAN BRIDLE

LEAD 25 lb
IRON BAND

LEIGH SHRIMP TRAWL

TRACED FROM DRAWING BY DON PATERSON

Edgar March
1957

Sketches of trim-tram and Leigh shrimp trawls

but only at the ends of the lower beam, to allow mud, stones and rubbish to escape; but shrimps, rising a few inches above the ground when disturbed, swam into the net, the meshes diminishing from $\frac{1}{2}$ in square at the mouth to $\frac{1}{4}$ in at the cod-end, 20 ft or so away.

At Leigh, the trawl had a three-span bridle made fast to the warp, two ends attached to the lower beam, one to the top of the stick. The trim-tram gear, with the warp fast to the iron shoe at the point of the triangular frame, was handy to use in busy, narrow waters, being quickly and easily hauled and shot again.

When hauling, as soon as the far end of the warp came up to the rail the hauling chain was cast off and hooked on to a tackle from the masthead; pulling on the chain now caused the whole frame to tip inwards and inboard to be lowered across the coamings with the heavy lower beam outboard of the rail. The net was not brought up over the beam as with a normal beam trawl, but the stick was removed from its chock and the belly part of the net pulled up and the shrimps shaken down and ladled out. For shooting again, the stick was refixed and the hauling chain made fast ready for hooking up on the next haul. The frame, still laid flat, was slid aft and squared over the stern. Hemp netting was used down to recent times, when it was replaced with cotton, dressed with cutch.

At Leigh, two to four nets were used by each boat and kept down for a quarter of an hour or longer, depending on the extent of the ground being worked, always towing with the tide. A man and a boy were sufficient crew as only one net was hauled at a time; the shrimps were immediately sifted and the small ones thrown overboard. Until well after the mid-nineteenth century the catch was kept alive in wells and boiled in coppers ashore. In 1865, a hundred gallons a day were not unknown, and over 144,000 gallons were sent to Billingsgate by Baxter & Son.

I was able to glean most valuable information from notes and a report which the late Dr James Murie was instructed to prepare, c 1900, by the Committee of Sea Fisheries, of which he was a member. Despite repeated requests, he never completed the report, and after his death at the age of 93 in 1925 his cottage at Leigh was searched and masses of papers were found. Fire had destroyed many. Bundles of galley proofs and sheets of manuscript, almost unreadable, were found under piles of coal and wood. Fortunately, Mr F. J. Lambert rescued this almost pulped mass. It was dried at Southend library and the librarian, Mr W. Pollitt, did his best to transcribe the papers, but many gaps had to be left. In July 1952, thanks to the courtesy of Mr Helliwell, I made notes of salient features and quote extensively from them.

Dr Murie is described by a colleague as 'a man of wide knowledge and great ability, but very difficult to get on with. Industrious and dilatory, broad-minded and opiniated, and disposed to present the side of his character most opposed to the views of those under whom he had to work . . . that he was correct there can be little doubt, that he was offensive, whether deliberately so or not, no doubt whatever.'

The fisheries at Leigh are of great antiquity and the rights frequently reverted to the Crown. In 1280, his ministers rendered accounts to Edward I, and earls and dukes to the queen of Edward IV in 1460. The wives of Henry VIII held the fishery as 'pin money', but in 1551 Edward VI gave it to Lord Rich. A century later the Earl of Warwick leased the rights to Anne Brand and others, and so it went on down the centuries until finally they came into the keeping of the Salvation Army—'from Royalty to the Submerged Tenth has been the fate of the old Leigh Fishery'.

Throughout, the Leigh fishermen waged a continual fight, insisting on their rights of free fishery. In one instance Baron Pollock wisely remarked on a case before him—'he feared that the fishery had gone to feed lawyers'.

It would seem this was not so at the time of the Norman Conquest, as in Domesday Book 1086 there is a mention of five 'bordarii' or 'cottar' fishermen families, with no land for cultivation, but poor, free fishermen. In 1891, one-third of the population of 2,108 were fishermen and their families.

In the 1840s, the inner creek harbour and embayment out to Leigh Road had plenty of water as far as Clamshell gut. The boats were chiefly pink-sterned, very few with square sterns, and the largest was about 4 tons. 'Pink' is an old name for a sharp stern. The boats lay well together, moored fore and aft, close alongside the quays, using legs to keep them upright when the tide was out . . . 'no small boats with them to land when tide was up, each craft paid a weekly sum to Sam Johnson who kept a small flat punt for taking crews aboard and ashore. Trading schooners and Alston's deep-sea oyster-dredging fleet of smacks anchored at Clamshell gut, where the depth allowed them to swing freely with the tide. None of the small fishing craft anchored outside in the Bay as is now the case.'

Until about 1820 the main catch was sent to Billingsgate by boat, or occasionally by cart:

> thereafter James Cook commenced to run vans nightly to London. Large, four-wheeled open vehicles carried shrimp 'pads', oblong-lidded baskets, bags of oysters and other fish. Each pad held eight to ten gallons of shrimps, packed one above the other, the lot covered with a tarpaulin, the driver on a high seat in front . . . started from Billet Wharf between 6 and 7 pm, even up to 9 pm, driven four-horsed up the steep hill out of the village; then two or three horses took on the load, according to its weight or the condition of the roads. Went by Wickford and Shenfield where the horses were changed, arriving at Billingsgate between 4 and 5 am. Cook fell from his van and broke his neck. W. R. Hay bought the vans which were licensed to carry passengers. Rival firm was commenced by Messrs A. Surridge and Sam Hong; the latter soon left and Hay and Surridge became partners, Hay running to Shenfield, Surridge from there to London.
>
> When the railway opened, c 1855, Hay split partnership, carrying fish from City Goods Station to Billingsgate. Surridge tried to compete with the railway but was compelled to give up, but van rates have never been reduced.

The shrimps were consigned to fish salesmen. At Leigh an agent or 'sender' received all goods and on Saturday evenings

o

paid over all monies received from the London salesmen, 'much found its way into the pubs'.

One activity was 'banding'—a modification for 'trotting'—for flat fish, especially flounders, and practised from very early times. The hooks were made from twigs of black or white thorn, cut from the hedges, each consisting of the sharp thorn and a small piece of branch—the shank—whittled down until it equalled the thorn in length, besides being carried beyond the junction of the branch and thorn by a 'knob'. The thorn and shank formed a wide angle, making a fair hook, which was bent on to a short snood of horsehair or twine; if the latter, the twine had a knot in the end and a double half-hitch secured it to the hook. 'The aim is by a knack in the turn that the angle be so gripped that the snood does not slip over the shank-knob, or the tackle will draw off altogether.' My informant laid stress on this point.

The old men made and sold these hooks at a penny a hundred, far cheaper than steel and, being lighter, they floated the bait a little off the mud. Snoods were about 6 in long, spaced just sufficiently not to entangle with each other and rove on a line some 17 fathoms long, carrying roundly a hundred snoods. The hooks were baited with pieces of lugworm, slipped first on the shank, then drawn right over the sharp tip, then again backwards towards the shank extremity and so held tight.

Fishing went on during the winter and spring when other fish was scarce. Three or four boats would go as far down as Foulness sands, a favourite ground being near Blacktail Swin, below the measured mile. Each line was laid on the sands at low water, pegged down with a peg at each end and one in the middle; other lines were attached to form a length of about a mile, say 5,000 to 6,000 hooks. The lines were carried in 'flaskets', the local name for a flat basket in which the 'bands' were laid to run out freely; each held about 15 to 20 bands.

When the lines were hauled, the fish were stripped off the line, hook and all, and fresh hooks tied on the snood for each fishing. In those days it was not uncommon to find a flounder on every hook; 'as soon as caught the flounder should be cleaned and backbone cut through just behind the head, otherwise so tenacious of life that hours after will jump out of the frying pan into the fire . . . can make rapid darts along the bottom and so are difficult to catch in a trawl'. The old name was 'fluke' or 'flowk' from the similiarity in shape to the fluke of an old-fashioned anchor.

The best fishing was when the weather was cold enough to stop the tidal wanderings of crabs which robbed the hooks the moment they were on the bottom. The procuring and putting on of bait was arduous, a sloppy, dirty job done indoors by the women who earned ½d per band of 100 hooks, 'many so dexterous and nimble-fingered as to make the task worthwhile. Finally the dearth of good baiters was the primary cause of the decline and ultimate extinction of banding at Leigh.' Flounders were seldom sent to the London market, but found a ready sale locally.

Lobster catching was governed by byelaws issued at a Court of Free Fishermen of the River Thames held on 29 July 1697—'no one to catch or expose to sale any lobsters of any less size than ten inches "whole ware" and nine inches "half ware" to be reckoned from snout, to the middle feison of the tail. Penalty 20s'. 'Whole ware' were egg bearers, 'half ware' were those without berry. The local supplies had to compete with lobsters from Scotland and Norway, brought by water, and many byelaws prohibited 'imports of live fish until reported at Nore or Gravesend'. Lobsters were stored in floating boxes, square trunks called 'corves' or 'hurleys', laid in long strings of 50 in a line at Queenborough and Old Haven. Henry Barber of Billingsgate had a large salt-water pond at Herne Bay, keeping up to 2,000 lobsters, 'now a swimming bath'.

Plaice were caught in trawls, by Peter net, banding, spruling and rod and line. Dabs frequented deep-water channels during the sprat season, being caught in stowboat nets at all depths, 'best in winter, a great reduction in summer, increasing again as cold weather set in'. Catches were mostly sold to hawkers.

Soles were abundant from Hole Haven to the East Girdler, chiefly from the beginning of June to the end of September, averaging 6 to 12 in in length, 'many up to 15 in and more, one pair 16 and 19¼ in long, 9 in broad, weighing 2 lb 9 oz, small soles—slips—are only used by fishermen families'.

Halibut were sometimes caught. In 1856 R. Johnson had one 3 ft long, caught on a line hook-baited with plaice, laid the night before, and sold for 15s at Billingsgate. In 1870 another weighing ¾ cwt fetched only 5s.

In the mid-nineteenth century turbot were plentiful in the Swin and along the Maplin sands, running up to 2 ft in length— 'magnificent ones at back of the Falls near Margate, but Leigh men seldom go there'. Smaller ones, common around Foulness, were stored in fish pits adjoining the seawall; string was tied round the tail root with a cork at the free end. In the autumn of 1870 one 2½ ft long was brought up when the bawley *Busy Bee* was dredging for five-fingers off Grain Spit; ten days later another big one was caught in her shrimp net and fetched 10s at Billingsgate. As late as 1900, a 13-lb turbot was caught in a stow net near the Knock Buoy. Brill were also taken at times, and '50 years ago a regular cod and skate fishery with long lines, commencing in November, ending in March, regular grounds for both fish between Oaze Channel and Naze, some to Orfordness, both inshore and seaward towards Long Sand and Kentish Knock, market cod 15 to 20 in and over . . . codling seldom brought ashore as not saleable'.

Whiting also abounded . . . 'in old times seldom sold, as part of fishermen's diet . . . at end of October 1867 immense numbers in the Thames, nearly 2,000 bushels caught and used for manure'.

Sprats were noted for their number and quality, 'immense shoals of adult sprats annual, but somewhat capricious winter visitants . . . juveniles at least nine to ten months in the estuary . . . S.E Kent sprats are big and plump, caught in large-meshed drift nets, not stow net as in Essex. Barely two seasons following resemble each other, plenty or the reverse, some years a glut . . .

one boat in 1877 caught £50 worth in a week, west of Tongue
Light. . . . Drawback in better-class households is strong, pun-
gent and penetrating oily odour given off in cooking, freely used
as manure.' Eighty tons a morning were sent to Billingsgate at
times.

Whitebait were then popular among gourmets, special
dinners being held at famous riverside hotels frequented by
Cabinet Ministers and lesser lights, but old Phineas Webb said,
'the poor would not give it belly room'. John Welch of Billingsgate had twelve boats at Southend, six at Gravesend and five at
Greenwich, paying out £60 to £70 a week in wages—from
£1,500 to £1,800 a year. At Queenborough, wages were up to
£40 a week: the season lasted from February to August, and up
to ½ ton was sold daily at from 1s to 2s a quart wholesale, about
204 fish making one shillingsworth.

James Cannon said that his grandfather was the first man in
1780 to bring in the fish to which he gave the name 'whitebait',
selling them to hotel and tavern keepers in Blackwall and
Greenwich. He had much trouble with the Thames Conservancy who alleged it was the fry of herring, shad and the like,
but the son, Richard, proved before the Lord Mayor that whitebait was a species of fish and not fry. 'In 1798 my father succeeded in the business, supplying HRH the Prince Regent at
Carlton House, and from 1820 to 1830 King George IV . . .
supplied royal tables every day during the season, the King of
the Belgians and most of the nobility. I have supplied Bruns-
wick Hotel, Blackwall for 35 years.'

Roker, a species of ray, frequented channels on the Kentish
Flats, Spaniards and in the Wallet when sprats were about. In
1870 on 28 lines 190 great rokers were hooked, and several lines
lost through the weight of fish on them. 'Fetched no money,
seldom sent to London, go to Sheerness and Chatham, some
crimped and sold locally, wings fried with eggs and bread-
crumbs make sweet eating.'

Mussels teemed in the brackish estuaries, clinging to iron
vessels, lightships and any suitable place. They hung in clusters

on harbour piles and old wrecks were literally covered with them. Enormous beds on the Flats yielded vast quantities for manure, and so abundant were they that efforts were made to send mussels for bait to Scotland, but rail expenses were prohibitive. Buying price was about 1s a bag or tub, 'men were employed to "set them out", then 6d a bag to pick them up, the bag cost 3d, carriage to London by sailing boat was 6d. Hence each bag cost the vendor 2s 3d, for which his return from the buyer, who paid steamer carriage north, was only 2s a bag. The reason for carrying on was it was more economical to lose 3d a bag and thus get rid of overstock, than otherwise to clear and clean the beds.' Hundreds of tons were dredged up by Faversham and Rochester boats for manure for Kentish farmers. Brightlingsea supplied Essex needs.

Cockles were prolific on all the sands in the vicinity of Leigh, the largest coming from Pollard inside the Columbine, Whitstable Bay, eight and nine years old. They found a ready sale to the stalls selling winkles and other sea delicacies to the day trippers who came swarming to Southend following the opening of rail communication with London. The enormous heaps of empty shells used to be one of the sights of Leigh and were sold by the barge load, crushed up to provide grit for poultry, and for use in garden walks.

The tastiest cockles came from the Maplin Sands, but collection was difficult as the beds lay within the Shoeburyness artillery range and cockles could be gathered only on rare occasions. It was necessary to go to the barracks to obtain the firing list for the week; a few foolhardy men took the risk, but a big shell landing in their vicinity shook them in more ways than one. The usual procedure when cockling was for the boat to stay out two low tides, gathering when the sands were bare, the beamy boats sitting almost upright while the cockles were flung into the well; many were bawley-rigged with no topmasts. In the winter, a start was made about daybreak and on arrival over a likely spot a lad with an oar searched the bottom as a rough test for numbers. The anchor was then let go, sails lowered and the men had a meal while waiting for the tide to fall, being warned by the bumping when the boat listed. Then a box or two was placed by the side of the boat and each of the crew took a basket and a couple of rakes. The iron one was to dig into the mud and sand to bring out the cockles just below the surface, piling them in a heap. Then the 'picker-up' was used to scoop the cockles into a net, the mouth of which was kept open by a stirrup-shaped iron; the bag was swished about in any convenient pool and then the contents were emptied into baskets, taken to the bawley and shot into the well or hold. At times the cockles lay so thick that they could be shovelled direct into the hold. Eighty baskets weighed about a ton, and it was essential to spread the cockles evenly. When loaded it was often a long wait until there was water enough to get the boat up the creek to Leigh. The channel was narrow and winding, and awkward to navigate on a dark night when the crude tree beacons were difficult to sight. Certainly it was a case of following the leader. If he went aground, it was full round and hope for the best; if beating up and a bawley touched the mud to leeward she would blow farther and farther in and be forced to wait for the tide to rise, but if on the windward side of channel might be possible to work clear.

Both the sands and the channels between them were constantly altering; mud and other material was brought down by the rivers emptying into the estuary, while wind and tide played their part in silting up once deep waters.

Shrimpers are forced to go farther out to sea because of the great increase of impurities and the disturbance of passing steamers. . . . The most serious drawback is the steady decrease in depth of water in an already shallow creek. Originally the 'Slade' near Southend Pier was the only entrance to Swatchway and the Ray . . . a gradual tendency to shallowing of the Swatch, Leigh Creek and the Ray, believed to be caused by mussel culture in Hadleigh Ray. During 1883–84 a narrow deep channel with bar entrance opened up rather suddenly across Marshend sand—the 'Low-way' about 100 yards below a previous gut, now the only entrance to Leigh and Benfleet, for during low tide the Swatch is nearly dry, yet 20 years ago smacks used to beat up regularly at three-quarters ebb, now cannot sail except at high water. . . . Chart corrected to 1879 says the Benfleet and Leigh Creeks discharged through a single channel with a bar of 11 ft at low water . . . in 1883 bar only 5 ft deep, Canvey Spit having been partly washed away in 1881 . . . in 1895 a reversion to the state of a century ago is manifest, Leigh Swatch and the Ray have again separate entrances. . . . Southend pier was erected in 1832 and some fishermen hold it was one cause of the change of the Swatch.

These conditions ruled the coming and going of bawleys; often a start had to be made well after midnight, or long after daylight, and the return was governed by the depth of water as the flood tide made. (Pictures, p 184.)

Each ground had its speciality and according to the season, state of weather, tide, or kind of fish sought, the men made their choice, long experience telling them that, given certain conditions, one ground was likely to be more successful than another. 'On other occasions, with fair weather, say near the Oaze or Girdler, two boats, may be fishing in proximity say a cable's length apart. One's catch will be chiefly big-sized, the other's small-sized shrimps.'

From very early times the Peter-boat was used by fishermen working in rivers and estuaries; double-ended, beamy, and without a keel, it had no gunwale or sheer, and the top strake ran perfectly horizontal. Amidships a well for live fish divided the boat into two compartments, the forepart for the rower, the after part for nets and the fisherman. The well was about 2 ft wide at the base, tapering to 1 ft at the top, and extended the full width of the boat. Its depth was just level with the thwarts and, when covered over, it formed an additional seat. The bottom of the well was pierced with a number of holes, permitting easy flow of water, and fish could be kept for days or even weeks providing the boat was always afloat in sufficient depth of water. At the stern was a raised platform on which the fisherman stood when shooting the net, and this enabled him to lift the cork line high enough to allow the net to run out freely.

A Peter-net was 20 to 25 fathoms long, corked above, leads

PETER BOATS c 1830. (After E.N. cooke) NOTE Koff in foreground and between boats Net drying over lowered sprit; rudder lying on after deck; well amidships

Sketch of Peter-boats, c 1830

below, 4-in mesh, and made of two-laid twine. These boats fished opposite Leigh eastward to Shoebury sands for plaice, dabs and flounders. 'Flat fish were so abundant on the Essex side that the men seldom, or never, fished on the Kentish side; this was used by London men, ie, Deptford, Greenwich and Erith. . . . Old regulations prohibit "fleeting for flounder with net in the night-time from sun going down to daylight the next morning between Michaelmas and Christmas because they make destruction of small flounders and carry them both un-seen and unknown".'

The Peter-boats carried a man and a lad and enough provisions for a week or so, being away:

short or long according to the catch . . . had wells or a 'koff' as additional receptacles for live fish as soon as captured. On return to Leigh the fish were transferred by dipnets from well to pits.

When it was deemed that enough fish had been got together in store pits to make a full cargo, the fish were drawn out by bagnet. The stiffly laden boat was soon away to Billingsgate, generally once a fortnight. By degrees the Peter-boats were enlarged until they became small smacks. In the old days, owners often lived and slept on board for six months in the year. About 1902 the last Peter-boat was eel fishing.

An ancient dug-out or log canoe found in Benfleet Creek may have been the aboriginal fishing boat, then clinker-built open boat, the pink-stern of Leighmen in form and build had its origin in Viking boats, Danish and Saxon settlements bordering Leigh Creek. Then followed square-stern bawleys. *Alert*, built at Leigh in 1832, was pink-stern and went shrimping. Later she was enlarged and given rounded bows to give more cabin room, then altered again to square stern, another owner rebuilt amidships and fresh lined or skinned and finally was likened to more recent bawleys, afloat in 1898 . . . was a lucky boat, so bit by bit was altered. Geo. Kirby says his father similarly converted *Lady Sparrow* over 50 years ago, others did likewise. The pink-sterns were originally open boats, small locker for'ard, stem and stern narrowed and sharp, hull shallow, drew little water. Later were 18 to 22 ft long, 2 to 4 tons capacity. Clinker-built, bow a trifle fuller and rounder than stern, later straighter with moderate rake, rudder hung outside, little sheer.

Then became half-, then whole-decked and latterly welled. From a diminutive cuddy forward it became a low-roofed very small cabin, if absent the 'Tilton-bails'—tarred canvas tents— used for temporary covering. Short bowsprits, at first no topmast, soon all had them. Some had spritsail, others gaff and trysail, also jib and stay foresail of very moderate size, a very small topsail with yard, a fore and main horse, no windlass, hand over hand raised anchor or net. As the boats increased in size the cabin was enlarged and gradually came the change to square-stern bawleys.

The man who sailed in her said the first Leigh square-stern smack was *King William IV*, belonging to James Plumb, who also owned *Good Intent*, a coasting sloop which brought oysters from Jersey. Date therefore *c* 1830. Four tons, so little bigger than some of the pink-sterns, in rig, but not spritsail, it agreed with them, so that the nearly vertical square stern and fuller bow were the distinguishing characteristic, both kinds were welled. Between 1831–40 only about half-a-dozen square sterns in the Leigh fleet, but numbers increased year by year and pink-sterns declined, but in the hands of poorer men hung on until the 'eighties. The last lay on the 'mush'—marsh—for some time in a disabled condition, finally broken up 1894.

Every new square-stern added to in length, depth and breadth, the mast became more massive, topmast and bowsprit lengthened, the spritsail became antiquated. Jib, foresail, mainsail and topsail augmented in area, the lofty sail and spinnaker an advantage in running to and from the fishing grounds. Greater capacity and speed, stimulus was necessary to catch rail and get the early market.

The bow has not much changed, though stern is more raking, still very little counter. One or two had a mizzen mast. Boomed mainsails not tolerated on account of interfering with trawling. The windlass has grown with the size of the boat, the earlier occupied less than half the bow, now right across and in some capable of heaving in two tons and more. Scuppers not used, an inch wide opening flush with deck along both sides.

Around 1858, a wink was placed aft of the well and a snatchblock on the midships gunwale for hoisting the trawl were introduced, previously all hauling 'knuckle-em-up'. Later the wells were abolished, the hold enlarged with moveable hatching.

The bawleys often went fish-buying round the Forelands in the early days, then built of oak to stand the knocking about, lasted longer than recent boats, many built of fir for cheapness and lightness. The Brightlingsea pattern and build, though more expensive, had a good reputation for speed and easy handling.

Size ranged from 24 to 30 ft, a few up to 38 ft. Tonnage, early 4, 5, 6 tons, increased gradually to 8, 9, 10 and 12, a few 15 and over, but these found to involve more labour, expensive in gear and repair. The tendency was to return to medium size, as handier to work, and easier kept in working order.

A medium-size bawley, Brightlingsea-built in 1889, was *Happy Home*, 10½ tons. Registered 30 LO. Owner, Robt Johnson. Crew 2. Beam trawl, shrimps and flat fish in estuary.

HULL	*ft*	*in*
LOA outside from stem to stern	34	10
Breadth about amidships	12	9
Depth, inside to top of kelson	5	2
Cabin, inside stem to bulkhead	14	–
Well on top of hatch or funnel, length	4	6
do. breadth of said hatch top	3	–

	ft	*in*
do. full inside dimensions fore and aft	4	6
do. port to starboard width	12	–
Hold length, inc. well	17	–
After sheets, fore and aft length	3	–
MAST and topmast, total deck to truck	50	–
Mast, length total to top of masthead	34	6
do. do. deck do. do.	28	–
Dia. made of pitch pine		8½
Topmast, heel to truck	26	6
Gaff, horns to guy end	24	–
Gaff dia. tapering from 6 in to 4½ in		
Bowsprit, full length, 4½ ft housed and		
17½ ft free	22	

SAILS

Mainsail, Mast rope 18 ft, head 23 ft, leech 35 ft, foot 19 ft, diagonal 26 ft. Spread of 105 yd, cut out dimensions. Material, Haywards No 1 double-thread coker canvas, 2 ft width.

Topsail, Stay 27 ft, leech 27 ft, foot 21 ft, 38 yd Haywards No 3 canvas, 2 ft width.

Storm Jib, Stay 19 ft, leech 16 ft, foot 10 ft, 17 yd ditto

3rd Jib, Stay 24 ft, leech 18 ft, foot 12 ft, 24 yd ditto

2nd Jib, Stay 33 ft, leech 26 ft, foot 16 ft, 35 yd Haywards Navy duck, 27 in width.

Stay Foresail, Stay 18 ft, leech 16 ft, foot 9 ft, 19 yd Haywards No 3 canvas, 2 ft width.

Balloon Foresail, Stay 18 ft, leech 22 ft, foot 16 ft, 30 yd Haywards Navy duck, 27 in width.

Spinnaker, Stay 40 ft, leech 36 ft, foot 24 ft, 60 yd calico, 34 in width.

Sprintle Jib, (local name) viz. fore topmast stay or flying jib, Stay 28 ft, leech 23 ft, foot 15 ft, 28 yd calico, 34 in wide.

The little pink-sterns had small wells, nearly amidships, separated athwart from cabin by a bulkhead and from afterhold by another. Bottom and sides pierced with holes. The top of the lower part of the well on port and starboard sides had a solid casing or well deck, 2 to 3 ft, beneath the main deck, the remaining mid-portion rises and narrows, opens by a square hatchway on deck in front of winch. The space between well deck and upper deck communicates with the after hold and is used for storage.

In 1898 only six or eight Leigh smacks have wells, but seldom used except in the hottest weather. Will be removed when opportunity offers as catch is now sent so quickly to market that wells are no longer needed, also tending to leakage.

Skiffs were the bawleys' small boats. Pink-sterns had no small boat and at certain states of the tide could not land catches. An old fisherman kept a small punt and acted as ferryman to the fleet as the boats then moored right up the creek abreast of the village . . . no boats for early square-sterns as they were deficient in sailing power, little steam traffic until after the 'fifties, no heavy trawl to work. The boats were shallow draught, easily handled and beached. As they became bigger, so began the practice of towing a small boat, now a necessity as the increase in size, shallowing of creek and guts means the bawleys have to anchor out in the Ray: going to Harwich and the vast increase in steam and river traffic makes for danger at times.

Skiffs are 13 to 15 ft long, beam 4½ to 5 ft, built at Leigh and elsewhere. Pin Mill the best though dearest . . . elm, heavy to row, very strong to stand heavy wear. All carry a lugsail, two oars with thole pins, rudder and tiller. With a 12 ft mast, the lugsail has 15 yd of calico, 34 in wide, tacked to stem, a few have the newer balance lug.

Leigh once had fish and shrimp 'koffs' similar to cod chests, but shape and use different. Only one now (1898) remains in the yard of George Kirby, but not used for many years . . . resembles a coffin and some think the name is an abbreviation, but it probably comes from the Dutch and German 'koffer', a chest or trunk. Made of deal boards ½ in thick, about 9 ft long, 2½ ft broad, 10 in deep. The prow is wedge-shaped, stern square, the sides and bottom pierced with holes 1 in diameter. The top has a square opening and lid is fastened by a staple and wooden plug, the bow has a ringbolt, a rope spliced in and the koff dragged astern of the boat . . . extra to well in pinks and in calms, when insufficient aeration of wells, the fish were transferred to the koffs. Shrimp koffs were similar, but 6 ft long, 1 ft deep and smaller holes.

The trawl winch by which the beam trawl is hauled in has the supporting upright post housed and socketed in the hold immediately abaft the well, 3½ ft above the deck. Near the top it is pierced fore and aft by an iron bolt 2 ft and over in length, behind, upright, is a small cog and pawl. In front two cog wheels work the barrel or drum. This short barrel is solid wood, 18 in in diameter and slopes so that the warp releases itself as it winds round. When wanted, a handle is fixed on the fore end of the iron bolt and this turns athwart the deck.

B. Baxter says this form of winch was taken from the Jersey pattern and first adopted by oyster dredgers who went there from Leigh. Previously bawleys had a bigger and longer barrelled unwieldy affair, the barrel perfectly cylindrical and at every few turns the warp had to be released by hand. The bolt passed right through the drum and two men were needed, each at a handle on opposite sides of drum.

The snatchblock is an oblong piece of wood, and the wheel carrying the warp works in a deep notch cut in the long diameter of the wood. Iron straps on each side of the block terminate below in a long, round bolt fitting into a hole in the gunwale abaft the shrouds. The bolt is inserted when wanted and unshipped when the trawl is got aboard.

The sounding lead is of ordinary shape, 7 to 8 lb in weight, on 12 to 15 fathoms of thin rope. When nearing certain beds it is continually heaved, for shades of depth mean good fishing ground or otherwise. The lead is seldom required in navigation unless in dense fog to ascertain whither drifting.

The cabin stove in pinkies was a small, moveable affair with a copper top, and when wanted was rigged in the cabin or other covering; when the cooking was done it was unshipped and removed outside. No room for a fixed stove, but as boats increased in size the ordinary cast-iron smack stoves were used. Nearly all have short chimneys so, with equally short funnels of boiler, under certain conditions of wind, smoke and soot abound.

A ship's carpenter's 'fire pan' was used to burn off old tar on a smack's sides, prior to new dressing. May also serve to get up a copper fire for boiling cutch in tanning small gear, oyster net bags etc. A semi-circular fire-box, 18 in by 11 to 8 in deep, front and bottom are grated, the curved sides of the sheet iron drilled with holes. Hinged to the fire-box is a strong shaft iron, 2 ft long, which widens into a conical socket to receive the 8-ft spar handle by which it is carried about. As the box swings it balances itself horizontally at whatever angle the handle is held. From the base of fire-box to socket is an iron guy rod furnished with hook and eye, which, when wanted, steadies fire-box as it is shifted about.

The whitebait board is a smooth surfaced board of deal, 4½ ft long by 3 ft broad, used for 'cleaning the bait' ie, knocking off nut-galls.

Smaller gear included buckets, formerly wooden staved with rope handles, now galvanised buckets, coal and salt boxes, iron bowl for skimming the brine as it boils and froths in the copper, furnace raker and a small iron-handled shovel.

BOAT BUILDERS

The most noted among the older men were Thos. Bundock & Sons; John and his father, famed for building welled smacks, followed Jas. Wiseman who shifted to Southend, T. Robinson, M. Heywood and Holden from Harwich and Burnham. Then came the four sons of John Bundock who, as a firm of five hands, carry on today (1898). The elder brother, Thomas, secured a medal at the Fisheries Exhibition for models of shrimper and stowboat.

The earliest sailmaker was Reynolds, then came D. Tomlin sen. J. Brown, P. Webster, H. Robinson and others. Churchyard sen. had sailmakers and his son built a commodious sail-loft. Now two lofts and five or six men constantly employed. Some fishermen make and mend for themselves. . . . Barnard and Partridge succeeded H. Churchyard and have one man from Yarmouth and others do the bulk of the fishing work; Angier from Brightlingsea and staff more for yachting.

Two forges, and five workmen employed, Geo. Bradley, foreman has a high local repute for trawl heads, anchors and boat work generally. Sixty years ago, before beam trawling, one blacksmith sufficed, his son still carries on.

Up to 1858 I. Balls made all sorts of baskets, also at Hadleigh J. Ridgewell supplied pads etc. Several firms of ship chandlers. After shrimping became a business factor salt was obtained in small quantities from London and brought down in smacks or barges and sold by general dealers. When the railway came Tomlin & Sons brought truckloads at a time, obtained direct from Bromsgrove or Droitwich, called 'broad salt' in Worcester but fishermen know it as 'rock salt' or coarse, but it is not in great masses as is the true rock salt of Cheshire. Coal for the coppers was taken out in sacks, consumption being one to two cwts weekly.

The coppers in which shrimps were boiled had three stages of development. First—the boilers when the shrimps were cooked ashore, ordinary cast-iron coppers, bricked up roughly and holding eight gallons, eight being situated in various parts of the village.

Second—George Emery had a boiler set up on board his square-sterned bawley *Surprise*. He remembers the circumstance perfectly well as he had an altercation with Kemp, the bricklayer, about the price. Also a claim by Fairchild to be the first. The copper was heavy cast iron, roughly bricked all round and 'took all the room of the boat'. Several followed suit, but the apparatus was too clumsy and heavy and bricked copper did not last above 12 to 15 months. Pinks were too small to receive them.

Third—George Churchyard set up as a ship chandler and first sold encased boilers akin to present pattern as little alteration since. The change, wrought instead of cast iron and latterly galvanised iron coppers. Size of first ones, about 1 ft deep, mouth 18 in dia, the separate iron casing somewhat reversed the boiler's shape, being now widest at the base, narrowing upwards so as to closely grip the boiler immediately underneath the flange . . . fixed in the middle of the hold, most are slightly towards the starboard side.

Old boilers were used for boiling bark or cutch, holding about eight gallons, but Baxter had a 12-gallon boiler and another man a 20-gallon one.

The sieves or riddles were instituted about 1830, the gauge should pass three pennies through for big shrimps, and a penny-farthing for small. A full-sized sieve will pass three pennies and a sixpence, about $\frac{1}{4}$ inch. Winter sieve must be a penny and farthing gauge, according to Abel Abraham Robinson, but the Fishery Officer states, 'In June mesh would be three pennies, in winter three halfpence . . . 3 pennies = 3/16 in, 3 and a sixpence = $\frac{1}{4}$ in, one penny and a farthing = $\frac{1}{8}$ in, three halfpence slightly over $\frac{1}{8}$ in.'

At Leigh there was no reduction of size of mesh from 1830 to 1898. Those sold now are 18 in dia, $3\frac{1}{2}$ in deep, 6 stout cross wires, and right angles are 63 to 71 thinner, more flexible wires, giving oblong spaces of $2\frac{1}{2}$ in length and $\frac{1}{4}$ to 3/16 in width.

From 1830 to 1856 shrimps were sent nightly to London by van in baskets called pads, oblong, flat topped, $2\frac{1}{2}$ ft long, 2 ft broad and $1\frac{1}{2}$ ft deep, two handles on ends, lid tied down. These held 8 to 10 gallons of shrimps.

From 1860 to 1898 (1) Originally made at Harwich, contained 18 to 20 gallons of shrimps, but size was reduced and now 10 to 14 gallons as handier to lift and carry full from boat to railway

station. Majority made at Harwich, a number at Hadleigh.
Shape differs, not flat and quadrangular, more oval hamper of
greater circumference above than below. No 1 was 2 ft 3 in high
and 27 × 18 in dia at mouth; No 2 18 in high. 22 × 17 in dia.

The flaskets used in Banding, and into which the baited lines
were coiled and taken on board, were open, long, oval, flat
baskets 9 in to 1 ft deep, 2 ft dia with handle each side, base less
than summit.

The whitebait boxes, used daily by morning train, were oblong,
shallow boxes, ½ in top, ¾ in sides of deal. Part of the top forms the
lid, not hinged, but slides into place by two fillets, no fastening.
Originally rail charge was by weight, afterwards so much per box.
One 2½ ft long and 17½ in broad, inside depth 3¾ in, outside
5 in, holds 16 to 18 quarts = 4 to 4½ gallons, quite full might
hold 20 quarts.

The second type 21½ × 18 in dia, inside 4½ in, outside 6 in, 20
quarts or 5 gallons, but 24 might be got in. Rail charge 10d for
small, 1s for larger box.

TANNING

The sails of the small pink-sterned bawleys were first dressed
with a watery mixture of red or yellow ochre, then while still wet
dogfish oil was brushed over with a mop. Then thoroughly dried
before being sent on board.

With the coming of the larger bawleys, the men used cutch for
dressing foresails and jibs, but with trysail nothing was done to
prevent it from mildew. Nowadays dogfish oil and ochre entirely
done away with and sails are dressed with cutch and grease, two
to one. Most of the smacks tan the jib, foresail, spinnaker and
balloon foresail, but not the trysail. Lugsails of the small boats
also tanned.

NET MAKING

In pre-railway days the village was not readily accessible, and
although so near London the people not so well off. Most families
made nets of one sort or other, the women grouped in friendly
gossip out or indoors while working, many very expert netters.
No net trade carried out of the village, except occasional sets of
hurdle nets for sheep folds, a cartload at a time to Foulness, main
work was for husband or parent's use. About 100 so engaged.

P

Then the girls took to domestic service and netting dwindled and so had to be procured, Bridport chiefly, but the men aver that nets factory made and sold by retailers are not nearly so lasting or of such good shape for trawl and many bought had to be altered, or a piece taken out of uppers and grounds and cod-end shortened. Now only eight to ten make nets.

Jerseys, stockings, mufflers and caps are home knitted and some sold away, but now little done, mostly bought readymade.

Formerly the stownets only were tanned with oakbark from trees in the neighbourhood, bark was beat up and then soaked for a week or more and afterwards boiled in coppers. The stownets were put into large tubs and boiling bark liquor poured on, covered over and left for four days to a week, then taken out, hoisted on board and there dried. Now nearly all nets are cutched. The cutch when broken up is added to boiling water in the copper, the amount varying according to strength required. The nets are dipped and then dried before use. Some men use a little tar with the cutch which hardens the net and dries it quicker.

FISH OILS

Dogfish oil was obtained from tope, the 'rig' of Folkestone men, which frequented Barrow and Black Deeps to near the Sunk, and ran up to 6 or 7 ft long. When longline fishing was in vogue the men took out the livers and on return home boiled them in a copper. The floating oil was skimmed off and put into one-gallon stone bottles, kept for a time to settle and clarify, becoming a clear, rich amber colour. Not for sale, but own use, dressing sails, it also softened thick leather sea boots.

Sting-ray oil, local name 'fire-slower oil', was valued highly for sprains, burns and bruises, also rubbed into sea boots. A fish of 2 ft, excluding tail, yielded about half a gallon of oil and more from its liver, a nut-brown colour.

STORE PITS

About 120 ft long, 30 ft broad, smaller ones 50 to 60 ft long, 25 to 30 ft wide, surrounded by high dykes or embankments, a few inter-connected. At high water the marsh was tongue-shaped, the creek on one side, a narrow deep gut on the other. Sea water entered at one end and passed through two or three pits, then into side canals to serve the middle ones. The puddled clay walls were 8 to 10 ft in height, the sea water about 5 to 6 ft deep, and so constructed that at high water the contents did not overflow the top of the walls . . . floor was mud, no food except what the fish could find burrowing, plaice and flounders sent to market every 10 to 14 days, but some flounders burrowed so deep as to escape dragnet and lived a long while. Byegone winters often severe, and when Thames icebound meant a harvest for Leigh men, the store pits were drained off, ice broken and fish dragged out in enormous numbers, big, plump flounders, high prices realised. Turbot sometimes had string to tail with cork at end to tell their whereabouts. Originally seven pits on the marsh, and two more on north side of creek . . . failed when tried to store shrimps as too little movement or aeration of water.

SHARES

There were several systems of sharing profits, or 'lay', none very complicated. One for shrimpers and fish trawlers, another for spratters or stow boaters, a third for whitebaiters, and a fourth for cockles.

SHRIMPERS. The captain was usually the owner, but whether he or an outsider, the vessel has one share, two of the crew share alike, irrespective of the more responsible position of master. No wages or extra to either skipper or mate, division of gross earnings all entitled to, so three equal shares whether profit or loss. Owner, whether master or outsider, is responsible for all tear, wear and other loss and supplies all fishing gear on like conditions. Fishing in the estuary and daily returning to Leigh, each man takes his own food from home. When pink shrimping from Harwich for the season, or out for days running into Sheerness or Chatham for sale of catch, the crew board together in common and pay share according.

SPRATTER AND STOW BOATING. In winter the usual crew was three, master, mate and third hand, equal shares, profit or loss, boat has share and half, whether master-owned or by outsider, so division into 4½ shares. In fitting out, additional expenses for gear, such as extra sails, nets or sundries, so owner gets a half share additional. The responsibility his, as with shrimpers. Men pay only for individual outfit, clothing, bedding, food, for latter a common fund. Captain is caterer and pays first costs which are refunded according to amount per share.

Spratters often combine in temporary companies, two, three, a dozen or twenty unite in a fleet and form partnership. Choice is made of the fastest sailing craft which act in rotation as carriers, passing from boat to boat, as soon as a full cargo, off to market, discharge and quickly return. The captains of boats who sell cargo receive moneys direct, at end of every week the returns are all put together and then and there divided equally, according to number of boats, irrespective of catch. Then each boat subdivided into 4½ shares.

WHITEBAITING. Several London firms engage at Leigh for the greater part of the year and arrange with a master and owner to hire his boat and crew at a stipulated sum per week, generally £4 10s to £4 15s. Firms pay expenses, dragnet, boxes and carriage to London, but fishermen provide crew, boat, stow net and minor apparatus and stand all wear and tear. The firm receives the daily catch, large or small, makes no difference to the men. Usually a crew of two. First a small sum is deducted for coal and oil, then divide into three shares, one for master, one for mate, one for boat, roughly 30s each. Using a dragnet a lad is necessary, paid a weekly wage 12s or 15s. This sum is first paid out of that received from the firm, what remains is then divided into three shares, so earnings are less when using a seine than stow net. Some firms allow a trifle for the lad, but not usual.

In May 1880, two Leigh whitebaiters dragging below Canvey Spit caught a 27½-lb salmon which was sold for 1s 9d a lb to the Rector. In June 1891, a 3-ft salmon weighing 33 lb was caught at the entrance to Hadleigh Bay and sold for 1s a lb to Mr Cadman who had it stuffed and now in the Board school.

SHRIMPING. Two kinds of shrimp were sought, the brown or true shrimp, brownish-grey when alive, and the pink, allied to the prawn, whitish-pink when living, boiling to a bright, reddish hue. The brown teemed in the estuary, the pink farther offshore, size varied according to the season and ground fished. The undersized brood, called 'dust' or 'smig', were supposed to escape through the meshes, the largest ran up to 3 in long, average market size 1½ to 2½ in. Fleets of smacks and bawleys worked all the year round, each catching from 30 to 50 gallons, 80 to 100 on red-letter days. Shrimps are very sensitive to temperature, and few are taken in frost. In 1868 catches were extremely poor until well into July and then only one to two gallons a day, the old men saying 'they were drove to bed somewhere'. A mixed bag of various sizes yielded about 1,250 to a half gallon, shrimps in a fresh state adjust themselves so that they take up less room in a measure than in cooked condition, after boiling half pint to one pint more to a gallon, accounted for by their bent condition. However, a number of smaller size now get through the sieve during the second riddling, an average would be 2,700 to 2,800 to a gallon.

In spring and summer the shoals dart about in shallow water, increasing in size, in late autumn as weather gets colder they go into deeper water. In an ordinary haul are shrimps of all ages, they are usually found near the bottom, but at times big catches were made in stow nets, taken from muddy grounds they are pale in colour and cook still paler, but on sand are more highly coloured.

The pink shrimp is variously known as red, soldier, rock, sea, Aesop's prawn, ringhouse prawn. They appear in great shoals from the Norfolk and Suffolk coasts and make shorewards and southwards among the various deeps and channels, being plentiful in Prince's and Queen's Channels off Kentish coast. Finally small groups head up the estuary, mingling with the brown species in the vicinity of the Nore, vanishing about end of November, returning to deep water for the winter.

A byelaw of 1697 limited the use of drag nets except between 1 November and Good Friday from Barking Creek seaward, but shrimp fishing at Leigh did not begin until much later. 'Old Stephen Frost, 65 or 70 years ago, went in his punt and small drag net in the Creek, boiled the catch in a big pot at home. Soon others engaged in the fishery until many boilers in backyards. . . . James Tyrell said as a boy of nine he went with his adopted father, J. Wilder, shrimping from the Nore to Holehaven. Craft was *Lamplighter*, 18 to 20 ft long, a pink-sterned bawley, spritsail-rigged, decked with a well, no cabin, only Tilton-tails, a shelter covered with a tarpaulin, c 1838–40, no shrimper with a beam trawl of present fashion.'

A Leigh shrimp net had a beam of oak or elm, 8 ft long, net 8 to 10 ft, mesh ½ in to over 1 in, warps 30 fathoms attached by bridles. 'Beam has two scores cut in it, and these are leaded. The upper thwart stick was about 3 ft long, and the upright— in local parlance 'right-up stick'—about 2 ft long, inserted in a hole in centre of beam, but there was no chock. The bridles were fastened a foot from the end of beam with staples, as was the net.'

In Yantley and inside the Blyth the net was kept down 1 hour, but in Sea Reach 2 to 3 hours. The Yantlet was then an open bay and could be fished at all tides, but gradually it became closed by sand. 'Ordinary catch 9 to 10 gallons, culled and turned alive into the well, when home, swept out by hand-net and brought ashore in boxes or baskets. Eight or nine boiling houses in the village, a copper bricked up with a furnace beneath, shrimpers took turns in their use, paying a halfpenny to a penny a gallon for boiling.' After cooling, the shrimps were put in flat baskets holding 6 to 10 gallons and sent by van nightly all the year round, there being no local sale.

When rail transport became available, the number and size of the bawleys increased but, owing to continual silting up, the procedure for fishing changed, the creek and flats now drying at low water.

In neaps have to anchor in Ray gut, in springs nearer the village when can leave at high water and fish ebb and flood, but at neaps have to leave considerable time before high water so as to drift the ebb, as have to return on flood to catch night goods train, so boats have to leave at all hours of the night. Seldom start in the afternoon.

At any hour after midnight a man gathers his kit and pads—baskets, the daily return of empties—and goes to his small boat drawn up on the hard, or moored to the wharf, rows to his smack, on a dark, foggy night this may be difficult to find. On board, the sails are set according to the strength of wind, heave in chain, weigh anchor, which ground to make for chiefly depends on wind and whether spring or neap tide. With a spring tide and wind easterly more often go downstream, choosing Essex or Kent shore according to season of year. If wind southerly Kent shore is preferable, westerly either can be worked if moderate weather, in strong wind Kent side best. If nor'west or northerly blowing strongly, Sea Reach is more frequented. With neap tides must leave two to three hours before high water to get upstream, for high water is best time at the Blyth and midstream at Hole Haven. A necessity, so that on the ebb the smack may reach port for at such times a risk of being too late for the goods train. Westerly winds preferable.

If start in early morning the fire is lit and tea made, the net prepared and trawl shot on reaching ground. Sails trimmed according to weather and boat drifts, either with the current which is preferable, or across or against as wind serves. While the trawl is down it requires constant watching, with extra breeze it may 'leave the ground'. Now and again the warp is felt and by its tremors judge if all well. (Picture, p 183.)

When it is time to haul the captain calls 'let boat come-to to haul'. The warp is put in the snatch block then round the winch, one man heaves on the winch, the other coils the warp. 'Bridles up', then the bridles are pulled on board, the tackle hooked to the fore trawl head, hoisted up, stopper rove under beam to pull aft end on taffrail. The helm has been lashed and the bawley looks after herself. 'Pull ground rope on board, gather in on the net', the catch is shaken all down into the cod, bit by bit, the cod pulled on board until the contents can be shot on deck, then if conditions are favourable the trawl is shot again.

It will be seen that the procedure with the ordinary type of beam trawl with iron trawl heads, as used towards the end of the nineteenth century, differed from that adopted with the trim-tram or the old pattern shrimp net. The catch was roughly culled on deck, then riddled and the siftings thrown overboard, ie, what passes through the sieve.

The brine in which the shrimps are boiled in the copper is made of sea water with a quantity of coarse salt added, the brine being very strong, the proper strength is when the shrimps float, too weak they sink. After boiling for a short time they are taken out and cooled before being packed in pads, landed and sent off by train.

For a time in the 1870s the Leigh men used the trim-tram for one summer, on the issue of an injunction for using a beam trawl within the Conservancy's limits.

Only about a dozen gave it a trial, found it most inconvenient to work, and the men apt to be thrown overboard by the clumsy iron-shod pointed wooden frame. The beam, of elm, 18 ft long, had screwed to the top two wooden bridles, the 'snooks', each some 8 ft long and 4 in wide, the 'point'—the heel or shoe—being iron-clad and pointing up, the warp being made fast to a ring. The mouth of the net was triangular, supported by an upright— the 'right-up stick'—centred in the 3 ft upper 'thwart stick', the net being 20 ft long. A fishing line fastened to an eyebolt at the apex of the snooks ran backward to a ring on the top of the upright stick and pulled taut, kept the net open when in use. In hauling in, this line was slacked, the net fell forward and was closed.

It was more popular in the upper reaches rather than in the estuary. The regulations stated:

> No trim-tram or four-beam net shall be used with a weighted beam of greater length than 21 ft, mouth greater in total circumference than 60 ft, netting not to exceed 30 ft from beam to extreme end of cod, not less than ¾-in mesh, knot to knot, measurement made when net is wet.

When two nets were in vogue, as originally in the old pink-sterns and the early bawleys, the captain stood right aft, the mate abaft the shrouds, each with a net in his hands. The one aft was shoved off, immediately followed by the fore, and the moment the fore net was overboard the mate jumped forward to the bow to check the net by the warp coiled at the head. When enough warp was out to both nets, each was 'boomed out' by booms 8 or 9 ft long, the end of the fore one being hitched to the fore horse, the aft one to the main horse. The outer ends of these spars had a cleat on the top and the warp ran in the cleft.

> When three nets, aft and fore were shot and boomed out, the third, or middle opposite the centre of boat, was not boomed. Spars were 12 to 14 ft long, but shorter than when four nets were used. Then the aft stern net was put over, and if the bawley was making good headway each net was slid gently overboard in a slanting direction backwards, 'then follows fore net by the mate, then aft middle, then fore middle, only the fore and aft nets being boomed. If vessel was drifting, then each net was more forcibly shot away at right angles to prevent any entanglement, 'sinking o' em away'.
>
> On heaving-in, the middle ones were first taken in, one after the other, then fore and aft are pulled up, both at once, each man his own net. The booms were now 20 to 22 ft long, no longer spars but builders' scaffold poles, so heavy affairs.

D. Ford says when he first went shrimping it was 'main strength and stupidness', the nets were first fixed to the boomers and then by main strength hauled out. A long while before they thought of first fixing boomers out and then easily running out nets 'good enough for fathers, good enough for their successors'.

The 'tell-tale' was a shovel-like instrument with a short net lowered at times to tell if shrimps were about; 'a mixture of dredge and hand-net, neither so heavy as one or light as other', being a rough twine net fastened to a stirrup-shaped iron into which a wooden handle was socketed, with 12 to 14 fathoms of rope as warp. Thrown overboard, it was dragged for a short time along the ground, and hauled at short intervals.

When three nets were worked, two had 9-ft beams, one of 12 ft amidships. The first bawleys to go to Harwich had beam trawls with iron heads, and soon they began to supersede the double-beamed nets. Each man had the irons made by the local smith to his own fancy, some choosing the stirrup-shaped Barking smack type, others favouring the Brixham pattern which predominated. A few tried quadrangular, but finally the stirrup was generally adopted. Beams were now 21 ft long, net 30 to 36 ft long, hemp, two-laid; when cotton tarred by the makers was tried, it proved unsatisfactory, but was better when cutched and tarred by the fishermen. With a larger mesh this trawl could be used for fishing for soles, plaice and the like, the net being 3-laid twine, the meshes following the regulations laid down in 1697.

A bawley's rig was eminently suitable for trawling as speed could be adjusted to a nicety. The loose-footed mainsail had an almost vertical leech, was high and narrow, with a long, high-peaked gaff. A brail led from the masthead through a cringle about halfway up the leech, back through a block at the throat and down to deck; this and the 'truss', or tack tackle, were in constant use in squally weather, quickly brailing in half the mainsail or more, or picking the tack perhaps halfway up the mast, leaving the rest of the sail standing. In a hard breeze the sail could be scandalised by settling the peak and tricing up the tack when coming up to moorings. If there was much traffic about, the first line of reef points was tied up to give a clear view ahead and to keep the foot of the sail clear of men working on deck. (Picture, p. 166.)

A bawley would handle beautifully under a brailed mainsail and topsail. The loose-footed sail stood fairly well on a wind, but was apt to bag when the sheet was eased off. The mainsheet, similar to that in a spritsail barge, had a heavy double block, with an iron pin through the sheave, travelling on an iron horse across the transom. Two single blocks were hooked in cringles, one in the clew, the other in the first reef cringle above, the sheet leading from the double block up to the clew block, back through the second sheave and up to the upper block, the fall belaying round the iron pin in the double block.

When reefing, the bawley was hove-to, the sheet slackened and immediately the sail shook the upper block was shifted to the cringle above, in line with the second row of reef points, and the clew block hooked in the cringle for the first line of points. The reef points were tied and the tack bowsed down with the truss. A danger was that if the heavy double block shot across the horse it could well knock a man out, or overboard; also if an accidental gybe, or caught aback, the sheet could then gather itself into a bight, possibly round the neck of the man at the tiller, and the gaff crashing over could tighten the sheet with murderous force.

The foresail, working on a horse, could be held aback by a stopper round the foremost shroud; with the sail just a'weather, the bawley would hold her course for miles unattended, assisted by the square forefoot and the long, straight keel.

The lower mast was short, with tackles for hoisting the cod end up to the masthead for emptying or drying the net. The topmast was long, in later days exceeding the length of lower mast; also the bowsprit, when reefed down a storm jib was set well inboard as the spar was seldom, if ever, reefed. In summer a huge jib, the spinnaker, was carried with its head right up the topmast. Altogether as handy a sail plan as could be devised,

but only suitable for work inshore; bawleys seldom ventured
round the Foreland. (Picture, p 183.)

With a hundred or more boats working at night in narrow
waters thronged with steamships, barges and other sailing craft,
collisions were not unknown, 'but few compared with Kent
district'. Fog was, of course, a nightmare, and sailing vessels
could then only drift, but many a steamer kept up speed to
avoid missing a tide. The many sandbanks claimed their vic-
tims in winter when smacks were caught out stowboating and a
gale suddenly blew up. Even well up river trouble could come
when a squall lashed down over the house tops, as was the case
with *Requital*. After delivering a catch of sprats at Billingsgate
she was returning down river when a sudden squall capsized her
near Woolwich, drowning her crew of two. On 4 October 1890
the bawley *G.M.A.C.* was coming home from trawling near the
Oaze as night closed in. Halfway towards the Nore the wind,
which had been blowing very fresh from the sw, without warning flew round to the NNW in fearful gusts. The boat instantly
capsized, George Cotgrove was swept away and never seen
again. His brother Alf grasped the shrouds and gained the topmast rigging as the bawley sank. All night he clung with fingers
so frozen that he thought he must drop. At daylight he was seen
by another smack and rescued. He spent three months in bed
and it was a year before he recovered, but was so unnerved that
he gave up fishing. A public subscription raised enough to buy
him a rowboat, which he let out on hire while he did odd jobs
ashore.

Abraham Cotgrove in *Renown* was dragged overboard by the
trawl rope and drowned near the Nore lightvessel. A year later
his son, William, in the same smack, met a like fate on the
Maplins. William Harvey went to rescue some yachtsmen in
trouble on the Middle Sand near the Spaniards. He saved them,
and with his bawley cruising close by, a sudden gust capsized
his small boat; the yachtsmen were saved but Harvey sank
before his smack could reach him.

Dr Murie writes thus of the Leigh men:

Of average size, muscular and well built, mainly home-loving, family men, seldom restless or wanderers, closely inter-married and clannish, truthful, but not sharp-witted, pushing or of keen business habits, but shrewd to take advantage of the main chance. A few boorish and suspicious of strangers.

Prior to the accession of residents, visitors from London and yachtsmen on Sundays, the boats seldom left shore on Sundays and the men had a strong objection to go on the water that day. Blue-jerseyed fishermen and their families flocked to church or chapel, the few backsliders lounged on the wharf or old market space. Night found the village quiet, the men home ready for a start at early dawn.

The first rule in the byelaws of the Company of Free Fishermen of the River Thames, issued 1697, read:

'That no person using the Art, Mistery or Craft of a Fisherman shall (below London Bridge to Yantlet and to N. Foreland and Harwich inclusive) use or practice Trincking, Stowboating, Trawling or Catching of Fish or Bait on the Lord's Day, commonly called Sunday, upon Forfeiture of Twenty shillings for every such offence.'

John Wesley's preaching had a lasting and beneficial effect on the Leigh fishing community and fishermen in the pulpit were not infrequent. The advantage of this life as compared with deep sea trawling was, seldom away from home except when spratting. A night, a day or two and home. In bad weather mend nets and gear, but few did any indoor work or cultivated a garden, hung about smoking and yarning, at night gathered in pubs, spending freely, played cards or dominoes, skittles or quoits. The Ship Inn a favourite, a fiddler came regularly from Prittlewell and rough dancing till early hours. Eight pubs throve in a population of 1,200 to 1,300 persons. Regatta with bawley races, at Leigh Fair in May for several days. Nicknames frequent as usual among fishing communities, essential with so many of same surname in a small village.

The men usually wore flannel shirt and drawers next to the skin, at sea 'fare-not' (fearnought) trousers, a thick, coarse felty flannel of a ruddy-brown hue, sometimes a pair of pilot cloth, in summer, tweed or 'gray-jane' material. A thick blue jersey or coarse, woolly checkered suit, in warm weather white calico jumper, but no vest or jacket worn. Caps of various sorts, a blue or coloured worsted muffler wrapped round neck and chest. Double stockings of wool, strong seaboots, pipe in mouth . . . the moderate weather working kit. In rain or storm (tempest) oil smock and oil petticoat trousers, sou'-wester, in cold weather thick worsted mittens.

In byegone days, shore 'togs' were plum-coloured cloth trousers, or pilot cloth, young 'swells' in white ducks. No white shirt or collar ever worn, a blue jersey smock or guernsey, peaked or billycock hat, shoes, bluchers or wellingtons imported from Rotterdam via Harwich. One character had ducks with fringed bottoms, zebra-striped smock with his full name across, a long red jersey cap, curly hair, white cotton stockings and slippers tied with ribbons.

The present craze for teenagers to have fringed jeans is not so modern after all!

Then came broadcloth of the latest fashion and cut, white shirt and studs, or yachting costume among the younger generation.

When cash was short, credit of most was good . . . hearty meat eaters, early marriage the custom, large families, but not such risk of widowhood as in North Sea ports. Women did the drudgery, banding etc, men prone to booze, but later money went in finery. Sixty per cent own their craft, some their houses, boat's share and family help in fishing always been turning point, leading to independence, want of them the reverse.

As in the Colne area, salvaging brought windfalls, but . . .

. . . sixty or more years ago, if a strong north wind, several craft would drop down to Blacktail Swin, (Maplins) and lay up idle. At night the crews kept a sharp look-out, then up lights in rigging to lead ashore collier brigs, timber or tallow men from the Baltic. Then the men walk across at low water or row out and proffer assistance, perks in coal, boards etc thrown overboard, Whitstable men also out. But bawleys often stood by vessels in trouble, the estuary not so well lighted as now, or steam common.

The Act of 1697 said all owners of such Trincke shall within the bounds of the Conservancy on dark and foggy nights hang forth out of his said Trincke boat one lanthorn with sufficient candle-light for the better and safer passage of ships, boats and vessels passing to and fro. Penalty Twenty shillings for every such omission.

Hence the men claimed they were only following this injunction.

Before the early 1860s no provision was made for any in-

surance. Then certain prudent men formed The Leigh Fishermen's Mutual Insurance Society in January 1866, the rules
being slightly modified in March 1872.

To provide against total loss of boats, members to be owners.
Annual payment not to exceed 2½ per cent of sum insured. Classi-
fication to hold good for five years. Legal advice as required.
Members to appoint five arbitrators, three of whom chosen by
lot, to settle every matter in dispute, half estimated value of boat
not to exceed £100. When compensation paid, but boat afterwards recovered, owner can again have boat at half estimated
value, otherwise to be sold, half going to owner, half to the
Society. If owner recovers damages he is to recoup Society what
has been advanced. Call to be made if Society short of funds. No
compensation for wilful neglect or carelessness.

During the first year 60 boats were insured for sums varying
from £15 to £45, and £50 to £100; very few over £100. At the
end of 1897, 62 were on the register, and there was only one
total loss in 32 years, *Perseverance* in 1871, costing £130. In
November 1897, when *Excelsior* was driven right over the seawall at Parkstone, £30 was paid for re-launching and repairs.
In 1866 the total funds were £84 9s 9d, rising to £507 6s 7d in
1897.

Oysters have been cultivated in Hadleigh Ray from a very
early date. Originally they may have been natural beds. 'In
1714 Sir Francis St John granted leases to William Utton, who
commenced oyster cultivation and made a fortune. This culture
excited the jealousy of Whitstable oystermen for a Kentish
armada of 100 smacks invaded the Ray with flags flying and
firing guns and carried off some thousands of bushels of his
oysters. They paid dearly for this . . . case tried at Brentwood
1724–25, verdict £2,000 damages.'

Other beds were established in Chalkwell Oaze and were in
the possession of Alston Bros, *c* 1856, although the Crown had
ineffectually tried to dislodge them. 'During the mutiny at the
Nore in 1797 Leigh men did a roaring trade with the fleet as the
man-of-war crews were short of provisions.' These beds were
restocked from time to time with various foreign oysters. Many

from the Channel deep-sea grounds, and from near the Varne and Ridge shoals, off Margate Sands and the vicinity.

In 1870 a good bed was found, news spread and 75 smacks from all quarters soon laid ground bare . . . for two months the dredger-men obtained very large, middle-sized and small oysters. Boats left Leigh at ebb tide, often returned with the flood . . . average take of each boat about three pecks a day, sent by rail to Billings-gate, 7s a peck, more in the market £2 a bushel. . . . J. Tyrell said 'Leigh men scooped them right completely up'. In 1901 a London firm of oyster importers offered to supply oysters for re-stocking at 4s 6d a 1,000 in baskets containing 1,500, 12s for 400, Portuguese, Britanny 10s and 24s . . . drainage from Southend increased the risk of pollution and beds moved to the Medway.

In the spring of 1883 several of the Emery family went to the Beachy Head grounds for scallops, but the venture was not a success. A more profitable dredging was for that inveterate enemy of the oyster, the star fish, or 'five-finger', 14 to 15 boats sailed regularly, dredging in spring and fall, two months at a time; at the Nore they 'swarmed on the ground'. On one trip a small bawley was loaded with about 2 tons in a couple of hours, sold for manure, another took 5 tons in as many hours.

At first sold at so much a bushel, afterwards by weight, so the fishermen hastened to sell before the moisture began to drain off. Average value £1 a ton, but in 1877 Mr Fitch purchased 70 tons at 16s a ton, all procured in the Blackwater . . . 30 to 40 boats at a time, but catches usually sold where the men came from. . . . The decline was due to guano and chemical manures, railways, wet seasons, depressed farmers . . . ceased about 1886, occasionally a crew went for a few days five-fingering if they heard of a farmer willing to buy. Used light oyster dredges, six a common number.

Eighty-six fishing boats were registered at Leigh in 1898, and of these, 42 went to Harwich after pink shrimps in the season. The oldest bawleys were *Alert*, a boomsail built at Leigh in 1832, and *Harvey*, built at Southend in 1848. The fleet included one yawl, 14½ tons, built at Harwich 1875, three boomsails, four half-sprits, all the rest being true bawley rig. Eight used the Leigh shrimp net, the rest the beam trawl, 25 the stow net.

George Kirby was the last man to use the old shrimp net in 1901.

My analysis of places where these bawleys were built gives: Brightlingsea 21, Milton, Kent 20, Harwich 17, Leigh 16, Southend 5, Shoeburyness 5, Maldon 1. In some instances the builders were unknown.

Motors were introduced during and after the 1914–18 war, many bawleys retaining a full sail plan, but gradually it was cut down until little, if any, canvas was spread.

The sturdy construction and conscientious work put into these humble craft is exemplified in *Honour*, 12 LO, built at Leigh in 1868 and still working in the Thames Estuary in the 1930s under a full spread of canvas, although fitted with the ubiquitous motor, and taking the ground at every tide.

GLOSSARY

NOTE: The same item was frequently known by a different name in various districts.

Apron. A backing or strengthening timber bolted behind the stem. In Yorkshire, called a stomach piece.

Bank. Single-banked when only one rower on each thwart; double-banked, two men on each thwart with an oar out each side, or two men to an oar.

Bench. The after thwarts; those extending along the sides are side benches.

Brail. A rope encircling a boomless mainsail to gather it up to the mast and gaff.

Breaming. Cleaning the bottom by fire to melt the pitch or other composition before scraping.

Breasthook. A stout knee bolted across the inside of the bow holding stem, shelf and frames together. Known in Shetland as 'a hinney spot'.

Build. Three methods of fitting planking. (1) Clench, clincher, clencher, clinker or lapstrake. (2) Carvel. (3) Diagonal. (1) In clench, the strakes overlap; (2) in carvel, they are flush with each other. The planks can be fastened only to the timbers and require caulking to ensure watertightness. Not so strong as clench built. (3) Planks are laid diagonally across the timbers and usually a second skin is laid over running in the contrary direction. Very strong, but heavy.

Bumpkin. A short iron or wooden bowsprit fitted with a hook to take the tack of a dipping lug, or foresail. If aft, it has a block or sheave to take the mizzen sheet.

Caulking. Stuffing the seams between the planks in carvel build with oakum and then paying them with hot pitch.

Clew. The lower after corner in a fore-and-aft sail.

Counter. The extension of the hull beyond the stern-post.

Covering board. The outside deck plank fitted over the timber heads. Also called the plank sheer.

Cringles. Loops or eyes formed in the bolt ropes of sails. Reef pendants pass through them if the mainsail has a boom. Iron cringles, as on the foresail, are called hanks.

Crutch. A prop or stanchion with a semicircular groove cut into upper end in which the foremast rests when lowered, or the boom of a mainsail when furled. On the East Coast it is called a mitchboard, at Hastings a match.

Cultch. Shells, stones or similar hard substance to which the spat—or spawn—of oysters adheres.

Cultick. A heavy knife used to remove oysters off cultch. In Essex it is called a cultar.

Dead rise. The approach the floor timbers make to the perpendicular.

Deadwood. Solid timbers bolted on top of the keel fore and aft to receive the heels of frames which do not cross the keel, also to take the ends of the lower strakes of planking.

Depth. In ships, the inside measure from the underside of the beams to the kelson; in open boats, the outside depth from the top of the gunwale to the underside of the keel.

Dipping lug. A quadrilateral sail bent to a yard which hooks to a traveller, set to leeward of the mast with tack to stemhead or weather bow. When going about—tacking—the sail has to be dipped—lowered—and the yard shifted to the other side of mast.

Doubling. A method of restoring old clench-built hulls by covering each strake with a feather-edged plank cut flush with the lands and forming a smooth surface.

Earings. Ropes attached to cringles in the head of a sail to fasten its corners to the yard.

Fall. The hauling part of a tackle.

Fashion timbers. The aftermost timbers to which the transoms are bolted, forming the shape of the stern.

Fifie. A Scottish boat with vertical stem and stern posts.

Floors. The lowermost of the various pieces of timber making up a frame and crossing the keel into which they are often recessed. Their moulding is the depth or vertical dimension, the siding the thickness in a fore and aft direction.

Floor boards. The loose planking lying over the floor timbers; they cover the ballast and keep bilgewater out of sight. In Shetland they are called tilfers.

Frame. One of the ribs or timbers of a vessel, made up of floor timber, futtocks and top timbers. Its moulding is the thickness athwartships, ie, between the inner and outer planking, its siding the breadth in a fore and aft direction. In Shetland, known as bands or baands. At Deal, as the futtocks.

Garboard. The strake of planking next to the keel into which it is rabbetted and fastened.

Gores. The angle at one or both ends of sail cloths to increase the breadth or depth of the sail.

Gunwale. In an open boat it is the top of the sheer strake—saxboard—or a timber above it, in it are holes for thole pins or rowlocks. In cobles, it is on the outside of the sheer strake.

Hoist. The length of the luff of a fore and aft sail. In Scotland, it is the name given to the luff, or weather, of a lugsail.

Hollow lines. The horizontal lines of a vessel which have inflections, where they change from convex to concave.

Horse. The iron bar running athwart a deck or stern upon which the sheet tackle travels. If a foresail, the sail is called a working foresail.

Joggles. The notches cut in timbers to allow them to lie flush in the lands of the planking in clench build.

Keel. The lowest and principal timber in a vessel, running in a fore and aft direction. Its moulding is the depth, its siding the thickness, or breadth.

Keelson (or Kelson). The timber lying on top of the floors and through-bolted to the keel. Its moulding is the depth, its siding the breadth. In Scotland, it was fitted below the floors in luggers; in East Anglia it is called the hog.

Kentledge. The pigs or shaped pieces of iron laid as ballast, fore and aft near the keelson.

Knees. Natural-grown crooked timbers with two arms used to connect beams with sides or timbers. In an open boat knees join the thwarts to stringer, lodging knees lying horizontal, standing knees with one arm vertical.

Knittles. Short lines used to bend the head of a sail to its yard. Also known as rovings, robands and yardbands. Sometimes spelt 'nettles' and used instead of reef points.

Lade-net. A long net on an iron hoop attached to a staff and used to pick up fish which had fallen out of the nets into the water. Known as a didlenet in East Anglia, a keep or kieve net in Cornwall, and a scum net in Scotland.

Lands. The overlap of planks in clench build through which the fastenings are driven and clenched. In Shetland, they were known as landings.

Last. An old herring measure, nominally 10,000 fish, about 2 tons, but actually varying in number according to how many fish were counted into a long hundred, 12,400 to 13,200.

Leech. The lee edge of a sail.

Leg-of-mutton sail. A triangular sail, usually set on the mizzen mast.

Lines. The drawings of the shape or form of a vessel. Hand lines, or long lines, used when fishing with hooks. Known in Scotland as taes, ground lines; haavres in Yorkshire; boulters, spillers, or spilliards in Cornwall; baak, balk or bale in the Isle of Man for deep-sea fishing.

Luff. The weather edge of a sail, also called the weather or hoist.

Lumber irons. Rings on the quarters in which oars, spare sails, spars, and boathooks are carried in East Anglian and Isle of Man boats. At Hastings, known as raft ropes; in Cornwall as crutches.

Mast case (or Tabernacle). The three-sided case on deck in which masts which lower are stepped. In decked vessels, the mast lowers back into a scuttle at Lowestoft, the lears at Yarmouth, feathers at Hastings, scottle in Mount's Bay, trunk or locker at St Ives, slides or guides in the Isle of Man, skegs or hitches in Scotland, and the gantry or gauntry in Yorkshire.

Moulded (or Moulding). The depth a timber is made between its curved surfaces, the side to which the mould is applied.

Nails. Clench nails have square shanks allowing them to be driven and withdrawn without splitting planks. Copper or galvanised iron, clenched over rooves.

Norman. A short bar thrust into one of the holes in a capstan.

Norman post. A vertical post nearly amidships round which a rope can be belayed when boat is being towed.

Oakum. The substance to which old ropes are reduced when unpicked, usually by prison labour, and used in caulking seams in planks in carvel-built vessels and in decks.

Parrel. A rope used to secure a yard at the slings to the mast, and rove through balls of wood—the beads or trucks—so that it hoists easily. Known in the Shetlands as a rakki and made from a cow or ram's horn. If an iron ring, it is called a traveller, and was often bound with leather, kept well greased.

Pawl. A small stop or catch which stops a capstan from running backwards.

Pay. To give a coating of tar, pitch, paint or other composition to anything requiring it.

Peak. The upper end of a gaff or lugsail yard.

Pendant. A rope to which a tackle is attached, that part of a rope which runs between the blocks, or short lines rove through luff cringles for use when reefing sail.

Platform. The floor boards over the ballast.

Rabbet. The groove cut in keel, stem, sternpost and deadwood to receive the edges or ends of outside planking.

Ribs. The timbers or frames of a vessel.

Rising floor. Sharp-bottomed on V-shaped floors.

Roach. The curve on the foot or leech of a sail.

Roost. The strong and furious tides which set in between the Orkney and Shetland Islands.

Roove (or Rove). The small washer placed over a nail before clenching.

Rovings (or Robands). Short lines by which a sail is bent to its yard; from the Norse ra-bands, 'ra' being a yard. In fifies are rovings, in zulus are yardbands.

Scantling. The finished dimensions of a piece of timber.

Scudding. Clearing herring nets over a pole above the hatch leading to the fish hold. In Scotland, it is known as reddin' the nets.

Sided (or Siding). The thickness of timbers between their flat surfaces, or parallel sides.

Sheet. The rope by which the clew of a sail is controlled.

Shelf. The longitudinal timber running the whole length of the hull inside the frames on which the ends of the beams rest. In Shetlands, the fasteband; in cobles, the inwire or in-wyver, on which the thwarts rest.

Skeg. The heel or extreme after end of the keel which sometimes projects slightly abaft the sternpost.

Snoods. The short lines to which the hooks are fastened at intervals on a long line. Known in Scotland as toms; in Cornwall as nessels.

Sprit. The diagonal spar across a fore-and-aft sail to extend it by the peak. The heel rests in the snotter, known as the shangie in the Orkneys.

Standing lug. A lugsail with its tack permanently fast to a hook at the foot of a mast. Invariably set on the mizzen mast. Often known as a Clyde lug if very high-peaked.

Stem. The foremost timber in a vessel or boat, usually having a strong iron band on the outer face to connect it with the keel.

Step. A timber bolted down to keelson or floors with a mortice to take the tenon in the heel of the mast.

Sternpost. The aftermost timber connected to the heel of the keel by tenon, with metal plates on which the rudder is hung, the gudgeons and pintles. Its moulding is the fore and aft dimensions, the siding the thwartship dimension.

Strake. A line of planking extending the length of a vessel. Sheer strakes are the uppermost planks, usually thicker than the remainder, and form the sheer.

Stretcher. The movable piece of wood against which a rower presses his feet. In Shetland, they are known as the pitlins.

Stringers. Strengthening timbers running along the inside of a boat to brace the timbers.

Tack. The lower fore corner of a sail.

Thwart. Transverse seats in an open boat; known in Shetland as tafts, and in Yorkshire as thofts.

Transoms. The timbers lying horizontally across the sternpost and bolted to it and the fashion timbers at the sides of the hull.

Tholes (or Thole pins). Pegs fitted into holes in the gunwale. If single, the oar is either held loosely by a grommet of rope—the humbleband in Shetland—or the fulcrum of the oar is so enlarged that a hole may be bored through it to allow the oar to be dropped over the pin. Known as cabes, or kabes, in Shetland. Can be removed when sailing.

Tye. A rope or wire attached to a yard and reeving through a sheave or dumb sheave in the masthead with a tackle at the lower end, the halyards.

Wash strake. A strake of plank, usually movable, fitted to the gunwale of an open boat to increase the freeboard. In it square openings are cut to form rowlocks.

Wheft, Waif (or Waft). A long streamer or piece of bunting used as a signal that the vessel requires the services of a beach boat or yawl.

Yawl. From the Norse 'yol', the name frequently given to a vessel on coasts where the Viking influence is strong; may be a cutter, as at Whitstable.

INDEX